On TARGET

MW01264547

On Target

Creating A Faith Development Plan for Your Church

J. Brackemyre

COLLEGE PRESS PUBLISHING COMPANY· JOPLIN, MISSOURI

DEDICATION

To Miriam Spaeth

For her gift of music, her godly heritage,

and her unwavering support in my ministry.

I love you, Grandma!

Toll-free order line 800-289-3300
On the web at www.collegepress.com

All Scripture quotations, unless otherwise noted, are from the
New American Standard Bible, © 1960, 1962, 1963, 1968,
1971, 1975, 1977, and 2005 by the Lockman Foundation,
and are used by permission.

Cover design by Mark A. Cole

Library of Congress Cataloging-in-Publication Data

Brackemyre, J. (Jennifer), 1968–
   On target: creating a faith development plan for your
   church / by J. Brackemyre.
      p. cm.
   ISBN 0-89900-940-9 (softback)
   1. Christian education of children.   2. Faith development.
   3. Spiritual formation.   I. Title.
   BV1475.3.B73 2005
   268—dc22

                                      2005026494

FOREWORD

As I sit here in my office, pecking away at the keyboard, I keep flipping back and forth from my word processor to MSN. I'm not normally a news junkie, but Hurricane Katrina just swept through New Orleans, the levee broke, looters are running wild, federal help is slow in coming, and a chemical plant just blew this morning. Reporters are calling this the worst natural catastrophe in the history of our country. Undoubtedly it is. Part of the problem is the unprecedented strength of the hurricane; the other part is the lack of preparation combined with the thousands who did not heed the warning.

The church is experiencing a spiritual catastrophe of equivalent proportions of Katrina—biblical illiteracy. It is rampant, it is devastating, and it is crippling. We are mastering megachurches and bemoaning the fact that our people are ignorant of the Word of God. We have perfected the Sunday Morning Seeker Event (for which I am, frankly, grateful), but our Sunday Schools have become ghost towns. It is not uncommon for vibrant churches to have 95% of the auditorium packed with only 30% of those people in any kind of a small group. Does this bother anyone?

Brackemyre has done the church a great service in this book . . . or should I call it a spiritual roadmap for a disciple's journey? This work will help your church develop an overall plan for Christian education. Instead of simply purchasing the latest curriculum based on snazzy design or colored photos, the author is helping you strategically target curriculum for various age groups. For example, when should you teach a child Apologetics? Well, when do they argue the most? Let's take a Jr. High kid's natural propensity to be cantankerous and baptize it for the glory of God! Let's take a fifth grade child's ability to memorize and get full chapters in their heads not just verses. Let's take a toddler's penchant for music and imbed sacred song into her soul!

This book will help you think through each age group at two levels. First, what developmental skills is the child experiencing at this stage of her life, and second, how can we capitalize on content during that period? The end result is a fully developed disciple by the time he graduates from High School. Rather than learning about Noah and Moses thirteen times, here is a holistic program of study throughout all ages and stages of development. This strategic plan is long overdue, and we here at College Press could not be more proud to present this tool and recommend its implementation in your educational program. This work will help you be not just as innocent as a dove but as shrewd as a serpent. Ok, if we haven't sold you on the book just yet, take a peek at Appendix D. That alone is worth the price of the book. May God exponentially bless your work in training up disciples.

Mark E. Moore
Ozark Christian College

TABLE OF CONTENTS

Chapter One

THE NEED FOR A BULL'S-EYE:
WHY HAVE A FAITH DEVELOPMENT PLAN?

As I walked to answer the front door, Justin's smiling face peeked though the window. I love it when the youth group members feel comfortable enough to just drop by the house, but Justin was always a special visitor. I have had the privilege of watching Justin grow up in our church. If the doors are open, he is there. If I had to choose one student who's had the full benefits of my ministry, I'd select Justin.

He didn't have to pick up his date for another half hour and decided to drop by. As we sat in the living room, the discussion turned toward Justin's future. "So, have you decided on a college?"

"Yeah, I think I'm gonna go to BGSU."

The twinge in my stomach was warranted. Bowling Green was my hometown. I had practically grown up on the state university campus. Flashes of outdoor frat parties, street madness, crowded downtown bars, and the hungover students going back to their dorms on Sunday mornings raced through my mind. I'd known several Christians who had lost their faith while attending BGSU. My words of wisdom?

"Justin, if you go there, you need to get into a campus ministry right away."

He agreed and asked, "What church did you go to when you lived there?"

I took the opportunity to tell him about my home church, but also explained that my home church and our current church don't hold the same beliefs on some issues. "You may feel more comfortable at a church that holds the same beliefs as our church."

He looked at me in frustration and said, "I don't even know what our church believes. I know there are Presbyterians, Lutherans, Church of Christ, Christian Churches . . . but I have no idea what makes them different from us!"

I was floored! How could he not know this, something so fundamental as what we believe? How many Sunday school, Sunday night, and Wednesday night programs had he been through, not to mention the conventions, retreats, and extra programs? He's getting ready to graduate and he isn't even equipped with the decision-making skills to choose a church.

After he left, I took a long look at my ministry. I have to admit that I felt like such a failure. I felt like I had spent the last fifteen years in youth ministry spinning my wheels. What did I want my students to know by the time they graduated and, more importantly, how was I going to get them there?

"If We Aim at Nothing, We'll Hit It Every Time"

We need to stop and ask two crucial questions of our ministries right now, "What do we want our students to know by the time they graduate?" and "How are we going to get them there?" By the time you finish this book, not only will you have these questions memorized, but the answers will transform your educational ministry. These two questions are the center of establishing a Faith Development Plan.

A Faith Development Plan is a roadmap, a plan of action, a game plan on how to get students from their present spiritual status to a deeper faith, a passionate, personal relationship with Jesus Christ. A Faith Development Plan is an instrument no Christian educator should be without.

> A Faith Development Plan is an instrument no Christian educator should be without.

In Psalm 127:3-4, David likens children to arrows. "Behold, children are a gift of the Lord; The fruit of the womb is a reward. Like arrows in the hand of a warrior, So are the children of one's youth." Of course David wasn't thinking about Christian education when he wrote this verse, but he gives us the visual image of children as arrows. Today, when we think of arrows, archers' targets come to mind; the great bull's-eye in the middle telling

Chapter One ◄ 10

the archer where to aim. Our children's and youth ministries should display this simple picture. Our students are the "arrows," and we must direct them toward a target.

In his video series, *Dynamic Communicator's Workshop*, Ken Davis tells of an experience he had as a child during an annual hunting trip with members from his congregation. As Ken and the other men began moving through the forest to begin hunting, a shot rang out. The bullet came less than four inches from his face. A second shot rang out and was again so close it hit a branch near him. The third shot didn't hit anything, but was so dangerously close to his ear he could not hear out of that ear for about fifteen minutes. As he dove to the ground, bullets began spraying everywhere. He instinctively buried his face in the mud, but seconds later there was silence. As he looked up from his position on the ground he could see a man standing on a rock, frantically reloading his gun. Ken continues with a comparison to today's youth ministry:

> Now I have a question for you. What was this man's philosophy? What was his philosophy of hunting? His philosophy went something like this, "There's deer in there somewhere. If I just shoot enough bullets into the woods, I might get me one." Would you want to be in the woods with this person? They should have never let this guy out of his pickup! Because he had an inefficient and in fact dangerous philosophy about hunting.
>
> Now what I would like to say to you is this, that all across the country, and I believe this with all my heart, there are well-meaning, dear-hearted, God-fearing men and women in youth ministry, pastors, youth pastors whose philosophy of communication is unconsciously the same philosophy.
>
> There are people out there everywhere, and they desperately need to hear the gospel of Christ. "If I just pump enough information in their direction, some of it is bound to hit." And nothing could be further from the truth . . . "If I just get them fired up enough, if I just say enough stuff to get 'em going . . . that something will stick, I'll hit something." The truth of the matter is this, "If you aim at nothing, you will hit it every single time."[1]

Is this your theory as a youth minister or children's minister? "I'll try this curriculum this month and we'll go from there. Hopefully something will stick with these kids!" Ask yourself, "Is this philosophy fair to your students?" When we total the hours our students spend on weekly activities, we see that we, the church, only have students 1% of their time. The other 99%

is spent at school, at home, on the internet, in sports, watching television and sleeping. This overwhelming statistic challenges us, the Christian educators, to make that 1% quality Christian education. What do we want to accomplish in the 1% of time we have with our students?

In his book *The Seven Checkpoints*, Andy Stanley says

Most of us have spent little time determining what our students need to know before they graduate from high school. Our days are spent planning activities and designing T-shirts. Often the core of what we want students to learn gets lost in the shuffle. Think for a moment about the class of students you just graduated from your ministry. What are the four or five key concepts, principles, or lessons you believe they walked away with as a result of their time under your leadership? As you consider that list, ask yourself: Are these the principles you set out years ago to instill in the hearts of the students under your watch? Or did they pick them up by chance?[2]

What Is Our Purpose?

Look at a web site, newsletter, or bulletin of almost any church today and you will see a mission statement. A mission statement is also known as an expression of core values. Take a look at any of the eighteen top visionary companies in America such as Johnson & Johnson, Ford, IBM, Motorola, Sony, or Wal-Mart and you will find one common thread: they have never strayed from their core value. Their methodology has changed with the times, but their core value remains the same.[3]

I have never seen the mission statement for our country's 9-1-1 emergency system, but I can share a time they seemed to forget it. "At about 5:00 a.m. on February 16, 2002, Karla Gutierrez was driving on the Florida Turnpike in West Miami-Dade when her car veered off the road, plunged into a canal and sank. The exact timing of the event is unclear, but Gutierrez was able to dial 9-1-1 and reach a Miami-Dade County call-taker, and speak for some 3½ minutes before her car submerged." The bone-chilling 9-1-1 call played on NBC's *Today Show* allowed the viewer to listen to Gutierrez frantically ask the operator how to get out of her rapidly sinking vehicle. The operator repeatedly asks Ms. Gutierrez to calm down and tell her where she is. Gutierrez cannot remember at what point she went off the turnpike; therefore, she doesn't know her location. As Gutierrez begins begging the operator for directions on how to get out of her sinking car, the phone call ends; Gutierrez is dead. "Gutierrez's fiancé was angry, and claimed the call-taker did not receive sufficient training; he said the unnamed dispatcher should have given Gutierrez instructions on how to escape from the vehicle rather than focusing on questions about her location."[4]

Without knowing 9-1-1's mission statement, I can guess that it has something to do with saving lives. On February 16, 2002, a member of the 9-1-1 system forgot the system's core value: to save lives. The astonishing truth to this story is this: in the investigation of Karla Gutierrez's death it was determined that the 9-1-1 operator followed the training protocol to a "T." However, the protocol did not lead to the saving of life. The 9-1-1 operator had the instructions on how to get out of a sinking car at her disposal, but chose to follow protocol.

We listen to a tragic story such as that of Karla Gutierrez and shake our heads at the 9-1-1 system, but what about the church? Have we forgotten our mission? We have, at our disposal, the instructions which will save students' lives, but many of us are too busy following the youth ministry protocol: "Sunday School is Bible study time, we have to fit a teen choir in some place, and Wednesday evenings are light, fun, and evangelistically oriented." Are we forgetting our core value?

In her book *Blue's Clues for Success* Diane Tracy conveys the importance of organizing a mission statement and the crucial role it plays in the overwhelming success of the phenomenal children's show, *Blue's Clues*. "If you could sum up the show's success in one sentence, it would probably be this: They are crystal clear about their mission; and they are vigilant in the ways they live their mission every single day. At *Blue's Clues*, everything begins and ends with the mission. Hardly a decision is made without testing it against the mission. It's a mantra to them, one that they guard with the fierceness of a lioness protecting her cubs."[5]

> **"Discipleship is not a program. It is not a ministry. It is a lifelong commitment to a lifestyle."**
> (George Barna, *Growing True Disciples*)

Can you say the same of your mission (growing spiritually mature disciples of Jesus Christ)? Are you "vigilant" in the way you live your mission every single day (I will do everything in my power to grow spiritually mature disciples of Jesus Christ)? Does "everything begin and end" with your mission? Are you "crystal clear" with your mission (My mission is to grow spiritually mature disciples of Jesus Christ)? Do your students and, better yet, your students' parents clearly know your mission? Do you "test everything" against your mission (Does this program help my students grow into spiritually mature disciples of Jesus Christ)? Do you make your mission your mantra? "My mission is to do my best to transform my students into spiritually mature disciples of Jesus Christ." "My mission is to do my best to transform my students into spiritually mature disciples of Jesus Christ." "My mission . . ."

<hr />

Imagine this conversation:

Jerry: Hi, my name is Jerry. Is this your first year at this convention?

Bill: (Shaking Jerry's hand) Hi, I'm Bill . . . and actually I'm the main speaker for the evening.

Jerry: Wow, that's great! What's your topic tonight?

Bill: "How to Produce the Best Salesmen in Your Company."

Jerry: That sounds very inspiring. What does your company do?

Bill: We sell car stereos.

Jerry: Wow! I can't wait to hear what you have to say tonight. What's your position with the company?

Bill: I am the executive in charge of training salesmen. I have about fifty salesmen under me and my main goal is simply for these guys to sell as many car stereos as they can. Our company motto is, "Everyone should have a car stereo."

Jerry: Great, great! How long have these fifty salesmen been with you?

Bill: Some of them are brand-new, but many of them have been with me, now, for nearly eighteen years.

Jerry: That is so impressive. I can just imagine the amount of stereos your salesmen must sell.

Bill: Well, none of my people have actually ever *sold* a stereo. You know, it takes a lot of guts to approach that customer.

Jerry: So, none of the fifty people under you have ever sold *one* stereo?

Bill: No, but I am very proud of my salesmen. I believe that people just know my guys are salesmen without them ever having to say a word. We say every morning before the store opens, "You may not have the guts to approach anyone, but that's okay as long as your inner salesman light is shining." I mean, not everyone is cut out to be a salesman. Sometimes the guys do get brave. If they meet someone who might want a car stereo, they invite them into the store, and I take it from there.

Jerry: But the goal of your company is for *everyone to have a car stereo?*

Bill: Absolutely.

Jerry: Do your salesmen believe in the product? Do they know the benefits of a car stereo?

Bill: Absolutely! I don't know of any of our salesmen who don't believe wholeheartedly in the car stereo market. And yes, they know every benefit, every bell and whistle.

Jerry: Well, the only thing I can tell you is this, you better adjust the price of those car stereos so your salesmen have better success.

Bill: (Laughing) It's Jerry, right? (Condescendingly) Jerry, you don't understand, our car stereos are free.

Obviously we are not in the car stereo business. But a quick change of some key words in this story, such as car stereo and salvation, would reveal a striking comparison to some youth ministries. We know our mission, but have become complacent about the end result. We have lowered the bar and the expectations for our students in regard to discipleship.

—·—·—·—·—·—·—·—·—·—·—·—·—·—

Our core value is actually the same as the 9-1-1 system: to save lives. However, our mission is not focused on saving people physically, but spiritually. Jesus clearly states our mission in Matthew 28:19 and 20, "Go therefore and make disciples of all the nations, baptizing them in the name of the Father and the Son and the Holy Spirit, teaching them to observe all that I commanded you; and lo, I am with you always, even to the end of the age." Our mission, our goal, our target for these arrows is to make them into disciples of Christ, mature believers that are able to reproduce themselves. Bill Hull says, "The church must produce people who reproduce themselves; any other kind of Christian is spiritually sterile."[6] We cannot produce true, spiritually mature disciples of Christ if we don't aim our students at this specific target.

Diane Tracy says, "Many companies have mission statements on plaques and pieces of paper; too few have them inscribed on the hearts and minds of the people whose job it is to actualize the mission. If you ask most people to recite the mission statement for their company, department, or team, they would be hard-pressed to do so."[7] Perhaps it is time for all of us to reevaluate our mission statements and intensely evaluate how we incorporate such goals into our ministry.

> Perhaps it is time for all of us to reevaluate our mission statements and evaluate how we incorporate such goals.

Is the Aiming-at-Nothing Approach Working?

In his *Youthworker Journal* article, "The Failure of Youth Ministry," the late Mike Yaconelli posed this question to his readers: "What is the most important function of youth ministry? A) Introducing young people to Jesus. B) Providing healthy activities. C) Involving young people in service. D) Abstinence pledges. E) Good theological training. F) Worship." His answer, "None of the above. The most important function of youth ministry is longevity. Long-term discipleship." He goes on to say, "Very little youth ministry has a lasting impact on students. I believe we're no more effective today reaching young people with the gospel than we've ever been . . . if we want to see young people have a faith that lasts, then we have to completely change the way we do youth ministry in America. I wonder if any of us has the courage to try."[8]

That is a challenge, a challenge that requires looking at our students as future adults. In their book, *Boundaries with Kids*, Dr. Henry Cloud and Dr. John Townsend spend the majority of their first chapter stating a fact we all know, but often forget: children are future adults.[9] We often overlook the fact that the students in our ministries are future husbands, wives, fathers, mothers, politicians, authors, and who knows what else. Our ministry goals need to focus on aiming these future adults, these arrows, at the target of spiritual maturity and discipleship; the target that says to students and parents, "I don't

> Our ministry goals need to focus on aiming these future adults at the target.

want the kids in my ministry to be just any husband, wife, father, mother, politician, or author, but passionate, sold out, disciples of Christ who have built their lives on the rock and will eventually reproduce themselves spiritually."

This challenge will require an investment of your time and resources; however, George Barna challenges us, "The more diligent we are in these efforts, the more prodigious a harvest we will reap. Alternatively, the more lackadaisical we choose to be in our efforts to raise up children as moral and spiritual champions, the less healthy the Church and society of the future will be. The choice is yours."[10]

The aiming-at-nothing approach of youth ministry, the sporadic throwing of a curriculum here and programs there, is not working. Mike Yaconelli hit the nail squarely on the head; "we have to completely change the way we do youth ministry in America." Not only are we, for the most part, failing to produce spiritually mature disciples, in general we are losing our post-high-school students to church all together. George Barna's statistic on twentysomethings says, "A new study . . . shows that millions of twentysomething Americans—many of whom were active in churches during their teens—pass through their most formative adult decade while putting Christianity on the back-burner. Many twentysomethings are reversing course after having been active church attenders during their teenage years. As teenagers, more than half attended church each week and more than 4 out of 5 (81%) had ever gone to a Christian church. That means that from high school graduation to age 25 there is a 42% drop in weekly church attendance . . . That represents about 8,000,000 twentysomethings alive today who were active church-goers as teenagers but who will no longer be active in a church by their 30th birthday."[11]

> In general we are losing our post-high-school students to church all together.

If this hasn't convinced you, listen to what churched teens have to say about their church experience. Barna research shows that a mere "one-sixth of today's teens (17%) said their church experience had imparted core religious beliefs from the Bible. One out of every five teens (21%) said they did not learn anything of value during their time attending Christian churches."[12] Or better yet, take it from your own students. The first step in developing a formal Faith Development Plan (about which I will go into specific detail later) is evaluation. Evaluation is often painful, but necessary. Before you can map out where you want your students to go, you must determine where your students are. There are a variety of ways to evaluate your students, one of which is a basic Bible knowledge test.

After we evaluated our students with a basic Bible knowledge test, we were astounded at their lack of basic Bible truths. In addition, not one of our students (or sponsors) said they knew all the books of the Bible. While I don't believe for a minute that a person's faith will be judged on whether or not he or she knows all the books of the Bible, it is impossible to produce spiritually mature disciples of students who do not know basic facts about the Bible and their faith.

How Do We Fix This?

Establishing a formal Faith Development Plan in your church will ensure that you have a plan for where your students can be when they leave your program and how you are going to get them there. It is a paradigm shift—from shooting your God-entrusted arrows randomly, praying by chance they will hit something, to an intentional plan of action, a goal for shooting arrows toward a target. A Faith Development Plan is an instrument, a spiritual targeting system, which every Christian educator should use to aim his or her "arrows."

You may be questioning my naivete at this point. "Are you crazy enough to think that this type of plan will transform every one of my students into mature, disciples of Christ?" My answer is "yes." I believe that establishing a Faith Development Plan in our ministries will significantly increase the maturity of the disciples we release by graduation from our ministries. I believe having a specific, intentional plan of action for our students will be more effective than leaving our ministries to chance.

> To question a Faith Development Plan in this manner is the equivalent of asking your minister, "Do you really believe all the time and work you put into your sermon will convert every sinner this morning?" Or asking the dean of a week at camp, "Do you really think every unsaved child will come to Christ through this week of camp?"

A story is told of a small northern town which lost several of its youth to drowning one summer. A group of adults from the town came together and developed a threefold plan of action to help prevent the loss of any more of these young lives.

1) The town would offer free swimming lessons to anyone, child or adult, who could not swim. These swimming lessons would be offered at the local YMCA at various hours to accommodate all schedules.

2) The group worked with the town to offer tax credits to all residents installing fences or automated pool alarms around their in- and above-ground pools.

3) Lastly, the group worked on a plan to go into the local schools and educate students in regard to safety around lakes and ponds, specifically those that are frozen.

Each member of the group worked very hard to set an effective plan in motion. The group of adults revealed their threefold plan to a packed town hall one Monday night in October. Smiling from ear to ear with pride for their plan, the chairman of the committee asked the residents in attendance if they had any questions or comments.

One townsperson spoke up first, "Do you really think that putting this plan into action is going to save every resident from drowning? You and I both know that is a ridiculous goal!"

The chairman's face turned sullen and cold as he answered the pointed question. "Maybe all of you here tonight have the same question, 'Are we crazy enough to think that we can save every resident of this town from drowning?' Well, I have coached junior high football in this town for the past fifteen years. In that time we have lost five of my boys to drowning accidents; accidents that I believe could have been prevented. I plan to live in this town for the rest of my life, retire here, and watch my grandchildren grow up here. And I want to know that this town did everything it could to stop preventable accidents. We've lost too many lives already. We don't want to lose one more precious soul. This is our plan of action."

We've lost too many lives already. We don't want to lose one more precious soul.

Every student in our ministries is a precious soul, and our goal should be the same as our Heavenly Father's, "not wanting anyone to perish, but everyone to come to repentance" (2 Pet 3:9, NIV). Idealistic? Yes. Realistic? Absolutely.

As Christian educators our first goal for students must be

saving their souls. But after they have made that life-changing decision to accept Christ as their Lord and Savior, we should remember Mike Yaconelli's word, "longevity." We should fight with all our strength against our students becoming another "twentysomething" statistic, dropping off the radar of church activities. We need to live out our beliefs when we tell our students in no uncertain terms that Christianity does not end at the baptistery. It is just the beginning of their faith life. We need to communicate clearly to our students, "My goal for each of you is that you become spiritually mature disciples of Christ. My specific goal for each of you is to have such a passionate, personal relationship with Christ that you will naturally want to pass your faith on to others, others who will eventually pass on their faith and lead others to a life of discipleship. My dream is to become a spiritual great-great-grandparent." We need to be passionate about our goal to produce spiritually mature disciples of our students. This passion *demands* intentionality in our curriculum selections and intentionality in every aspect of the goal setting for our students' faith development.

So, Are You Ready for the Challenge?

Are you ready for the challenge? Are you ready to rethink your ministry approach? Are you ready to look at the students in your ministry as future adults, as arrows? Before you read another chapter in this book, consider spending some focused time in prayer. Take time to pray for transformation in your ministry, a transformation that changes your children's and youth ministry into a strong, healthy place where students grow into passionate disciples of Christ.

NOTES

1. Ken Davis, *Dynamic Communicator's Workshop*, Youth Specialties.

2. Andy Stanley and Stuart Hall, *The Seven Checkpoints* (West Monroe, LA: Howard Publishing, 2001).

3. James E. Collins and Jerry I. Porras, *Built to Last* (New York: HarperCollins, 1997).

4. http://www.dispatchmonthly.com/miami/miami_incident.html.

5. Diane Tracy, *Blue's Clues for Success: The 8 Secrets behind a Phenomenal Business* (Chicago: Dearborn Trade Publishing, 2002).

6. Bill Hull, *The Disciple Making Pastor* (Grand Rapids: Fleming H. Revell, 1998) 133.

7. Tracy, *Blues Clues*, 24.

8. http://www.youthspecialties.com/articles/Yaconelli/failure.php.

9. Dr. Henry Cloud and Dr. John Townsend, *Boundaries with Kids* (Grand Rapids: Zondervan, 1998).

10. George Barna, *Transforming Children into Spiritual Champions* (Ventura, CA: Regal Books, 2003) 42.

11. http://www.barna.org/FlexPage.aspx?Page=BarnaUpdate&BarnaUpdateID=149.

12. http://www.barna.org/FlexPage.aspx?Page=BarnaUpdate&BarnaUpdateID=143.

Chapter Two

ALIGNING THE SIGHT:
CHILDREN NEED A SOLID FOUNDATION

Most of us have gone through a faith crisis. I remember one of mine vividly. It was the summer before my freshman year of Bible college. I was working at a movie theater. It was the end of the night and time to count my drawer. My manager said he had heard I was going to Bible college. I told him that he had heard correctly. What proceeded out of his mouth was a blur, but I do remember the gist of it. "Did you know that Jesus Christ never lived? Did you know that the stories of the Old Testament including Jonah, Noah, and Adam and Eve are all folklore and I can prove it? Christianity is a farce." I distinctly remember keeping my head down and trying not to show my fear as he went on talking, but my mind was racing, "What is he talking about? He said he could prove it, and he seems like a pretty smart guy. I mean after all he is the manager of a movie theater!" I really began questioning my faith. Was my faith my own or my parents'? Did Jesus Christ ever live, or had I been brainwashed all these years?

What allowed me to survive this, and other faith crises throughout my life, is contained in this chapter. It goes beyond defending your faith; it is the crux of developing a formal Faith Development Plan. We need to aim our arrows toward the target of spiritual maturity, toward true discipleship of Christ. The results can be a foundation so deep our students will be equipped to withstand any faith crisis.

Our job as Christian educators is to give our students a strong foundation that will allow them to confidently and firmly withstand any storm or faith crisis coming their way. During Jesus' Sermon on the Mount, He told the story of the two foundations. "Therefore everyone who hears these words of Mine, and acts upon them, may be compared to a wise man, who built his house upon the rock. And the rain descended, and the floods came, and the winds blew, and burst against that house; and yet it did not fall, for it had been founded upon the rock. And everyone who hears these words of Mine, and does not act upon them, will be like a foolish man, who built his house upon the sand. And the rain descended, and the floods came, and the winds blew, and burst against that house; and it fell, and great was its fall" (Matt 7:24-27).

What is threatening the foundation in this passage? Storms. The storms are described in respect to floods, rain, and winds. Obviously these storms were very strong because the house on the sand fell, "and great was its fall."

A faith crisis can come in all shapes and sizes. It can come in the form of parents divorcing, the death or sickness of someone close, an unplanned pregnancy, or losing the trust of someone for whom we care deeply. For young people it can even materialize when they witness a "professing" Christian who turns out to be no different from the non-Christians they know. A faith crisis is a specific point in time in a person's life when he or she questions everything he or she believes. Unfortunately, it may happen more than once.

I recently spoke with a close friend and inquired why her husband is so adamant about not attending church. She told me a tragic story. Her husband had grown up in the church. His mother and father made sure he was present every time the doors were open. He attended every VBS and loved church camp. His family began having some problems and went to an elder in the church for counseling. The elder was very demeaning and condescending. He was brutally frank with the mother and father and blamed their family trouble on poor parenting skills. A few months into their family counseling, my friend's husband saw this elder at a video store renting pornographic movies. Her husband vowed he would never step foot in a church again. "I'm not going to a church where the people who judge me are bigger sinners than I am." Unfortunately, this type of scenario is very common.

Another faith crisis may be finding out a minister has had or is having an affair, discovering an elder has embezzled money from his or her company, or seeing a youth sponsor at a baseball game drinking beer and smoking. Perhaps a student loses a close friend or relative in an accident and the oft-asked question is raised, "Why would a loving God allow something like this to happen?"

Despite our desire to shelter our students from these storms, they will come. Just turn on CNN and read the news banner at the bottom of your screen. It is a nonstop message board of evil and strife happening around the world at any given moment: murders, kidnappings, bombings, abuse, corporate corruption, sexual immorality, and deception.

ACKNOWLEDGING YOU HAVE AN OPPONENT

Before we continue with the steps to fortify your students against these storms, we must stop to understand their origin. Who brings on these storms? Acknowledging and knowing your opponent is the necessary first step in any battle. In his book *Waking the Dead*, John Eldredge shares, "To live in ignorance of spiritual warfare is the most naive and dangerous thing a person can do. It's like skipping through the worst part of town, late at night, waving your wallet above your head. It's like walking into an al-Qaida training camp, wearing an 'I love the United States' T-shirt. It's like swimming with great white sharks, dressed as a wounded sea lion and smeared with blood. And let me tell you something: you don't escape spiritual warfare simply because you choose not to believe it exists or because you refuse to fight it."[1]

In a strange set of circumstances while attending an Easter Pageant at a large church in Fort Wayne, Indiana, I found myself with my six-month-old daughter in a cast room off the stage area. After arriving at the pageant an usher quickly informed me that children under five were not allowed in the sanctuary. I was invited to join the cast members, watching the pageant on closed circuit television sets in a room directly off the stage.

As I was sitting watching the pageant on the televisions, I noticed something odd out of the corner of my eye. Coming into the room were several scary looking demons. I tried not to stare as they chatted and laughed. After several minutes one of the demons came and sat behind me. Before I knew it, this demon was playing peek-a-boo with my daughter. I smiled nervously at the demon. Several more minutes went by when the demon asked me, "Do you mind if I hold her?" Lying through my teeth, I answered, "No, I don't mind." More time went by and the demon asked, "Do you mind if I take her over with the other cast members?" (She meant the other *demons*!) Again I lied, "Sure, no problem." I watched very intently as the demons fussed and played with my infant daughter.

Eventually the head demon himself, Satan, came into the cast room. Apparently Satan loves babies! Satan was delighted to see Sydney in the cast room. He went over to the other demons and held her hand, smiled at her and talked baby-talk to her. Within seconds Satan was holding my daughter. At that point I was forced to stand up and briskly walk across the room. I distinctly remember saying, with some humor of course, "Satan, I'll take my child back now!"

Christian educator, please believe me when I tell you that Satan would like nothing better than to have your students in his hands. First Peter 5:8 tells us that the devil "prowls about like a roaring lion, seeking someone to devour." Note he did not say, "seeking someone to get in his teeth and play around with for a while." No, he says the devil is "seeking someone to *devour*," demolish, and destroy. John 10:10 tells us, "The thief comes only to steal, and kill, and destroy" (NIV).

Ephesians 6:11 says, "Put on the full armor of God, that you may be able to stand firm against the schemes of the devil. For our struggle is not against flesh and blood, but against the rulers, against the powers, against the world forces of this darkness, against the spiritual forces of wickedness in the heavenly places . . . in addition to all, taking up the shield of faith with which you will be able to extinguish all the flaming missiles of the evil one." What these verses promise is that the devil is "prowling around" with the specific intent to "kill and destroy us" by launching "flaming missiles" of evil.

Erwin McManus tells a story of an interesting encounter he had with his son one evening. After coming home from a week of church camp his son was uncharacteristically afraid to have the lights turned out. After pushing his son as to the reason for his fears he finally came to the conclusion his son must have heard about Satan and his demons at camp.

"Now, I thought, 'Man! This is why I need to send him to a good pagan, secular camp!' Because if I sent him to a good secular camp, they tell him ghost stories and I could say, 'There are no such things as ghosts.' And he could say, 'Oh, daddy. Go ahead and turn off the light.' But what am I supposed to say? 'Yes, son, there are demons. They are everywhere.'

"I was so upset I didn't know what to do. And he said, 'Daddy, daddy, daddy, pray that I would be safe. Pray that I would be safe.' And I looked at him and said, 'Aaron, I will not pray that God will make you safe.' I said, 'I am going to pray that God will make you dangerous. So dangerous that when you enter the room all the demons of hell will run in fear.' He goes, 'Okay, but pray that I would be really, really dangerous, daddy!'"[2]

What a tremendous testimony that drives home this point: we cannot tell our students they will be safe in this storm-filled world, but we can train them to be dangerous. We are at war. Satan is constantly attacking you and your students. He would love for you to have a lukewarm youth ministry, growing lukewarm Christians who grow to be lukewarm spouses and lukewarm parents. He would dance with joy to see a student go through your ministry and abandon the church all together. It gives him absolute pleasure to see your students, with eighteen years of church under their belt, fall to a faith crisis or storm. He would high-five his demons if your ministry turned out spiritually mature Christians who never passed on their faith or reproduced themselves. And most importantly he would love for you to shoot your arrows anywhere but at a target. He does not want you to develop a solid Faith Development Plan because he knows your goal would be victory for the Kingdom. He *loves* to see you spinning your wheels in youth ministry. Don't let him have that joy!

UNDERSTANDING THE FAITH TABLE AND IMPLEMENTING IT IN YOUR FAITH DEVELOPMENT PLAN

THE FAITH TABLE

The following table is the foundation of the Faith Development Plan. The tabletop represents a student's faith. The six legs underneath the table represent different areas that support a student's faith. These six areas are: Bible knowledge, family, experience, feeling, science, and history. The Faith Development Plan makes use of of all six of these legs. The purpose of this table is to create a foundation for your students that will allow them not only to survive a storm, faith crisis, or any attack by Satan, but to be spiritually mature disciples of Jesus Christ. We must be extremely intentional with the limited time we have with our students. That time must be spent equipping them with the tools to withstand a faith crisis.

BIBLE KNOWLEDGE

Bible knowledge is the first leg for an obvious reason: knowledge of the Bible, or an understanding of God's Word given to us, is absolutely essential for any Christian's faith. Colossians 3:16 says, "Let the word of Christ richly dwell within you." Bible knowledge is central to a student's faith in God; but frankly, the church relies on it too heavily. Our young people need to be lifelong students of the Bible. They need to be challenged in daily devotions and serious study of scriptural content. However, the Christian faith needs to stand on more than Bible knowledge. Maybe when you picked up this book you thought to yourself, "This is basic scope and sequence. Our curriculum provides this for birth through high school. I don't need a Faith Development Plan." A Faith Development Plan is comprehensive, and Bible knowledge, or curriculum scope and sequence, while crucial to a growing disciple, is only one piece of the foundation.

Our young people need to be lifelong students of the Bible.

Let's take a look at students who have only Bible knowledge supporting their Christian faith table. At some point they may run into a person like my movie theater manager who could kick their Bible-knowledge leg out from under their table. They are at the risk of falling. They will fail their faith crisis like so many other students. Any table standing on one leg is performing a risky balancing act. It is not stable.

The Bible knowledge leg can also become shaky when a student starts to think about the stories in the Bible with superficial logic. I mean, come on, Jonah was really in the belly of a big fish and then spit out? That is really unbelievable. Students start looking around the church and saying to themselves, "These people are crazy for believing this stuff! It just couldn't happen." Such questioning is a natural part of human development. But without intervention at such times, a student can dismiss the Bible altogether as unreliable history.

As Christian educators we can be slaves to curriculum. We rarely think about changing publishers. We order faithfully every quarter or, better yet, have a standing order with the local bookstore. How many times have we visited a classroom with this message for a teacher, "Here's your curriculum, Karen. If you have any questions, give me a call"? It's a no-brainer. Our students are learning whatever comes next in the curriculum when half the time we don't even know what that is.

George Barna speaks to this very point in his book, *Transforming Children into Spiritual Champions*: "I also have discovered that most churches are interested in acquiring a turnkey curriculum—resources that require minimal administration by the church, minimal preparation time by the teacher, minimal prior knowledge by the students and the provision of all the ideas, materials and directions needed to fill the entire class time."[3]

He goes on to share findings from his research, "We also learned that while many churches feel vindicated in their approach by the fact that many of their children can identify the basic contours of the stories and can describe some details related to the key characters, the young people are clueless regarding the fundamental principles and lessons to be drawn from those narratives."[4]

We sadly found Barna's research to be true in our ministry. After evaluating our junior and senior high students for our Faith Development Plan with a basic Bible knowledge test, we discovered something alarming. The highest points scored on the tests were in the area of Bible knowledge. Some of the Bible knowledge questions required students to match the Bible character with a phrase. Most students could match every pair: Jonah—belly of the whale, Noah—ark builder, Joseph—colorful coat wearer, Adam—may not have had a belly button, Daniel— survived the lion's den, Jacob—twin brother to Esau, Moses— led the Israelites out of Egypt, Matthew—former tax-collector, Stephen—stoned to death, Cain—killed his brother Abel. For the most part, the students knew all the basics to the stories they had heard over the years.

But when we asked our students other questions such as, "If you committed a sin and died, would you go to heaven?" "If you died right now, would you go to heaven?" "Which of the following best describes your church? Protestant, Atheist, Catholic, Calvinist." "If you had a friend who wanted to be a Christian, could you tell them how and give Scripture to back it up?" The answers were alarming. Almost all the students answered incorrectly, including those who had been Christians for several years.

Our conclusion? Most students in our ministry were only receiving a narrow scope of information from their time at church. Based on our experience and Barna's research, it seems that the youth in most congregations are hearing the same stories over and over again with no more depth from one time to the next. They are not going any deeper than the surface of these stories.

If our youth ministries are only focusing on Bible knowledge, we are doing our students a tremendous disservice. When they leave our programs, they may know all the books of the Bible, every story in the Bible, the ten commandments, the twelve disciples, the major and minor prophets, the twelve tribes of Israel, the plan of salvation, the Beatitudes, the fruits of the spirit, the 23rd Psalm, and 50 verses by memory. They may have even been baptized and have repeated the good confession in front of the whole church, but if this is all they know of their faith, they are balancing the tabletop of their faith on only one leg.

FAMILY

The second leg of this table is family, a leg some students will have and others will not. Students with a solid family leg under their table will be more dangerous. We've mentioned that statistically we only have

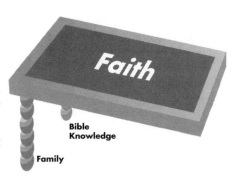

students 1% of their time. But often, spiritual training of children has been placed on the shoulders of the church. This is the shopping mall mentality for parents: "I take Johnny to school for his social, emotional, and cognitive development. I take him to soccer for his physical development, and I take him to church for his spiritual development." This mentality reduces parents to chauffeurs, chefs, and housekeepers. The simple fact is that in all my research I have never found a verse in the Bible that supports the mentality that a child's spiritual training rests solely on the church.

In fact, the biblical mandate is for parents to be the spiritual trainers in their home. Deuteronomy 11:18-20 beautifully teaches, "You shall therefore impress these words of mine on your heart and on your soul; and you shall bind them as a sign on your hand, and they shall be as frontals on your forehead. And you shall teach them to your sons, talking of them when you sit in your house and when you walk along the road and when you lie down and when you rise up. And you shall write them on the doorposts of your house." Ephesians 6:4 says, "And, fathers, do not provoke your children to anger; but bring them up in the discipline and instruction of the Lord."

The Scriptures are very clear: raising children in the ways of the Lord is the responsibility of the parent. George Barna explains a key which parents can use to begin raising spiritual champions, "One of the key elements . . . is the acknowledgment that the spiritual development of children is first and foremost the responsibility of parents and that a church is best poised to assist rather than lead in that process. . . . In other words to equip and reinforce rather than lead in this dimension. As the director of children's ministry of one congregation put it, 'Our goal is to become the greatest friend and best support a parent has ever had.'"[5]

However, some churches do not apply these commands the Bible lays out for parents. They send a very specific message to parents, verbally or otherwise: "Just leave your child here with us and leave the Bible teaching to the experts." Barna speaks frankly about such churches. "When a church—intentionally or not—assumes a family's responsibilities in the arena of spiritually nurturing children, it fosters an unhealthy dependence upon the church to relieve the family of its biblical responsibility. . . . Thus, a majority of churches are actually guilty of perpetuating an unhealthy and unbiblical process wherein the church usurps the role of the family and creates an unfortunate and sometimes exclusive dependence upon the church for a child's spiritual nourishment."[6]

The ideal for the students in our ministries is a tandem philosophy of parent and church. If we desire to create a fertile soil in which our students' faith can grow, we need to send messages to the parents: "The church serves as a reinforcement of what should be taking place in the home, not a replacement." This next quote should be typed, printed, and hung on the walls in your offices. Barna says, "The beauty of this process is that when it is working well you cannot tell who is really leading—the church or the parents. There is such a symbiotic relationship between the two that their progress seems carefully coordinated—which, of course, it often is. The result is a powerful two-fisted punch that has a synergistic impact on the children."[7]

If you are serious about making your students dangerous, I propose that you spend at least 50% of your weekly time training, communicating with, encouraging, and supporting the parents of your students. Train the parents to take the spiritual reins in their home and make raising godly children a lifestyle. The Deuteronomy passage instructs parents to talk about godly things with their children when they are sitting in the house, walking on the road, lying down or waking up. When we consider this passage, there isn't much more a parent does during the day. The spiritual training of children is a lifestyle, not an extracurricular activity like dance, soccer, basketball, horseback riding, camp, or Boy Scouts.

Some of the points in the Faith Development Plan are designed to strengthen this paradigm shift. For example, if we want our students to begin daily devotions, our best strategy is to get the parents on board with family devotions first. Children model their parents' behavior. If we decide not to train, communicate with, encourage, and support the parents of our students, we may be spinning our wheels. One percent is not a lot of time. The church that devotes itself to raising up godly parents will be placing a strong leg under their students' faith tables.

The church that devotes itself to raising up godly parents will be placing a strong leg under their students' faith tables.

Strengthening the family leg under your students' faith table also requires presenting them with God's design for their families. It involves clearly defining God's desire for each member of the family. It calls for teaching your students the scripturally stated roles for members of the family and teaching God's view on divorce. As future adults we want them to be godly husbands, wives, sons, daughters, mothers, and fathers. This important concept will be presented in greater detail throughout the proposed Faith Development Plan in the following chapters.

> **What about the kids whose parents do not attend or do not believe? Extra time should be spent with them. These students have a hard road ahead of them because they are missing a leg. They need our time, prayers, support, and encouragement.**

EXPERIENCE

Do you know of someone who came to Christ through an experience? Perhaps it was at a revival meeting, a week at church camp, a youth conference, or possibly the sad events of September 11th. Seeing a sinner come to salvation through an experience is an experience in itself. You will often see brokenness, humility, and genuine surrender to Christ.

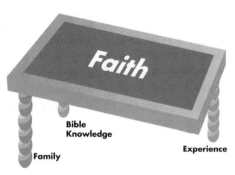

Experience is a powerfully important leg for our students' faith tables. It can be something they have done, some place they have gone, something they have seen which solidifies their faith or stabilizes their faith table. It is a memory they can recall or replay in their mind as they are facing a faith crisis. It is a specific point in time they remember so vividly they tell themselves, "I saw God at work. It was real. It had to be a God thing."

Proverbs 22:6 says, "Train up a child in the way he should go, Even when he is old he will not depart from it." Charles Swindoll sheds some light on the term "train" in this Scripture passage. He says it is similar to "a Hebrew midwife's actions as she dipped her fingers into the juice of dates and began to massage the newly-born infant's palate so that he would learn to suck."[8] This image of massaging the palate to create a desire for nourishment is something all Christian educators should desire to emulate. We must strive to create an insatiable desire for spiritual matters in our students' lives. And this very desire is brought about by providing activities inside and outside the church building so they may experience God.

This past year we began a new ministry with our junior and senior high school students called t-tag. T-tag stands for "testimony tag" and is played on the computer. We first sent out an e-mail invitation to all students and sponsors and also announced the game in class. After formulating our players we sent them the rules for the game. Everyone playing would have a list of players. When one person was tagged everyone would know. That person would have one week to send their testimony to me, the host, for my review and to let me know who they wanted to tag from the list. After I had reviewed the testimony, I would send the player's name and testimony out to everyone. Everyone had to be tagged once before the "game" started over.

To be honest I fully expected the students to struggle with this whole idea. I imagined myself e-mailing them after a week with a message like, "Hey, just wanted to remind you that you were tagged in our t-tag game, and I need to hear from you soon." Quite the opposite. The kids were so excited about sharing their testimonies we were averaging about four a week. And the testimonies these kids shared were unbelievable. I finally decided to ask one of our elders to join the game as an observer. He mentioned to me several times how impressed he was with these students' testimonies and their faith.

We really stressed one thing with this t-tag game: God is working in your life. God is working in the lives of the people around you. You need to start realizing all the wonderful things He is doing and acknowledge His goodness. This is how you experience God.

What can Christian educators do to strengthen the experience leg of their students' faith tables? One way is through servant evangelism projects, where youth filter into the community providing a service such as free window washing. When the recipients ask if they can pay the students, they answer, "No, like the grace of God, this is free. We're with the First Church of Smithville and here is our address. If you are ever looking for a church home, please come visit us." Through this simple activity your youth will see changed lives and share unbelievable testimonies.

Another great way to provide a faith-building, life-changing experience for your students is through mission work. My eleven-year-old son just came back from a mission trip to Uruguay where he helped renovate a church and minister to low income children in a Christian preschool. When he came home, the first thing he said was, "When are we going back?" I believe strongly this is the age to get your students interested in mission work. If we wait until high school, it gets harder to sell them on the benefits. Throughout the Faith Development Plan you will see suggestions for mission trips at different ages. It is imperative to offer family mission trips for all ages. If mission trips are life changing, which is how they are often described, why wouldn't parents want to experience this with their children? It will undoubtedly strengthen the family leg, too.

Often the church is guilty of limiting students' faith development to the walls of the church. If we want our students' faith to grow, we must be willing to get them out of the church building as often as possible. Failure to do so fosters the mentality in your students that Christianity is only for the church building. By getting your students out of the church and into different areas of service, they will inevitably see the power of prayer and experience God. They will see answers to prayers that can only be a "God thing," see God through people, and hear what God is doing in everyday people's lives. Actually witnessing the power of prayer and experiencing God's hand is essential to faith development. It is very hard for people to discredit a God that they have seen move.

> By getting your students out of the church and into different areas of service, they will inevitably see the power of prayer and experience God.

Experience is a powerful way of strengthening our students' relationships with God. However, it is also something on which to keep a watchful eye. For example, how many times have we seen an adult, teenager, or young child decide to make the choice for salvation through a powerful experience and days, weeks, or months later forget it all?

Large teen conferences are an example of this phenomenon. A powerful speaker comes to the stage and delivers a challenging message right on the students' level. As he moves through the message, he begins challenging the students to make decisions. As the speaker concludes, the lights fade, the music starts, and the students begin filing down the aisles toward the front. Those left in the seating area look around, to the left, the right, behind them . . . everyone is gone. What should they do? They can't go forward to accept Christ. They're already a Christian. "What to do? What to do? Think fast! Ah, I'll recommit my life." And the student hurries down the aisle toward the counselors in the front.

After the music stops, when the students are back home away from their friends and the magic of the convention center or campgrounds has worn off, they forget a commitment was ever made. I have even seen a broken teen go forward to accept Christ, decide to begin attending church regularly, and, after talking to the youth minister about her decision, arrange for a baptism the following Sunday. Unfortunately the teen never followed through. To the youth minister's astonishment this teenager not only failed to contact anyone, when contacted she replied, "Oh yeah, right! I guess I just forgot." No one at the church has seen or heard from her since. Once she was out of the experience, she fell. She accepted the call to salvation on the leg of experience before anyone had the chance to stabilize her table of faith, so it fell.

You may be wondering if I feel such events are wrong. Of course not. In large convention or camp situations it is impossible for the staff to follow each convert home, making sure they get into a small group, begin daily devotions, and grow in their faith. Their goal is presenting the gospel, planting the seed. It is a parent's, the youth minister's, the youth sponsor's, or the Christian educator's job to follow up with these students and ensure these seeds are watered and growing.

It is, however, tragically wrong for the staff of such events to play on students' emotions and purposefully aim to stir them into coming down the aisle or make a decision without a plan for follow up. If the staff's goal is to partner with the adult sponsors in a seed-planting, seed-watering situation, the results can be astronomically powerful and the Kingdom will no doubt be advanced from their efforts.

FEELING

If you came to know God through a feeling, you no doubt realize that strong emotions can be overwhelming. But for those who never moved on in their spiritual development, never added any legs under their table, those people will inevitably be disappointed when the feeling goes away.

I was talking to a friend recently who is a young Christian. His conversion definitely fell under the feeling category. When he started going to our church, it was because of the "feeling" he received when he heard the preaching. He hesitantly confessed he was leaving our church.

His reason? "I just don't have that feeling I used to have when I first came here."

Christians who are balancing on the feeling leg are on shaky ground and will fall. Feelings are unpredictable. Feelings change from one day to another. Feelings get hurt. And it is not fair for the minister of any church to bear the pressure of sustaining the congregation's feelings. It is an impossible goal for him to achieve.

The feeling leg is built and strengthened by allowing your students to feel God's presence. If your students' plan to leave home at some point, which their parents pray they will feel inclined to do, there will come a time they find themselves alone. Loneliness is a powerful feeling, yet Christians are never alone. If students have made a decision for Christ, they have the Holy Spirit, the Comforter. Our students need to know how to tap into His blessing and power.

I believe one of the saddest predicaments we find long-time church attenders facing is this very idea of living their entire Christian lives without ever "tapping into the Holy Spirit." How tragic for the ninety-year-old woman who finally realized she had electricity in her house for the previous fifty years. Oh, the things she could have accomplished with that powerful source. How tragic for an eighty-year-old man, lying on his deathbed, feeling the comfort of God's Holy Spirit around his frail body, turning to his son and saying, "So, this is what the comfort of the Holy Spirit feels like!" Oh, the things he could have accomplished with that powerful source.

Unfortunately, there are students and adults in your congregation who do not fully comprehend the fact they are Holy Spirit-filled vessels. They have missed the verses in the Bible which call us to put off the "old man" and put on the "new man." "Therefore if any man is in Christ, he is a new creature; the old things passed away; behold, new things have come" (2 Cor 5:17). Once we have emptied our sinful vessels at conversion, we are to be Holy Spirit filled. We have the power of the Holy Spirit as a guide and comforter. What a powerful source!

If you are at a point in your ministry where you cannot decide what to teach next, stop. Take the time to teach your students about the Holy Spirit and how they can tap into this Source living in their hearts, minds, and spirits. Share testimonies with them of how the Holy Spirit has guided or comforted you.

Some of my strongest leadings from the Holy Spirit have come in the late evening, or should I say early morning, through sleep deprivation. One night while pleading with God for some sleep, I asked Him simply to tell me what it was He wanted from me. I heard a clear voice, "I want you to write a book." I laughed to myself, "I can't write a book. I'm not a writer." When I began questioning what the topic of this "book" would be, another clear voice came to me, "Write a book about developing a Faith Development Plan." It *was* a passion of mine and I *had* done research on the subject, but again I was not a writer. After sending away to different publishers for applications, I set all the material aside assuring myself the voice I heard was just a product of my imagination.

One month later I was teaching a week-long intensive youth ministry course at a Christian college in Lansing, Michigan. On my last day at the school through a series of unexplainable coincidences and blunders I was invited to sit in on a meeting with the college faculty. My jaw dropped to the floor when I realized the reason for the meeting; a recruiter from a Christian publishing company was at the school looking for writers. How odd. I had never even met a person who worked for a Christian publisher.

Experiences like this give us a wonderful picture of God sitting in heaven on His throne with a conductor's baton. He is looking down at the earth with a concentrated smile. He has just sent His Holy Spirit to earth to orchestrate events in a musical fashion only He can pull off. He is waiting for instruments to play through, and when they listen to Him, He sits back on His throne smiling and directing and listening to the extraordinary swell of perfect harmony while He watches His Kingdom advance.

One of the greatest ways for your students to feel God is through quality worship. This is the time our students are invited to approach the throne of God. I once heard a worship leader lead a congregation in worship by prefacing the time with these words, "I want you to imagine that right in this sanctuary, up near the ceiling, is a large gold throne. On that throne is God, and sitting at His right hand is Jesus Christ. Lift your voices to Him now and praise Him for His power, His goodness and His never-ending love." I have never forgotten how simply that worship leader led me to the throne of God that day. It has forever changed my worship.

Throughout the Faith Development Plan you are encouraged to seek ways for your students to participate in opportunities to "feel God's presence," to "tap into" the Source they have in the Holy Spirit.

You are encouraged to seek ways for your students to participate in opportunities to tap into the Source.

SCIENCE

Did you know the earth weighs 6.588 billion trillion tons, its rate of rotation is precisely 23 hours, 56 minutes, and 4.09 seconds and its angle of planetary axis a perfect 23.5 degrees? Did you know if the earth were any closer or farther away from the moon we could not survive? Did you

know that every day the earth experiences over 10,000 thunderstorms whose powers are equivalent to a 100-kiloton nuclear bomb?[9]

How about the uniqueness of animals? Did you know "each animal has been designed by God with the abilities and physical attributes necessary to survive the challenges and demands of its everyday existence?"[10] The spider's silky webs are more durable than the fibers used in a bullet proof vest and are stronger than steel of equal weight. The bald eagle uses its razor sharp talons and its eyesight, eight times keener than humans, to spot a trout from 200 feet in the air, while flying at a rate of 50 miles per hour. Pacific salmon, who range in weight from 2 to 100 pounds, ascend waterfalls up to ten feet high to complete their circle of life and migrate to the exact waters where they were born.[11] These are just some of the awesome ways God has uniquely and powerfully designed the animals of His world.

And what about the human body? Did you know that only seconds after you were conceived, your height, eye and hair color, and capacity to think, learn, and speak were determined? When you were no larger than a drop of water, your heart beat for the first time and has remained constant since that time. Did you know that your "body's entire outer layer of skin is exchanged every two to four weeks? Your skeletal system is completely regenerated over a twelve-month period. And regardless of its purpose, before wearing out, a cell reproduces itself to exact specification." In fact your body is constantly regenerating; however, your uniqueness remains constant. You are receiving new "parts," yet look just the same.[12]

The complexity of the human body is a miracle. Sadly, "we go about our lives, for the most part, seldom acknowledging the spectacular reality of who and what we really are."[13] We are miracles of God's creation. We are walking, talking miracles of God. This intricate machine we call our body is simply further proof of God's existence, power, and love for his children.

All of these areas show God as an Almighty, Supreme Creator, Designer, and Sustainer. Werner von Braun, the German rocket scientist instrumental in America's space program, said it beautifully, "One cannot be exposed to the law and order of the universe without concluding that there must be design and purpose behind it all. Through a closer look at creation we ought to gain a better knowledge of the Creator."[14] Sir Isaac Newton penned these words, "This most elegant system of suns and planets could only arise from the purpose and sovereignty of an intelligent and mighty being. He rules them all as the sovereign Lord of all things."[15] This is not the science that most of your students will learn in public school. This is the Science that acknowledges God as the Supreme Orchestrator of creation.

From the law and order of the universe we conclude that there must be design and purpose and by looking closer we ought to gain a better knowledge of the Creator.

The real fact is there is no science apart from God. As our students learn about godly science, it will change the way they think about God. Introducing your students to godly science *will* solidify and ultimately change the way they worship. Picture if you will David as a shepherd boy. He is lying on his back staring in awe into the expansive sky. Listen to what he knows of God's creation and how it affects his worship.

> "Bless the Lord, O my soul! O Lord my God, Thou art very great; Thou art clothed with splendor and majesty. Covering Thyself with light as with a cloak, Stretching out heaven like a tent curtain. He lays the beams of His upper chambers in the waters; He makes the clouds His chariot; He walks upon the wings of the wind; He makes the winds His messengers, Flaming fire His ministers. He established the earth upon its foundations, So that it will not totter forever and ever. Thou didst cover it with the deep as with a garment; The waters were standing above the mountains. At Thy rebuke they fled; At the sound of Thy thunder they hurried away. The mountains rose; the valleys sank down to the place which Thou didst establish for them. Thou didst set a boundary that they may not pass over; That they may not return to cover the earth. He sends forth springs in the valleys; They flow between the mountains; They give drink to every beast of the field; the wild donkeys quench their thirst" (Ps 104:1-11).

David obviously had a great appreciation for God's creation and was able to express that admiration through song and prayer. Look how it affected his worship of the Creator.

Our students must be taught simple facts such as our Creator made nature, animals, and the human body with absolute perfection. (And that all powerful God wants to have a personal relationship with them. What an honor!) There is no reasonable explanation for creation beyond that of a Divine Creator. Appreciation of this fact will solidify the faith of our students.

HISTORY

The last leg of the table is history or, as we say in our house, "His story." The History of Christianity web site promotes Christianity as a faith based on historical fact. There is no history apart from God. He was before history, and He

will be after history is done. "History of Christianity—did it all really happen? At first glance, the history of Christianity's origin may seem like nothing more than a fairy tale. Many feel that it's just implausible, and even intellectually dishonest, for people living in the 21st century to believe that these events actually took place. However, the Christian faith, unlike any other religion, hinges on historical events, including one of pivotal importance. If Jesus Christ died and never rose to life, then Christianity is a myth or a fraud. In I Corinthians 15:14 Paul exhorts his readers to grab hold of this central truth, that 'if Christ be not risen, then is our preaching vain, and your faith is also vain.'"[16]

Our students need to learn how history supports, corroborates, and verifies the Bible. Do your students know that there is archaeological evidence supporting much of the Old and New Testament writings? There is an abundance of historical evidence supporting the Scriptures, and our students need to know about it. Exposing them to these facts will help to solidify their faith.

Our students should also know the history of Christianity and the history of their fellowship. This information is particularly helpful to a high school graduate, such as Justin, who needs to choose a church away from home. Knowing such key figures in church history including, but not in any way limited to, St. Augustine, Martin Luther, John Calvin, and Alexander Campbell will help your students better appreciate their Christian heritage. Our students should know of historical figures who made significant differences in the Christian faith such as Billy Sunday, Corrie Ten Boom, and Billy Graham. The testimonies of these historical figures are shining examples of how God works through willing vessels. Most importantly they need to know the history of the Bible writings in general. They need to know how the books were chosen and other details about the forming of the canon. This information will eventually assist them in defending their faith. If we do not present this information to them, where will they learn it?

How Did I Survive?

How did I survive my faith crisis? I had strong legs. I knew my Bible (**Bible knowledge**) and how to defend it. I had strong Christian parents (**family**) who looked at spiritual training as a lifestyle. My parents had provided me with **experiences** where I witnessed the power of prayer and saw God move. My youth sponsors had provided me with conventions and retreats where real worship (**feeling**) took place, and I saw the Holy Spirit working in my life. I knew there was **historical** proof to support the Scriptures, and through an appreciation of God's world (**science**), I saw His unmistakable design.

LEGLESS

Can our students survive without one of these legs? Absolutely. I have seen Christians live their lives standing on one, or even two, legs; however, the Christians I have witnessed with the strongest unwavering faith have all six legs in place. A successful Faith Development Plan works against any temptation we might face to teach the same information and Bible stories over and over without thought or regard to where we want our students to end up. A plan like this forces us to set intentional goals for the 1% of time we spend with them.

Before you go on, consider again the prayer challenge at the beginning of this book.
1) Pray again that God will speak to you during the reading of this book.
2) Pray that the Holy Spirit will show you the direction you should take with your youth ministry in establishing a Faith Development Plan for your students.
3) Pray for your students. Pray that through your Faith Development Plan they will become dangerous, able to withstand any faith crisis that comes their way.

Notes

1. John Eldredge, *Waking the Dead* (Nashville: Thomas Nelson, 2003) 152.

2. Erwin McMannus, National Youth Leaders Convention, 2003.

3. George Barna, *Transforming Children*, 39.

4. Ibid., 110.

5. Ibid., 98.

6. Ibid., 81.

7. Ibid., 99.

8. Charles Swindoll, "Know Your Child," *You and Your Child* (audiocassette series) (Fullerton, CA: First Evangelical Free Church, 1973) Tape 1.

9. *The Wonders of God's Creation: Planet Earth*, A Moody Institute of Science Presentation (Chicago: Moody Institute of Science).

10. *The Wonders of God's Creation: Animal Kingdom* (Chicago: Moody Institute of Science).

11. Ibid.

12. *The Wonders of God's Creation: Human Life* (Chicago: Moody Institute of Science).

13. Ibid.

14. *The Wonders of God's Creation: Planet Earth*.

15. Ibid.

16. http://www.history-of-christianity.com/.

Chapter Three

TAKING A SOLID STANCE:
A FIRM UNDERSTANDING OF THE GOAL

*Where do you want your students to be by the time they graduate,
and how are you going to get them there?*

During the organizational stages of the Faith Development Plan
for your ministry there are some important questions to ask and concepts to consider. These are key ideas to hold in the back of your
mind throughout the process.

1. CONVICTION

Each of us is well advised to ask ourselves an important question
before organizing a Faith Development Plan: "Am I convicted to
begin a Faith Development Plan in my ministry?" If you are not convicted to implement such a plan at this point in the book, I want to
encourage you to stop now and reread the first two chapters. Too
often, Christian educators read or hear of a new philosophy in ministry and jump on the bandwagon before experiencing any sense of
conviction. **Please do not mistake the conviction to try something
new in your ministry with the conviction to develop and implement a Faith Development Plan**. At the end of
the book, specific, field-tested and practice-proven
step-by-step instructions are provided for anyone
who chooses to successfully organize and implement a Faith Development Plan. The first step is
having the individual and personal conviction *yourself* such a plan should be in place.

> Please do not mistake
> the conviction to try
> something new with the
> conviction to implement a
> Faith Development Plan.

2. ARROWS UP

Hebrews 6:1 gives us a perfect example of the need for your arrows, or students, to be moving up, "Therefore leaving the elementary teaching about the Christ, let us press on to maturity, not laying again a foundation of repentance from dead works and of faith toward God, of instruction about washings, and laying on of hands, and the resurrection of the dead, and eternal judgment." How many times do we teach the same things over and over, recycle the curriculum or have the children tell us the stories? This Scripture is clear. Once the foundation has been laid, we need to move on to other matters of spiritual maturity.

First Corinthians 3:1-4 says, "And I, brethren, could not speak to you as to spiritual men, but as to men of flesh, as to babes in Christ. I gave you milk to drink, not solid food; for you were not yet able to receive it. Indeed, even now you are not yet able . . ." Are you still giving your students milk when they are ready for meat? Many of the students in your youth ministry want it and are ready for it. Several of our high school students recently attended a convention in Michigan. After looking at the list of electives offered for the students they looked at their sponsor, Lori, in disbelief. "We already know all this stuff. Can we go to the adult elective with you?" They went to the adult elective on discipleship and couldn't stop talking about the information all week. Lori told me, "They didn't want that milk stuff; they wanted meat!"

You might be familiar with the five areas of development: physical, emotional, social, cognitive, and spiritual. Now picture this scenario: you are teaching a high school Sunday school class when a six-foot, sixteen-year-old comes in with a pacifier in his mouth. He is hanging on his mom's leg, crying, begging her not to leave him in your class. He cannot walk, so he crawls in. He pulls himself up to the cookies and begins shoving all the cookies in his mouth, crumbs raining out. When you ask him his name, he says, "Tom, but don't ask me to spell it, I don't know how."

Picture this scenario: a six-foot, sixteen-year-old comes in to class with a pacifier in his mouth.

What would be your initial observations of this child? Is he delayed physically? Yes, he is sixteen, and he can't walk. Is he socially delayed? Yes, he can't seem to eat properly and still sucks on a pacifier. Is he emotionally delayed? Yes, he has some attachment issues. Is he cognitively delayed? Yes, he can't spell his first name (which is only three letters). Are you worried about this child? Uh, *yes*! Yes, he is not where a sixteen-year-old should be developmentally.

Think now of how many students you have in your ministry who are spiritual two year olds. They are doing well in four of the five areas, but are severely lacking in spiritual development. They have been in the church since birth, maybe sixteen years, and still don't know who wrote the Pentateuch. (Your students might be one of several students who would answer, "Penta-teuch? I think my friend has their latest CD!") Are you worried about them? You should be. We can do more than worry, though. We can offer them a ministry focused on a commitment to their spiritual development.

George Barna states, "I have been discouraged to discover that most American adults—including most parents—see spiritu-al development of children as a value-added proposition rather than the single most important aspect of children's development. You are invited to reconsider the priority of spiritual growth in the lives of children and to accept it as being more important than intellectual, physical and emotional development."[1]

What would happen if we refused to say "mission accom-plished" at the point where students walk down the aisle, con-fess their sin, and are buried in baptism? Instead, we encouraged students to "use their new commitments to Christ as a launching pad for a lifelong quest to become individuals who are completely sold out—emotionally, intellectually, physically, spiritually—to the Son of God."[2]

> What would happen if we refused to say "mission accomplished" at the point of salvation?

The "arrows up" concept is key to your Faith Development Plan and should be the backbone of the goal for your targets. When deciding which lessons or activities to implement with your students, you must constantly ask yourself, "During their time at this age level, did I bring them significantly closer to my goal of producing spiritually mature disciples of Christ by the time they graduate?"

3. REPETITION

Repetition seems contradictory to the "arrows up" theory, but repetition in this sense is brought to light in an air of expectancy. When my son was four years old, we enrolled him in a private Christian preschool. After months on the waiting list we finally had the opportunity to visit his prospective class. The teacher, Mrs. Ross, spoke very confidently of how our son, by the time he graduated from preschool, would know these facts: all the Presidents of the United States in order, all the books of the Bible, all the states and capitals, and all the dates the states came into the union. I tried to hide my utter shock but it must have shown on my face. Mrs. Ross reacted by asking, "Do you believe me?" I stumbled for an answer and muttered, "It *is* hard to believe." She clapped her hands and the class lined up. I stood in awe as every child in the class knew everything she had described. On the day of graduation, she was right; my son knew all those things, too. (He was a hit at all the family gatherings!) Sadly, the only evidence we have of this knowledge today is his preschool graduation videotape. Of all the information learned in preschool, he only remembers the books of the Bible.

How did he learn all the information Mrs. Ross described? Through daily repetition of the information. Why did he forget the information? Because he never used it again. This is the same for the information described in the Faith Development Plan. It will be learned through a variety of methods, but without repetition it will be lost.

For example, if you begin teaching the books of the Bible to the first-grade students and they have mastered them by the time they reach second grade, they should be expected to look up a Scripture verse. This means that the second grade teacher does not Xerox the page in the Bible where the Scripture is found, but expects the students to know what they learned in first grade. (If you think about this theory, it is used in public schools all the time, especially in the areas of reading, math, and writing. This is why most of us would miserably fail a third grade science or history test. We learned this information and rarely need to use it again, unlike reading, math, or language arts.) If your Faith Development Plan is working correctly, students will continue to reinforce the skills they have learned in previous classes to enhance retention. The second-grade teacher does not reteach the books of the Bible, but helps them retain what they learned previously by exercising skills they have already been taught.

If your Plan is working correctly, students will continue to reinforce the skills they have learned.

Thom and Joani Schultz tell us in their book *The Dirt on Learning*, "Research shows that retention is dramatically increased by what's called 'interval reinforcement'—review or use of the material repeatedly over a period of time. If the brain registers information just once, less than 10 percent of the message is likely to be retained. So why is this simple principle so often ignored in the church? Teachers and leaders have a strong desire to impart a lot of good information. The thought of returning to already-covered information seems a waste of time when there's so much new information to cover."[3]

Andy Stanley says, "Leaders often question the wisdom of repeating the same things over and over. The concern is that repeating the same principles year after year spells doom for keeping students' interest in the things of God. True, repetition can lead to boredom over time. But the assumption is that repetition is the reason students get bored. In most cases the problem is not the repetition; it's the *presentation*. It has been my experience that two things cause boredom in teenagers: a lifeless presentation by a teacher and the attempt to cover too much information in a short amount of time. Repetition has little to do with it. I have never met a student who, after hearing one talk or lesson on trusting God, fully understood the depths of that issue and obeyed the Lord for the rest of his or her life. Repetition has never hurt anyone, but it has transformed many lives spiritually, emotionally, and physically. You don't need to fear repetition!"[4]

4. DEVELOPMENTAL PACE

While studying the age-specific chapters of this book, it is important to remember that children develop at different paces. I have seen children in our nursery start walking at seven months and others who couldn't walk well until they were almost two years old. Amazingly, by age twelve both children ended up on the same basketball team, and their physical development is virtually identical. I have seen children who know all their letters by the time they are one year old, and I have seen children who struggle with their letters until first grade. By fourth grade they were both earning the same grades.

It is also important to note that some children are simply more advanced than others, while some children fall behind most of their time in an educational setting. In each of the upcoming chapters a fictional scenario of a child from each age group will be presented. Although the fictional child's *family situation* may not be "normal," the scenarios are meant to be that of a "developmentally average child" in the targeted age group. These scenarios are in no way meant to serve as a measurement tool for reliably evaluating the children in your ministry. All children develop at different paces, but most psychologists, physicians, and teachers would agree that there is a norm for children, and from this norm these scenarios are presented.

5. Good Soil

After reading through the information on the various age levels you will begin to organize your Faith Development Plan.

After reading through the information on the various age levels you will begin to organize your Plan.

Please keep in mind that a "top notch" plan, designed to ensure that "no child will be left behind," may follow all the steps for developing an ironclad Faith Development Plan, but these steps, by themselves, will not guarantee spiritual formation or faith development in a program or in individual students. However, it is important to remember, God is the only one who can ultimately grow the faith in your students. It is our job to create the best soil for God to come along and water those seeds, growing them into the disciples He intends. First Corinthians 3:6-7 says, "I planted, Apollos watered, but God was causing the growth. So then neither the one who plants nor the one who waters is anything, but God who causes the growth."

Note who is credited for the growth in this verse: God. The parable of the sower is found in Matthew 13:1-23 and is the first parable of the New Testament. The parable speaks of a "sower" who "went out to sow." Jesus tells of the four different types of soil the seeds fell upon: the path, the rocky ground, the thorns, and the good soil.

Obviously the best soil Jesus describes in this parable is the "good soil" which "brought forth grain, some of hundredfold, some sixty, some thirty." Our ministries can be fertile soil, **intended for growth produced by God** in our students. Our ministries can be a soil, plowed and enriched, in which the seeds of God's word can take root and bring a multiplied increase, resulting in students who grow into spiritually mature disciples of Jesus Christ, not through our power but through the power of God.

Our ministries can be fertile soil for growth produced by God.

6. The Basics

We know the goal for our students is for them to leave our program spiritually mature and continuing to be involved in a passionate relationship with Jesus Christ, a relationship so strong they will be actively telling others how they, too, can have the same relationship. When you picture the students in your ministry who have made a decision for Christ and are passionate in their relationship with Him, what are your minimal expectations for them once they leave your program?

Let me suggest four foundational blocks which will be laid at the bottom of the proposed Faith Development Plan and ultimately your students' relationship with Jesus Christ. These four blocks are habits we can seek to instill in your students from an early age. The blocks are daily Bible reading, daily prayer time with God, regular church attendance, and evangelism. We will begin developing these habits in the Faith Development Plan during the nursery years. Don't forget, aiming your students at a target requires you to view them as future adults.

We can imagine our students in their college dorm room or a military bunk house. Assuming they have made a commitment to accept Jesus Christ as their personal Lord and Savior, what do you want them to habitually do with this relationship? We can hope for them to choose the blessings which come from regular church attendance, interaction with God in daily Bible reading and prayer to ensure their ongoing spiritual growth, and involvement in some type of personal evangelism or discipleship activity.

Ideally you would like them to be on the mission field and involved in some type of Christian service, and this, too, will happen with some of your students. However, we can focus on those four blocks because they are fundamental in our students' spiritual maturity now and after they leave our programs. Throughout the Faith Development Plan a typical student will learn much more than these four foundational blocks, yet intentionally stressing the importance of these four blocks from year to year will help our students maintain the foundation once they leave our programs.

Intentionally stressing the importance of these four blocks will help your students maintain their foundation.

Developing these blocks as habits in your students involves a combined effort on the part of Christian educators, teachers, or sponsors, and hopefully the parents of your students. These four blocks should be shared with your leadership, your teachers or sponsors, and the parents of your students. When a parent comes to you and says, "I know Jeremy made a decision last year for Christ, but he seems to have forgotten that commitment. What can I do as a parent to make sure he is growing?" Our answer will include these four basic faith-building blocks, "Keep encouraging him to come to church regularly, even when he is too tired or complains about what is offered. Encourage him to set aside a time each day for daily Bible reading and prayer with God. And do whatever you can to make sure he is taking that time for growth. Encourage him to pass on his faith to others, even when it is hard. Ask him to invite someone he knows who is not a believer to church."

As with all of the concepts mentioned in the Faith Development Plan, your student's building blocks will be more easily developed and strengthened if the parent is practicing and modeling them for the child. It is very rare for a child to rise above the level of their parents in regard to any of these blocks. Parents who are sporadic church attenders cannot expect their child to go off to college and attend church each week. They cannot expect their child to go out and share their faith with all their unbelieving friends when they have never modeled this in their own life. We all know this is possible, regardless of the parents' model at home, through the Holy Spirit; however, it is much more of a challenge for us as Christian educators.

7. REMEMBERING THE FAITH TABLE

You must also keep the "Faith Table" in the back of your mind. Filling your students with knowledge of the Bible is wonderful, and providing activities in and outside the church in the areas of "Feeling" and "Experience" are essential too. Also, remember to spend a good part of your work week training and equipping the parents of your students to take over the spiritual reins in their home. When we factor in the 1% time limitation we have with our students, it quickly becomes obvious just how important it is to also invest in the spiritual lives of parents. Lastly, the legs of "Science" and "History" will provide your students with further evidence to support and solidify their lives of faith.

Perhaps your faith-table concept differs from the one I explained in the last chapter. If you do not subscribe to this table, subscribe to *some* type of table which has more than one leg. Maybe you can think of some extra legs you would like to see your students stand on, or possibly some legs you feel are not necessary in a faith table. The questions to ask when determining these legs are, "What supports my student's faith?" and "How am I going to make those legs strong enough to withstand a crisis or storm?"

Feeling overwhelmed? Not to worry. Before you ever opened this book, I prayed for you and asked God to give you strength in putting together your Faith Development Plan. This book is specifically designed to assist you in organizing your Faith Development Plan. Each chapter will encourage you to consider, or perhaps reconsider, the capabilities and limitations of your ministry model for various age groups in your ministry.

At the beginning of each chapter you will be given an age-appropriate fictional scenario that encompasses a typical student's physical, social, emotional, cognitive, and spiritual development. These scenarios are presented for two reasons: 1) Some readers love charts. Just show them a chart and they have all the information they need. Other readers learn better through illustrations. The following chapters will present you with both charts and illustrations to facilitate various learning types. 2) The scenarios are intended to help you, the Christian educator, realize how the child's home life effects his or her spiritual development. The children in our ministries come from a variety of home situations. Realizing how home life affects a student's spiritual life is vital to their faith development.

> At the beginning of each chapter you will be given a scenario that depicts a typical student.

In the following chapters you will also be given a skeleton outline of a formal Faith Development Plan you can implement in your ministry. It is a *skeleton plan* and should be viewed as such. At the conclusion of this book I will discuss twelve steps for creating your own Faith Development Plan. Please resist the temptation to skip these steps and simply copy the proposed plan for your use. The steps mentioned, including evaluation, are essential for you to examine and consider for use in your own ministry.

NOTES

1. George Barna, *Transforming Children*, 14.

2. George Barna, *Growing True Disciples* (Colorado Springs: WaterBrook Press, 2001) 2.

3. Thom & Joani Schultz, *The Dirt on Learning* (Loveland, CO: Group Publishing, 1999) 79.

4. Stanley and Hall, *Seven Checkpoints*, 13-14.

Chapter Four

EVALUATING THE ARROWS: NURSERY

Where do you want your students to be by the time they graduate,
and how are you going to get them there?

Brandon is six months old. He has two brothers: Ben, age six, and Charlie, age four. Brandon was four weeks premature and still shows signs of this by his tiny legs and arms. He has the most perfect head with absolutely no hair, which makes him the spitting image of his bald father, Kevin. Kevin buys cute little baseball hats to match Brandon's outfits.

Brandon attends daycare during the week while both mom and dad work full time. His parents also teach Junior High Sunday school each week. Brandon is used to seeing Mr. Gene and Miss Sharon every Sunday when he comes to church. He also visits the nursery on Sunday and Wednesday nights during the school year. Brandon's parents read to him each night before he goes to bed. They show him pictures of Jesus and church while smiling. Every night before he goes to sleep, they sing "Jesus Loves Me" to him and pray over him.

Brandon loves to sit in an ExerSaucer, a swing, or a bouncy seat, anything that allows him to put some weight on his legs. But his big milestone is rolling over. Mr. Gene and Miss Sharon sometimes lay Brandon on his back on a blanket on the floor. Brandon loves to grab one end of the blanket and roll until he has curled himself into a cocoon. He loves to play with his hands and can hold small things such as rattles and pacifiers. He loves to listen to music and look at brightly colored pictures and books. Brandon knows that church is a place where his parents are happy and he is safe. He feels safe with Mr. Gene and Miss Sharon and knows they will take care of his needs, which include warm bottles, cereal, diaper changes, and love.

One half hour into church time Mr. Gene places Brandon and his classmate, Conner, into ExerSaucers while the other workers keep a watchful eye on the infants. He places several Cheerios on the ExerSaucer trays and folds his hands in prayer. "Dear God," he prays with an enthusiastic smile, "Thank You for our food! Amen!" Brandon and Conner watch Mr. Gene through the entire prayer, never once closing their eyes or folding their hands, but Gene is not discouraged by this. He has worked with this age for many years. He knows by the time they leave his nursery, they will fold their hands and close their eyes for prayer time.

Mr. Gene has a wonderfully melodic voice. Every Sunday at this time he sings with the children, "Jesus Loves Me" and "God Is So Good." Again, neither Brandon nor Conner sing with him or utter a sound. They eat their Cheerios and stare at him, mesmerized by his interaction with them. Mr. Gene is not frustrated with their lack of participation. He can see in these children the seeds of faith development and is confident from past experience the children will participate in some form by the time they are ready to leave the nursery.

> Mr. Gene is confident from past experience the children will participate in some form by the time they leave the nursery.

After singing two songs, Mr. Gene reads Brandon and Conner a simple book about God and His creation. He has large pictures of happy children going to church with their mommies and daddies, and he talks with smiles and enthusiasm. Mr. Gene and Miss Sharon have visited the toddler room next door to see their "Jesus Time." They are confident the concepts that they are teaching Brandon and Conner at six months will be reinforced and built upon in their next age level.

How can a child begin faith development at this young age? What can a six-month-old child possibly learn? Should we sit him at a desk, encourage him to bring his Bible each week, and expect him to tithe on a regular basis? Absolutely not. That is absurd.

What we can expect from a child of this age is limited. However, if you look at the children's section in a large bookstore, such as Barnes and Nobles, you would find greater expectations than are commonly pursued in our preschool ministry strategies. For example: Baby Einstein products have become a popular buzzword for new parents since its founder Julie Aigner-Clark started the company in 1997.[1]

The Baby Einstein web site offers a large selection of products for children ages birth to five years old. Several of these products are books and DVDs specifically designed for newborns. "Today, Baby Einstein is a world leader in developmental media products for babies and toddlers with sales topping 18 million dollars."[2]

In addition to Baby Einstein, the Infant Learning Company's founder Dr. Robert Titzer has developed a video curriculum, *Your Baby Can Read*, teaching babies to read. Anyone who questions the validity of these programs can visit their website at **www.infantlearning.com** and view the testimonials. As astonishing as it may sound, according to this material, *infants are capable of learning to read simple words prior to their first birthday.*

Another interesting early childhood developmental phenomenon is in the area of infants and sign language. Several books have been written showing the effective benefits and tangible results of teaching sign language to infants before they can speak one word. Baby sign language is an effective means of communication. Infants can learn to communicate through simple sign language.

Maybe you have had the dizzying experience of visiting a baby specialty store such as Babies R Us. Choosing the correct bedding, wall hangings, or mobiles has now become much more complex. We now have to ask ourselves, "Which of these wall hangings and crib bumpers is the most visually stimulating for the baby?" "Which of these mobiles plays music that accelerates cognitive development?" In the "olden days" we would simply choose items which matched the walls.

In light of this information, the question must be asked, "If researchers, new parents, and child care providers believe that children can develop cognitively before their first birthday, wouldn't the same be true for their spiritual development?"

At six months old your precious little ones are at optimal age to begin faith development. One of the biggest mistakes any Christian educator can make with the children in their nursery is to underestimate the little ones' needs and potential. Fight the urge to simply view your nursery as "child care." Instead, we can encourage dramatic results by viewing these infants as seeds in God's hand which will grow into beautiful flowers given the right love, care, instruction, and direction, or as

At six months old your precious little ones are at optimal age to begin faith development.

arrows that are just being placed on the bowstring, ready to be aimed at a target. These little miracles are God's gift to their parents and your church, the people to whom He has entrusted them.

The following are age-appropriate faith development activities for children in your nursery beginning at age six months.

- ✔ Most children, at six months of age, can sit up by themselves or with assistance. At some point during the nursery class time the teacher can sit the child in a safe seating position. This may be an ExerSaucer, high chair, or specially designed table with built-in seats for babies and toddlers. Teachers should do four things at this time.

- ✔ Give the child something to put in his or her mouth. For younger children this may be a pre-refrigerated teething ring or age-appropriate toy. For older children this may be several Cheerios or an age-appropriate snack. (Out of respect for parents and concerns about allergies, never give an infant any snack without obtaining permission from the parent or guardian first.)

- ✔ Have a brief time of prayer. If children are old enough, help them fold their hands and bow their heads. Fold your hands and talk to God with energy, enthusiasm, and smiles. "Thank you, God, for this day. Thank you for our food. We love you, God, Amen." **(Experience)**

- ✔ Choose one or two simple, short songs such as "Jesus Loves Me" and sing them with the children. Energy, enthusiasm, and smiles are the keys. Most of the children will not sing with a teacher, but older children may hum or make music in their own way by singing musical notes with no words. Once you have chosen two songs that the children enjoy, sing those songs in repetition for several weeks. Babies love repetition and routine. **(Experience)**

- ✔ Read a simple book to the babies such as *God Made Kitties* or *God Made Me* with energy, enthusiasm, and smiles. An alternative to reading a book is using a nursery curriculum with large, colorful pictures or posters of children at church, children praying, children sharing, or children helping others. **(Bible Knowledge)**

The infants in your nursery department are taking an important faith-building step: learning to trust. Infants become familiar with

The infants in your nursery department are taking an important faith-building step: learning to trust.

the nursery workers and facilities and quickly learn to trust them and feel safe and secure in the nursery setting. (Feeling)

Brandon is in a healthy faith development situation because his parents and church are working together to help him grow from a seed to a sprout.

Do not resign your nursery department to child care. More important than teaching infants to read or learn sign language is teaching them of God's love.

Nursery Learning Goals

The following are simple goals you may include in your Faith Development Plan for your nursery department. By the time an infant leaves the nursery department at the Community Christian Church he or she will:

- See the church, specifically the nursery, as a safe and happy place.
- Through the realization that his or her needs are met in the nursery, learn to trust the nursery workers.
- Learn basic songs of God, Jesus, and Their love.
- Learn the basics of prayer by folding hands and thanking God for various things.
- Be familiar with basic books read in the nursery about God, Jesus, and Their love.

Things a Parent Can Do to Reinforce

What Is Taught in the Nursery (Family)

- Attend church regularly so the infant can develop a healthy routine.
- Leave the infant off in the nursery with a smile and a reassuring kiss, even if the child is crying.
- Provide church workers with all supplies necessary to ensure the baby's individual needs are met during his/her time in the nursery.
- Regularly read books about God, Jesus, church, and the Bible at home.
- Sing songs about God, Jesus, church, and the Bible at home.

- Pray before all meals and at bedtime, folding your hands and speaking in short easy-to-understand words, avoiding recited prayers.
- Make praying for your child a part of your daily prayer journey. Pray specifically for your child's spiritual growth from this point on.
- Try to make Sunday mornings a happy and peaceful time for your child. Lay out clothes the night before and set alarms early enough to give plenty of time for the morning activities. Infants are very intuitive and will pick up on any stress you are feeling.

NOTES

1. 01-02_history.asp/Store/Default.asp/Family/03-01_family.asp.
2. http://www.powerhomebiz.com/vol98/moms.htm.

Chapter Five

EVALUATING THE ARROWS: TODDLERS

*Where do you want your students to be by the time they graduate,
and how are you going to get them there?*

Stephanie is one and a half and proud to tell anyone who asks. She has long curly brown ringlets of hair and pudgy little legs, arms, and cheeks. Her mother clothes her in the most adorable frilly dresses with matching tights, shoes, and hats. Stephanie is an only child whose mother stays home with her during the week. Stephanie is not used to anyone watching her but her mother and father. She comes to church in a different mood each week. One week she barrels in the door, twirling her dress, smiling and eager to give her teacher a big hug. The next week she comes in hanging on her mother's leg. On such Sundays Stephanie will not look at the teachers and eventually launches into a screaming fit as her mother tries to leave.

Within five or ten minutes Stephanie's teachers have her in a routine. Regardless of how Stephanie comes to church each week, within five or ten minutes her teachers have her in a routine: play time, prayer time, story time with snacks, song time and more play. Stephanie is soon smiling and happy.

Stephanie has a normal vocabulary for her age: about 20 words.[1] She is still taking two naps a day; one in the morning around 10:00 and one in the afternoon around 2:00. She does not know how to say, "I'm tired," but it is hard to miss the signs: rubbing of the eyes and crying over very small things. She can drink well from a sippy cup and eats regular table food. She is still teething, which causes a lot of pain she has trouble identifying and processing. She is not quite ready to go on the potty, but is noticeably uncomfortable in a messy diaper. Her parents are beginning to wonder if the "terrible twos" possibly begin at one. If she does not get her way, she throws temper tantrums which include falling limp on the floor and yelling "Stop!" at the top of her lungs. She has no pride and will throw these tantrums wherever and whenever she feels led. This includes the grocery store, a restaurant, or at church. She is testing her parents and her teachers to see what they will do if she misbehaves. Both her parents and the church teachers use time-out for bad behavior.

Stephanie struggles greatly with the idea of sharing. She doesn't care for it at all, but she can tell you what sounds all the animals make, can identify all major parts of her body, and generally speaks in two-word sentences. She is motivated by praise.

Stephanie's Sunday school teacher, Miss Donna, is always smiling and energetic. She places great importance on the idea that all children entering her classroom feel it is a happy place. As the children enter the room, they are greeted by Miss Donna or her assistant teacher at the door. One teacher stays on the floor with the children as the other teacher greets children. Both teachers always make sure to bend down to the child's eye level. The children feel at ease coming into the room through the sound of upbeat Sunday school songs played on the CD player.

If a child is having a hard time adjusting, Miss Donna's assistant is there to rock and cuddle him until he is comfortable joining the class. Both teachers simply redirect students' attention away from the absence of their parents by offering toys or snack.

The toddlers in this room have a regular routine. After entering the room they play for almost fifteen minutes. Next, they clean up the toys and sit down for a snack at the table. Before they eat their snack, the teachers help them fold their hands and lead them in a short prayer. During the snack time one teacher reads the children short Bible stories from a preschool Bible. She points to pictures and tells the children about Jesus, God, the Bible, and church while smiling. After the snack time they sing simple, upbeat songs about Jesus, God, the Bible, and church. Next, if weather permits, they take the children outside, stopping to talk about all the wonderful things God has made. When they come back, they are allowed to play with the toys.

Miss Donna has gone to great lengths to ensure the toddler classroom is safe for curious little ones. All the toys are age appropriate and cleaned regularly. She and her assistant teach in this class each week, first hour, so the children establish a degree of trust. Both teachers handle any discipline problems by redirecting the children to another area of the room.

When we speak of toddlers, we are referring to one-year-old children who can walk well. These children have figured out how to use their legs and are ready to go, go, go. This age group should have one of the largest classrooms available. They need room to explore and use those large muscles.

Toddler-age classrooms, like the church nursery, are often viewed as mere babysitting or childcare. This is a terribly tragic mistake for any children's ministry. Toddlers are full of energy, and although they can't verbalize it as such, desire to know as much of the world around them as possible. They have to touch everything! This is why most parents despise taking their toddler to the grocery store or mall. A toddler can't keep her hands off anything.

> Although toddlers can't verbalize it as such, they desire to know as much of the world around them as possible.

This is the ideal age to begin teaching precious little ones that the world they are learning about was made by God. Hands-on learning is essential for these children, and they can learn simple Bible truths if these truths are repeated over time.

—··—··—··—··—··—··—··—

The following are age-appropriate faith development activities for toddlers:

- ✔ Weather permitting, take the children outside to look at trees, flowers, grass, bugs, the clouds, the sky, and the sun. Energetically tell the children that God is so good, He made all these things. (Science)
- ✔ Serve the children snacks and read them simple Bible stories from a toddler Bible while sitting at a table. Point to the pictures and ask the children questions about the story. Always refer to the Bible as a happy book and smile while you speak of the stories. Young children will associate your facial expressions and attitude with an object such as the Bible. (Bible Knowledge)
- ✔ Take a short time to help the children fold their hands and pray. Show them how you bow your head and close your eyes. Pray simple prayers with enthusiasm and smiles. Refrain from rote prayers such as, "God is great, God is good . . ." Pray from your heart. Children are more likely to understand these types of prayers. Remind children each week that praying is talking to God. We can talk to God anytime we want. (Experience)
- ✔ Sing simple songs about God with the children. A child

this age does not care if you use a piano, CD, or live band. Singing a capella is fine with them. It is imperative you carefully consider the words of the songs you teach this age group, as well as all preschool children. Songs such as "Climb, Climb Up Sunshine Mountain" and "Deep and Wide" are classic children's songs; however, they hold no meaning to toddlers and ultimately confuse them. Purchase band instruments and allow the children to play while you sing. Teach the children to praise God through singing and playing their instrument. (Experience)

It is also crucial to a toddler's faith development to ensure the classroom is a safe and happy place.

- Children must feel safe in the church environment. Workers should greet children at the door with smiling faces and open arms. The room should be warm and inviting to help the children feel comfortable in their surroundings.
- The toddler classroom should be one of the largest rooms in your church building.
- Toddler rooms should be equipped (at minimum) with rockers, changing tables, a table and chairs, age-appropriate toys (which should be cleaned at least every other week), and a CD or tape player.
- Children should enter the room to upbeat music playing softly in the background. Music is inviting and helps sooth children's fear of separating from their parents.
- Teachers in toddler classrooms must be prepared to get on the floor with children. This may require female teachers to wear pants, instead of dresses, on their teaching days.
- When children enter the room, teachers should kneel or bend down on the children's level to help them feel less intimidated. A wonderful exercise for all teachers this age is to enter the classroom on their knees. Look around the room and see it from a child's perspective
- Make sure that diaper-changing experiences are positive for the child. Smile, talk lovingly, and let the child know their needs will be met at church.
- Be willing to give children hugs or cuddles as you rock them during class time; however, it is very important

that this is not overdone. Some toddler teachers feel it is their job to rock and hold toddlers the entire time they are in their care. This philosophy does not help the child. On the contrary, it creates a dependency on that teacher and prohibits the child from getting down on the floor and participating in the classroom activities or any form of faith development.

✦ Toddler classroom workers should be as consistent as possible. Toddlers recognize and trust teachers they see each week. Heavy turnover in this area causes anxiety for children and can prohibit faith development.

✦ Teachers in the toddler area should remain as consistent with the morning schedule as possible. Toddlers pick up very quickly on routine and may suffer mild anxiety if it is changed.

✦ Redirection should be used frequently in this classroom. If a child is starting to fight with another child over a toy, do your best to interest her in another toy or area of the room. At this age, sitting children down and explaining God's desire for them to share is not something they are ready for developmentally.

✦ Redirection should also be used when a child is struggling with the absence of his/her mother or father. Often these children will sit in an area of the room where they can see the door, waiting for their parents to return. Each time the door opens and the child does not see her/his parents, the crying will start again. Try to redirect the toddler to an activity, a toy or another part of the room to focus her/his attention away from the emotion.

✦ Television, DVD, and video tapes should not be used in a toddler room. Most children this age watch several hours of television each week at home. Television is frequently used as a babysitter in homes. If these children are at church 1% of their time, they do not need to spend half of that time watching a video, even if it is Bible based.

TODDLER LEARNING GOALS

By the time a toddler leaves the nursery department at the Community Christian Church he or she will have:

- ✔ Continued learning that church is a happy place.
- ✔ Continued learning that the nursery is a safe and happy place.
- ✔ Continued realizing that his or her needs are met in the nursery, therefore learning to trust the nursery workers.
- ✔ Continued to learn basic songs of God, Jesus, and Their love.
- ✔ Continued to practice prayer times as a class and learn that praying is how we talk to God.
- ✔ Learned to recognize a picture of Jesus and know He is a good man.
- ✔ Learned what a Bible looks like and understands that it is a happy book.
- ✔ Begun to view creation as something special made by God.
- ✔ Begun to appreciate the outside world God made.
- ✔ Learned the basics of worship by praising God with his or her voice and instruments.

THINGS A PARENT CAN DO TO REINFORCE THE CONCEPTS

TAUGHT IN THE TODDLER ROOM (FAMILY)

- ✔ Continue attending church regularly so the toddler can develop a healthy routine.
- ✔ Leave your toddler off in the nursery with a smile and a reassuring kiss, even if the child is crying.
- ✔ Provide church workers with all supplies necessary to ensure your child's needs are met during their time away from you.
- ✔ Regularly read age-appropriate books about God, Jesus, Church, and the Bible at home.
- ✔ Sing songs about God, Jesus, Church, and the Bible at home.
- ✔ Pray before all meals and at bedtime, folding your hands and speaking in short easy-to-understand words, avoiding recited prayers.

- Make praying for your child a part of your daily prayer journey. Your prayers are essential for the faith development of your child.
- Try to make Sunday mornings a happy and peaceful time for your child. Lay out clothes the night before and set alarms early enough to give plenty of time for the morning activities. If toddlers are in a stressful environment before church, they will relate this experience to their feelings of church.
- Take your child to the zoo or for long walks stressing the beauty of God's creation.
- Allow your child to work in the garden and talk about the different flowers God made.
- Periodically take your child into the worship service during the singing time. Children need to see their parents worshiping and praising God.

NOTES

1. K. Eileen Allen and Lynn Marotz, *Developmental Profiles: Birth to Six* (Albany, NY: Delmar Publishers, 1989) 63.

Chapter Six

Evaluating the Arrows:
Preschool
Two- through Five-Year-Olds

Where do you want your students to be by the time they graduate and how are you going to get them there?

Zachary has just turned three years old. He is very energetic and built like a tank. He has jet-black hair, brown eyes and a very dark complexion. Zachary is an only child, for the time being. His mother is pregnant with twins and is due in three months. Zachary's father does not attend church, but does not object to his wife attending. Zachary's mother grew up in the church and his grandmother and grandfather both attend the church, too. His mother happily brings him to church and can frequently be seen breaking into a run for her Sunday school class after dropping him off. He keeps her on her toes. She is very soft spoken and is not quick to discipline him.

Zachary has finally mastered the art of going to the bathroom. (Seemingly much later than the girls in his church class.) No diapers for this guy! He is all boy. He is very cognizant that he is a boy and enjoys telling the girls in the classroom they can't play because "Girls can't be pirates!" Zachary loves to wrestle and play rough. He loves to run, jump, bounce, scream, and talk very loud. It is very hard for him to sit still for story time at church. He loves the singing time as long as it is loud with lots of big actions so he can jump and move his arms.

Zachary knows his dad does not go to church. Zachary understands that Jesus, God, church, and the Bible are things that make us happy.

He is very independent and wants to pick out his own clothes and dress himself every morning. His vocabulary is average for his age as he is able to understand more than 600 different words. He loves to talk and will occasionally break into a nonsense baby talk for amusement.

His teacher, Miss Linda, is very enthusiastic and keenly aware of a preschool child's limitations. She greets him at the door and notices he has brought his Bible. She smiles and tells Zachary how happy she is that he remembered his special book. She immediately helps him put his offering money in the basket. Zachary's mother gives him simple chores each week and allows him to use that money to put in the basket. The teacher directs him to a center which introduces the lesson that will be taught later.

When the weather is nice, Miss Linda takes Zachary's class outside for walks to talk about different things that God made. Sometimes they look at pine cones or leaves to see God's special design.

After learning centers, Zachary's class joins the four- and five-year-old children in their class for singing time. Miss Karen leads the singing and carefully chooses songs the children will understand. She chooses a mix of slow songs and really fast songs which provide opportunities for Zachary to jump, shout, and dance. One of Zachary's favorite songs is about heaven. Miss Karen talks with smiles and enthusiasm. Each of the children tell what they are looking forward to in heaven or what color their mansion will be. At the end of song time the teacher allows two or three children to pray and then she closes with an age-appropriate prayer.

After song time the children go back to their individual classes for story time. The children sit on carpet squares as Miss Linda, a wonderful storyteller, tells the story of Noah and the ark. Miss Linda has her Bible open to the story of Noah and her assistant helps all the children find the same story in their Bibles. All eyes are on Miss Linda as she excitedly tells the story and uses flannelgraph figures to help the children conceptualize what she is saying.

When story time is over, she helps the children review their books of the New Testament with a song they sing with a CD. Miss Linda has developed different hand motions, one motion for four consecutive books, and Zachary loves to sing his books of the New Testament and do the hand motions.

As story time closes, the children sit for a snack as Miss Linda talks to them casually about the Bible story and teaches them a simple Bible verse. She reads the story again from a children's Bible, showing the children the pictures. She also encourages them to tell someone about Jesus after they leave church.

Two Things Can Be Said about Preschool Children

Two- to five-year-old children are quickly changing in many respects. Their bodies are growing rapidly, their cognitive skills are changing, their social and emotional skills are being refined, and they have many, many questions to consider and ask.

> Two- to five-year-old children are quickly changing in many respects—physical growth, cognitive skills, social and emotional skills, and with many, many questions.

There is typically a considerable difference between two- to five-year-old girls and boys of the same age range. Boys tend to be more vocal in public and exhibit much more energy in a classroom situation. Girls tend to be more reserved, especially with teachers or students with whom they are not familiar or comfortable. For the most part, girls will sit still for longer periods of time and can keep quiet for longer, too.

Two things can be said about children between the ages of two and five: too much and too little is expected of them. Let me explain.

Too Much Is Expected

Some time ago I visited the public library in our town to use the computers. The woman at a computer next to me had a child who looked to be between the ages of one and two. The mother was talking to someone in an on-line chat room with the child on her lap. The child sat for a long period of time while the mother chatted, but eventually began to squirm. The mother stood the child up, spanked him, and sat him forcefully back on her lap as she began to type on the computer. This "battle of wills" went on several times. Over and over the mother scolded the young child for wanting off her lap. At one point the child started touching the keys on the keyboard. The mother immediately slapped the child's hands, followed by a scream from the child, and mom went on with her typing. This woman was on the computer before I started working on my research and remained there long after my thirty-minute session was done.

Last year, while visiting a bowling alley one afternoon with my children, I noticed a child around the age of two walking into the bowling alley with some other adults. The child seemed very excited about being in the bowling alley, visibly stimulated by all the lights and sounds. The adults rented their shoes, chose their bowling balls, and went to the alley. After all the set up, they sat the child on a chair. It became obvious they were not going to let this little child play. After a few minutes the child climbed off the chair. One adult immediately spanked the child and after scolding the little boy (loud enough for the whole alley to hear), set him back in his chair. As in the library this scene repeated itself over and over while the child cried in frustration.

During one of our ministries I had the opportunity to teach in a toddler classroom. Children were promoted to this class when walking steadily on their own and left well into their twos. A certain mother would come in each week with her two-year-old son. Every week she would bring him to the check-in counter, and every week he would grab her neck tightly and cry. No matter how at ease I tried to make him feel he did not want to come to this class. The mother would say something along these lines, "Okay, fine! If you aren't going to stay in here, you'll have to go to my class. But you better be good!" I came to realize after several weeks of this routine that this speech was for my benefit, not the child's.

One Sunday I was given a break in the toddler class and took the opportunity to visit an adult Sunday school class. This mother was sitting in the back of the room with her son on her lap. At the beginning of class he seemed quite content to sit with his mom; however, after his sitting limit was up, he tried to climb off her lap. The mother would stand the child up, spank him, and sit him back on her lap. Over and over the cycle continued: she sits him soundly on her lap, the child tries to get off, the mother becomes upset, she stands him up and spanks him, the child screams, the mother puts the child back on her lap. I looked at my friend next to me wide-eyed. She leaned over to me and said, "This happens every week."

Let me offer a question at this point: Who benefited from this situation? The mother? No, she seemed to get nothing out of the class time. The child? Absolutely not. He was miserable and not getting much in the area of faith development outside his class. The people in the mother's class? Not even close. We all wanted to walk out! The fact is, no one benefited from this situation.

Maybe you have witnessed scenes similar to those I have mentioned—young children forced to conform to adult environments. These situations are developmentally inappropriate for small children. An adult should no sooner expect a two- or three-year-old child to sit perfectly still than they would a new-born baby to be potty trained. Why? Because it is not developmentally appropriate.

God gave preschool-aged children a spirit of laughter, a spirit of movement, an inquisitive spirit, a spirit of love. To expect more of children than they are developmentally capable of quenches their God-given spirit and their God-designed stages of growth.

> God gave preschool-aged children a spirit of laughter, a spirit of movement, an inquisitive spirit, a spirit of love.

Perhaps you have seen the following scenarios played out at your church. Teachers insist on using the lecture method with no visuals for their students. Well-intentioned adults structure their preschool-aged classroom with sit-down activities such as coloring sheets, play dough, and puzzles. Teachers instantly begin reprimanding little ones as soon as the child starts raising his or her voice or getting "too rowdy."

Preschool age children have energy to burn, and their desire is to burn it until they are too tired to go anymore. Additionally, when preschool children come into a social situation with five to ten of their peers, the energy is exacerbated. Not only do they want to move and talk, they want to do all this with their friends or while their friends are watching.

Does that mean we should not expect a child to sit still at all? No. We should expect children to have the capability of sitting for short periods of time, even sitting quietly. But sitting quietly for an hour is an entirely unrealistic developmental expectation for a preschool child.

TOO LITTLE IS EXPECTED

Looking at the scope and sequence section of any Bible-based curriculum is sometimes amusing. For the entire four years of a child's faith development the writers may set goals such as, "Children will learn that God loves them, the Bible is a good book, and God made the world." Christian Educator, please be warned: these minimal objectives are a total underestimation of what preschool children are capable of learning. These objectives are better meant for a toddler class rather than preschool. Preschool children are capable of learning concepts beyond what you or I could ever dream. They are extremely intelligent and setting the bar so low for them is hampering their potential faith development. Expect more and you will be pleasantly surprised.

> So what are preschoolers capable of learning?
> Lots! See the end of the chapter for suggestions.

PRESCHOOL BIBLE STORY TIME

A MASTER STORYTELLER

College education classes frequently teach a formula for calculating the average person's attention span in minutes. Simply figured, it is one minute for each year of age. Following this formula we would quickly figure that the attention span of a two- or three-year-old child is two or three minutes. I have heard other teachers generously double this formula for the first twenty years of life. Thus, a ten-year-old child could pay attention for a maximum of twenty minutes and a twenty-year-old could pay attention for twenty minutes, twenty-one-year-olds, twenty-one minutes and so on.

Several examples could quickly squelch this theory, but I will concentrate on the popular children's television show, "Blue's Clues." Any of us who have ever had the privilege to "experience" "Blue's Clues" have probably noticed that the thirty-minute program flies by quickly. Preschool-aged children can sit and watch this entire show, interact with Steve or Joe and not realize they have been learning for thirty minutes.

In her book *Blue's Clues for Success*, Diane Tracy shares the research of Dan Anderson, a professor from the University of Massachusetts at Amherst in regard to retention and attention spans. "He . . . found that preschoolers could and would pay attention for long periods—more than short three- to four-minute segments—if they were told an interesting story by engaging characters."[1] This research revealed that children could sit for long periods of time if they were told a story by a "master storyteller." Please do not assume that children and adults can pay attention for longer lengths of time only with the assistance of television, video games, movies, and the like. A "master storyteller" is someone who can tell a story and captivate an audience, teaching them with laughter, serious thought, and creativity.

Among his other talents Tommy Oaks is a preacher and

Children can sit for long periods of time if told a story by a "master storyteller."

teacher who is also a master storyteller. I once heard him speak on the account of Esther and her life. I can't even remember breathing for forty-five minutes. After several minutes I suddenly realized my mouth was hanging wide open as I listened intently to his paraphrase of this account. Not only did he hold my attention for forty-five minutes, I can tell you every detail of the story he shared from Esther's life and the thesis statement from his sermon. "Esther was placed in her position to fulfill the plan God had for her life. What is God's plan for your life?" It was awesome. I was not watching television or a movie, playing Pac Man, or watching a Broadway show. I was simply listening to another human being tell a story, and it was wonderful.

Perhaps you have such storytellers in your congregation, maybe not as well spoken as Tommy Oaks, but someone who has the gift of storytelling. Perhaps this person is an elderly woman or gentleman who would welcome the opportunity to tell a Bible story once a week to preschool children while showing them pictures or manipulating some flannelgraph pictures. (For those of you who are laughing at the idea of a flannelgraph, stop. A flannelgraph is an excellent resource for teaching young children simple Bible stories while maximizing attention and retention.)

It is worth your time to seek out such persons in your congregation. The benefits are threefold:

1) The children in your ministry will learn and retain more of the Bible stories with one "master storyteller" than with several different teachers who love children, but become frustrated during story time.

2) Your teachers will welcome the addition of a permanent storyteller, taking the burden of story time off their shoulders. Eliminating story time in their job description may even aid in recruiting teachers.

3) Incorporating a "master storyteller" helps us in our mission to "grow spiritually mature disciples of Christ," providing children with the basic Bible stories of faith they will recall for years to come.

DRAMA

The alternative to the "master storyteller" idea is presenting the Bible story as a drama. Children love drama and will sit for longer periods of time during a dramatic presentation.

Presenting a Bible story through drama is very powerful for any age child, preschool included.

Presenting a Bible story through drama is very powerful for any age child, preschool included.

However, caution should be taken to ensure the story or principle is told with respect to biblical truth and fact. A trend for curriculum publishers is for stories to be told by puppets or in a cartoon video. Please be warned: presenting Bible stories in this manner confuses children who are bombarded with cartoons, videos, television, and other fantasy characters such as those brought to us by Walt Disney. As Christian educators and teachers we are called to "rightly divide the word of truth." This command is the same for the senior minister standing behind the pulpit as well as the preschool teacher. The stories of the Bible should be presented as factual, historical events on par with the Civil War and September 11th.

In the July/August 2003 edition of *Children's Ministry Magazine*, William Chad Newsom wrote a brilliant article on the importance of this very issue. "'I know Jesus said he had all the power, but is that the same power that Pokemon and Digimon characters have?' 'Moses parted the Red Sea, but have you seen what Harry Potter's done lately to Voldemort?' 'And, of course, it wasn't a big deal for the big fish to spit out Jonah. He also did it for Pinocchio and Gepetto.'"[2]

Children growing up in today's culture are inundated with such myths. It is no wonder that children have such a hard time distinguishing truth from myth. Newsom writes, "With amazingly realistic and believable visual storytelling (television and movies), it's getting harder for children to distinguish reality from fiction. . . . Those of us concerned with teaching the Bible to children seek new ways to clear up this clouding of truth and imagination."[3]

This challenge is of utmost importance when relaying the message of Jesus and the historical figures mentioned in the Bible to preschool children. It is essential that the children are told repeatedly, "The people I am going to talk to you about today are not pretend. They were real people who had skin."

The overuse of cartoon Bible stories, cartoon looking pictures on flannelgraph, and puppets only solidify the message many children are receiving, "Jesus, Paul, and Moses are just the same as Superman, Blue from 'Blue's Clues' and Scooby-Doo." It is imperative that you choose your curriculum and teaching methods wisely for this age, or you could be doing more harm than good. No teacher wants their students to view the Bible stories as fiction, but unfortunately if we're not careful about our teaching methods, we run the risk of fostering this very view.

> As I pointed out in teaching toddlers, the same is true for preschool classrooms: television, DVD, and video tapes should not be used. Most children this age watch several hours of television each week at home. Television is frequently used as a babysitter in homes. If these children are at church 1% of their time, they do not need to spend half of that time watching a video, even if it is Bible based.

CONCEPTS AND FACTS PRESCHOOLERS CAN COMPREHEND

CHURCH IS A HAPPY PLACE (Feeling)

In the nursery and toddler rooms, we presented the idea that young children must realize that church is a happy place. Preschool children still need to be reassured of this very fact. Smiling teachers greeting children at the door with age-appropriate learning activities help to develop this concept in young children. Preschoolers need to feel a sense of warmth while participating in the various activities in their classroom. This will, however, be the last age group for this step. After preschool age the idea that "church is a happy place" will be implied and supported by the other steps in the Faith Development Plan.

TRUSTING CHURCH WORKERS

As with the "Church is a happy place" concept, we have been building trust in church workers since the child was placed in the nursery. Trust in teachers and classroom surroundings is essential in working with children of any age.

One key area in the development of trust of church workers by preschool children is the control of turnover in teachers. Recruitment is not easy. People are simply very busy and service in the church is suffering as a result. Children's and youth ministers are reduced to breaking down Sundays to find workers. "I'll teach one Sunday a month, but that's about all I can at this point." I even approached a woman at one of our ministries asking if she would teach only fifth Sundays in the toddler department. After much thought she gave me her answer, "I've decided. I'll take half of those Sundays." She would take half of the fifth Sundays, which is two Sundays the entire year. That is rough!

Unfortunately our children feel the ramifications of busy church members as well. Overly busy church members who only serve one Sunday a month without a doubt do not bond as well with their students as those who will commit to teaching every Sunday for a certain length of time. Encourage teachers to make a year-long commitment to teaching the same hour every week. The result is a child's trust in their church workers.

Church members who only serve one Sunday a month do not bond as well with their students as those who commit to teaching every Sunday.

Like the "church is a happy place" faith development step, this is the last time we will include this step in the suggested Faith Development Plan. I would encourage you to read "Discipline in the Classroom and Faith Development" in Appendix B to further understand the importance for all students to have trust in their church workers.

HEAVEN (Bible Knowledge and Feeling)

One topic the church in general does not speak of enough is heaven. Sad as that may be, it is true. Preschool children can begin to learn that heaven is a special place. Heaven is a place we go when we die, but it is not a sad place. There is no crying in heaven and no darkness. If a person has "Jesus in her heart" she will have a mansion and be listening to a heavenly host of angels. She will be able to see Jesus and because it is never dark, no more going to bed or naps!

Heaven is a topic I believe should be discussed with preschool children every week. We frequently ask our preschoolers what color their mansion will be in heaven. Several of our girls will say without hesitation, "Barbie pink!" (I'm sure we will be able to spot their mansions in heaven without any trouble.)

Recently an elderly gentleman from our church passed away. As the mother of one of our preschooler's was crying at home, her five-year-old said, "Mom! Heaven is a *happy* place!" Heaven is our hope. It is our prize, our reward. It is something wonderful and a place where we anticipate spending eternity. Children of preschool age are at exactly the right age to begin appreciating how wonderful heaven can be.

A wonderful way to reinforce the hope of heaven is to host

an annual "Heaven Celebration." This can quickly be transformed into a cross-generational activity, including everyone from senior citizens to preschool children. "Heaven Night" can start with a pitch-in meal with all dishes reflecting a "heavenly" theme. Angel hair pasta, angel food cake, and heavenly hash are some ideas. Prizes could be awarded for the best theme dish. After the meal, a singing time could include old hymns and praise choruses dealing with heaven. (We even allowed one full month for the congregation to vote on their favorite "Heaven Song." The votes were tabulated into a top-ten list and sung during the service.) Perhaps a few special numbers could be added, Scripture verses describing scenes from heaven, and a time of remembrance for those in your congregation who went to heaven during the past year.

However it is presented, "Heaven Night" can be a time for preschool children to see the importance heaven has on those in the congregation. Through such a service they will undoubtedly see that heaven is a special place where they definitely want to go.

TITHING (Bible Knowledge and Experience)

These words are frequently used in preschool church classrooms, "Who has money for Jesus?" or "Would you like to give money to Jesus?" Unfortunately this is a concept most children cannot understand without at least some explanation. If children can't see Jesus, how can they give Him their money? They have come to understand that "Give your money to Jesus" means putting their money in a little basket or plastic church bank. They probably have figured out that putting money in these receptacles is a good thing, because their teacher smiles and says "thank you" when they do it. But after they put their money in the basket by the door, what happens to that money? How does it get to Jesus?

One Sunday I decided to ask my preschoolers what it meant when we said, "money for Jesus." I asked them, "How does Jesus get your money?" Taking the offering basket off the countertop I put all the offering money in my hand and threw it up in the air asking, "Do we throw the money up to Jesus so He can grab it and take it to heaven?" All the children laughed. One girl said, "No silly! The angels come down and take it up to heaven!" When I really pressed them for an answer to this question, my usually talkative group had no answer. They had no idea how Jesus ended up with their money.

Preschool age is the best time for children to begin learning about giving, specifically tithing. Children as young as two years old can learn the importance of tithing and giving. Imagine the impact this could have on the future church if we could start our children in the habit of tithing when they are two! By the time they are married, wouldn't they be more likely to be regular, "cheerful" givers?

Take the time to introduce these young children to the concept of tithing. Most curriculums have at least one story of Peter and John going to pray or the widow's mite, which illustrates how God feels when we give. Once this story has been presented, reinforce it each week by reminding these precious souls how their money is being used for Jesus. A missionary home on furlough can come to the preschool class and thank the children for their offering, showing how the money they gave bought Bibles for children in a village to learn more about God's love and heaven.

One of the best ways to teach children about giving is to ask parents of preschoolers to begin implementing a chore system for their little ones. You may question the feasibility of a two-year-old child doing chores; however, it is not only feasible but a great learning exercise. Parents can fill out a chore chart and set a certain amount to be given at the end of the week in return for the work. If the child earns $1.00 for a week's worth of chores, the parents can pay the child in dimes, preceded by an explanation of saving, spending, and giving. The child would then take that dime to church the very next Sunday and place it themselves in the offering basket. This method creates a sense of accomplishment for the child as opposed to parents reaching in their pockets at the last minute each Sunday, smiling, and saying, "Here's your money for Jesus. Don't forget to put it in the basket."

An excellent resource for parents in this area is "My Giving Bank" by Larry Burkett. The bank has three separate areas for money: a bank, a store, and a church. Children can separate their money into the three different buildings and begin to learn to manage their money. There is even an ATM which serves the same purpose. "The Learning ATM," by Larry Burkett allows parents to preset limits for their children in spending, saving, and tithing. If the child only has one dollar in the bank and wants to buy a piece of candy for $.95, the bank will not let the child take the money out. (I once found my daughter trying to pry open the money door of her "The Learning ATM" with a butter knife!)

PRAYER (Feeling and Experience)

Another skill that should be further developed during the preschool years is prayer. Following the Faith Development Plan, we know these children learned in the nursery and toddler class that prayer is folding our hands, closing our eyes (or whatever posture you've chosen to teach them), and talking to God. During the preschool years it is very important that we demonstrate to children how to pray. Preschoolers learn volumes by watching others, especially adults. It is essential that church class time is not limited only to children praying.

Frequently allow time for teachers to pray, as the teachers can use this opportunity to demonstrate how they pray to God in a conversation format.

Some children in your preschool program may hear only memorized prayers in the home. "God is great, God is good . . ." and "Now I lay me down to sleep . . ." Encourage your children to "pray from their hearts." In the Faith Development Plan, we encourage them to talk to God as they would their parents. This is the first step in allowing the children to discover that they can have a personal relationship with God, which includes talking to Him anytime they would like.

The ministry model also encourages and demonstrates to preschool children that prayer includes praise, petitions, and asking for forgiveness. Too often our preschool children, and some adults for that matter, get into a rut of asking God for something every time they pray. While it is not wrong to ask God for something, it is wrong to present children with a God that is the equivalent of Santa Claus. We must allow them to see us praise God and worship Him through our prayers.

A great way to encourage parents to pray with their children at home is to organize monthly prayer calendars for them to hang in a visible place in the home. Every day offers different ideas for prayer time: pray for someone you know who does not go to church; praise God for the people in your family; pray for the senior minister, the church leaders, your sisters and brothers, a missionary; pray for someone who is mean to you; praise God for something you saw outside today that He made. These are meant to be "prayer starters" and are wonderful for parents who do not know where to start with their children.

Such calendars can be done with simple publishing software and completed in a few minutes or compiled by hand. The benefits are worth whatever time is expended. Print several copies each month and display them at the welcome center for parents to take at their leisure.

EVANGELISM (Bible Knowledge and Experience)

Preschoolers are known to say anything. On several instances we have had children spill the beans on many family secrets during church time. Young children do not realize there are things you say and things you do not say and, for the most part, they are not inhibited to tell people what they know. They are not embarrassed to invite their friends to church because they have not developed any insecurities in doing so. What a great time to place the seed of evangelism in their heart. Motivating them to tell others about their church, the Bible, and God are vital steps in the process of raising them up to be disciples of Jesus Christ.

Time should be taken each week in church class to challenge young children to share their faith. One way we encourage our children to tell others about Jesus is through the simple song, "It's Bubbling," which tells about how exciting it is to have Jesus in your life—so exciting that it comes bubbling out of you and you just have to express it to everyone you meet. We purchased a very inexpensive bubble machine and allowed the children to sing the song and pop the bubbles at the same time. We repeatedly explain, "If we are friends with Jesus and love Him, we need to be happy and tell others about Him. We 'just can't keep it quiet!'"

Another way of encouraging preschool children to share their faith is by giving them something tangible to assist them. Occasionally you may give children five pennies to take home. We encourage them to put the pennies in one pocket and every time they tell someone God loves them, they can move one penny to the other pocket. If they move all five pennies from one pocket to the other, they have shared God's love with five people each day. This is a good exercise for elementary children also.

One of the best ways for preschoolers to see the importance of evangelism is through the model of their parents or grandparents. When a child witnesses his parents sharing their faith with an unbeliever, he sees evangelism in action. I am so fortunate to know several people who have come to Christ through the testimony and disciple-

One of the best ways for preschoolers to see the importance of evangelism is through the model of their parents or grandparents.

ship of my parents. It has undoubtedly left a mark on me that will last a lifetime.

SERVICE (Bible Knowledge and Experience)

Most young children love to help. They are full of energy and bask in the praise they receive from helping mom, dad, or teacher. Preschool is the optimum age to affirm and develop the desire to serve. Children are more than happy to take a dust rag and walk around the church dusting pews. They love to use their energy by picking up trash in the church yard.

Take at least two weeks to present lessons for preschoolers on people in the Bible who served and how Jesus served. Allow certain times for children in the preschool class to participate in acts of service around the church. This may be a wonderful fifth-Sunday alternative tradition to begin. Give each child a dust rag, a paper towel, or a broom to walk around the church and serve. While you are walking explain to the child how God is pleased when they help others this way.

Perhaps one Sunday every quarter you can choose two or three preschool children to help pass out bulletins. Maybe one Sunday you can make cards or cookies to take to a nursing home. Group Publishing has a book entitled *Service Projects Preschoolers Can Do*.[4] Use this book as a resource for choosing service projects for your preschool students and incorporating them in the preschool area of your Faith Development Plan.

Again, one of the best ways for preschoolers to see the importance of service is through the model of their parents or grandparents. If these children do not see their parents serving in any capacity, they will struggle to see the importance of it in the future.

Strongly encourage parents to choose an area of service beneficial to the Kingdom where they can serve alongside their child. Perhaps the parents can sign up to clean an area of the church building once a week. Maybe they can deliver wheeled meals once a month. Soup kitchens are always looking for volunteers to help serve, and even the smallest child can hand out napkins to those in need. Servant evangelism projects are a perfect way for parents and children to work together in service in such activities as: handing out water bottles with the church address and service times at a local park, washing car windows in a grocery parking lot while placing advertisements for church services, sweeping a sidewalk, or raking some leaves for a neighbor, who does not know Jesus. All are great ways for parents to model service to their children. Who knows, you may be raising future missionaries for the Lord.

BIBLES ARE IMPORTANT (Bible Knowledge and Experience)

If you grew up going to church, you might remember when you loved to bring things from home to church—stuffed animals, Barbies, purses, blankets, cars, and trading cards? Preschool children love to bring things from home to church and back again and sometimes they need help from mom and dad to remember these items.

Bibles are no exception. There is no better time than preschool to begin expecting children to bring their Bibles to church each week. There is no need to bribe children by rewarding them with candy; they will do it just for the sheer joy of bringing their own Bibles.

> There is no better time than preschool to begin expecting children to bring their Bibles to church each week.

Most churches provide children with a Bible at some point in their Christian walk. Some receive their Bibles at birth, others when they start reading, and still others at conversion. Whatever time children receive their Bible, it is imperative they learn to value it and treasure it. An excellent Bible for two- and three-year-old children is *My First Bible*[5] by Kenneth N. Taylor. Each Bible account is written on a preschool age level with easy to understand words. The pictures in this Bible are very realistic as opposed to other preschool Bibles which use cartoons. One of the most wonderful features of this Bible is the built-in handle. This is a wonderful addition for little hands. Consider purchasing a copy of this Bible for each of your two- and three-year-old students. Make sure to have plenty of extras of these Bibles in the classroom for children who forget theirs and for visitors.

The Beginner's Bible by Karyn Henley and Dennas Davis is an excellent Bible for four- and five-year-old children. Although it has cartoon like pictures of the historical figures of the Bible, it is an excellent resource for preschool children. Consider investing in a copy of this Bible, or another Bible you feel is better for your children, for each child entering your four- and five-year-old class.

Encourage children and parents to bring their Bibles to church each class time. When a story is told from the Bible, not only should the teacher have her Bible open, she should take time to find the story for the children in their Bibles, and allow them to have it with them during the story time.

Ask the parents of your preschoolers to read the story they learned in church throughout the week and go back through their Bibles reinforcing the stories learned in the past. Suggest that parents choose key words from each story to leave out. Allow children to fill in the blank as an interactive experience. "Abraham married _____" (SARA) "and they had a son named _____" (ISAAC). This is a creative alternative to parents simply reading them the stories over and over.

As with everything we have introduced at this developmental level, it is most important that the children see the importance of the Bible in their parent's lives. Do these parents bring their Bible to church each week? Do the children see their parents using their Bible at home during the week, or only at "special times"? Encourage parents to set the example with their children and treat their Bibles as the most important book ever, God's Word.

> Encourage parents to make their child's first Bible very special. Setting aside a special afternoon to visit a Christian bookstore for the specific purpose of choosing their child's Bible and taking the child out to lunch afterwards is something parent and child will always remember. Also, encourage parents to choose a Bible on their child's level. Several of the children in our preschool class have children's Bibles, pink with cute pictures on the front, but the inside is the same translation their parents are using. Sending a child to church with a translation meant for adults is the equivalent of sending your child to kindergarten with a college textbook. She may hold it, look at it, and love it, but it will not make any sense to her.

BOOKS OF THE BIBLE (Bible Knowledge)

Contrary to what some people may believe, preschool children can learn, at a minimum, all the New Testament books in order. It is also possible for them to learn their Old Testament books, if it is done properly.

Most children and adults memorize volumes of information through song lyrics. It is why most of us reading this book know the preamble to the Constitution. It is why we know a "story 'bout a man named Jed" and can tell anyone word for word "a tale of a fateful trip that started from this tropic port, aboard this tiny ship." It is why the stories of Zacchaeus, Ananias and Sapphira, and Peter and John going to pray are so familiar to many of us.

Taking a visit to a Christian bookstore in your area will no doubt show you many possibilities for teaching your children the books of the Bible in song. For the purposes of this Faith Development Plan I will suggest teaching the two's and three's class the books of the New Testament and teaching the four's and five's class the Old Testament while reviewing the New. It can be done. Don't underestimate your preschooler's intelligence.

> **When we evaluated our junior high and high school departments for our Faith Development Plan we learned none of our students or sponsors knew all the books of the Bible in order.**

SCIENCE AND PRESCHOOLERS (Bible Knowledge and Science)

Preschool children are forming their own mind-sets on many things they see on a daily basis. They are determining how they view the world around them, even in the aspect of creation. Preschool is the best time to help children formulate the mind-set of God's master design in the creation of nature, animals, and our bodies.

Preschool is the best time to help children formulate the mind-set of God's master design in creation.

There are several ways to foster this view with God and nature. Permanent nature centers can be set up as part of your preschool classroom. Bring in collections of leaves, pine cones, pictures of lakes, rivers, and mountains to show these little ones how powerful God must be to make these things. The more enthusiastic the teacher in this area, the more amazed the children will be. "Can you believe how beautiful God made each of these leaves?!" "I love the fall! I love to see God's world and how special it is, all the different colors of red, orange, yellow, and brown!" Preschool children will pick up on that enthusiasm and will have a deeper appreciation for their world as a gift from God.

Several things can be done to show God's design for the human body. Allowing the children to put their fingers in ink and look at their fingerprints is a wonderful way to show them how special God made them. Repeatedly tell the children how special they are and point out different features in different children to show how we are all different because God made us special.

Showing God's design for animals is wonderful to see through a preschool child's eyes. If you know of a Christian veterinarian, he or she can bring in an animal such as a dog or cat and show how God specifically designed that animal to live and function. The veterinarian may show the cat's claws or the dog's paws and tell how God made them special.

Another great way to show the wonderful designs of animals is to provide bug catchers for the children. Children can go outside with specially designed bug catching scissors and holders to find ants or other things God has made. Our preschool children have found broken robins' eggs and put those in their holder. After they have had time to catch several things they can stay outside and observe how special God made them.

However you choose to introduce your preschoolers to the wonders of science and God, it is important to take the children outside, weather permitting, for a short time each Sunday. Children must realize that learning about God is not confined to the four walls of the classroom or even to the church building. Taking the children into God's wonderful outdoors is the best way for children to actually see God through his creation.

BASIC BIBLE STORIES (Bible Knowledge)

Of course preschool children can comprehend basic Bible stories. If you use a "canned" curriculum, you will follow those stories in order. If you choose to write your own curriculum, the "Curriculum" section at the end of this chapter will help you determine which stories you can use with specific elements of the Faith Development Plan.

BIBLE VERSES (Bible Knowledge)

Children are wonderful at memorizing things, especially when facts are put to song. We can see dramatic, positive results when we take time to teach our preschoolers basic Bible verses and continue repeating these verses throughout the year to aid in retention. Visit the local Christian bookstore and invest in some Scripture CDs. There are several musical CDs and tapes with upbeat rhythms and melodies for little ones to enjoy.

WORSHIP (Feeling and Experience)

You rarely meet a child who does not love to sing and dance. Preschool age is a wonderful time to begin introducing the word "worship." Each week we can tell the children that we "worship" God because we love Him and want to thank Him for all the good things He does. A child who hears that explanation accompanied with "hands on" involvement every Sunday for four years will begin to know and experience the meaning of worship.

During "worship time" sing a mix of slow songs and fast songs with a lot of actions such as jumping, shouting, dancing, reaching high, going low, and twisting. Allow time for children to play instruments in praise to God. At times just allow children to lift their instruments up to God and play to Him. "Let's lift our instruments and praise God for our mommies and daddies!" (bang, clang, boom, ring). "Let's lift our instruments and praise God for the beautiful sun out in the sky!" (more clangs, ringing cymbals, and bangs).

Caution should be used when choosing songs for this age group. Only use songs whose meanings the children will be able to understand. Songs such as "Heavenly Sunshine," "We Are Climbing Jacob's Ladder," "Father Abraham," "I'm in the Lord's Army," "Deep and Wide," and "One Door and Only One" are very difficult for some older children to comprehend, let alone a preschool child. These songs can do more harm than good if the child is confused by what he is singing.

CONCEPTS AND FACTS PRESCHOOLERS STRUGGLE TO COMPREHEND

THE TRINITY

We all do it, often without even realizing it. We use different terms for God like Heavenly Father, Jesus, Lord, Savior, and even Holy Spirit. We do it when we pray, and we do it frequently in front of our preschoolers. This is a concept so frustrating to preschoolers that they literally give up trying to understand it. Listen to this prayer: "Dear Heavenly Father, we are so thankful for all the boys and girls in this classroom today. God, we thank you for all the good gifts you give us. And, Lord, we thank You for being our friend. In Jesus' name, Amen." This sounds like a very nice prayer in a preschool setting, right? Very simple and easy to understand. Now ask yourself, to whom was this person praying? We know. This person was praying to God. We know that God, Jesus, the Heavenly Father, Lord, and Savior are all one person. But think about this prayer from a preschooler's viewpoint. In their eyes, to whom was this person praying? Four different people: God, Heavenly Father, Lord, and Jesus. (I recently met a woman who came to Christ in her adult years. She distinctly remembers leaning over to a friend after her first month in church asking, "Who am I supposed to pray to?" She had heard so many different references to God even *she* was confused.)

The concept of the trinity is very hard for a typical preschooler to understand and it demands an explanation. As Christian educators we owe young children an explanation. We should not sit back and expect them to figure out such complex ideas on their own for fear of the conclusions they may reach. Many times this concept is overlooked because it is not a Bible story. Tragically it is not included in most curriculums. Did Jesus heal the blind man or did God heal the blind man? Yes. How can that be? They are the same person.

May I suggest two solutions for this predicament:

1) For the two- and three-year-old children, ask teachers to consciously use the same name for God when they are speaking or praying. For example, the prayer previously used would sound like this, "Dear Jesus, we are so thankful for all the boys and girls in this classroom today. Jesus, we thank you for all the good gifts you give us. We thank You for being our friend. In Your name we pray, Amen." That takes a lot of confusion out of the prayer.

    Or when telling a Bible story, not only say that Jesus healed the blind man, continually refer to Jesus in the story without bouncing back to God. Another possibility would be to say, "Jesus healed the blind man. And God healed the blind man too, because He used Jesus to make him better."

2) For the four- and five-year-old class, begin each school year (August or September) with the reading of the book *3 in 1*.[6] It is a wonderful resource that uses the three parts of an apple to illustrate the fact God is "three in one." God, Jesus, and the Holy Spirit are all the same, just as the flesh, peel, and core are all an apple. When we presented this concept to our four- and five-year-old class, we actually peeled an apple and

let the children see the three different parts. Later, we ate the apple for snack. After playfully quizzing the children several times, we realized they seemed to understand the concept as well as any preschool child could and that the confusion in this matter would be limited because of the lesson.

PERSECUTION

When my coteacher and I began working with the four- and five-year-old class, we strongly encouraged the children to tell others about God and His love. Each week we would enthusiastically ask the students who they were going to tell that week about God and His love. We explained that God wants everyone to be in heaven, and we want all our friends and family there, too. The children would smile and energetically yell names when we asked who they would tell about God that week.

Two months into the year I noticed the children had changed their attitude about evangelism. When asking them if they were going to tell others about Jesus, they all but shook their heads no. They looked timid and scared and often would stare at the ground.

After several weeks of this curious change of heart I decided to think about why all the children were behaving so strangely. After evaluating many of the things we did with the children, I zoomed in on our lesson series. We were studying about Paul and his many trips to jail. The curriculum called for emphasizing how horrible the conditions were in prison. The pictures included in the curriculum showed dirty Paul in a cold cell with rats around him. No wonder the children didn't want to tell anyone about Jesus after that story. In their minds, if you tell people about Jesus like Paul did, you could go to jail. They cannot separate in their minds that this was another continent at another time. And we cannot tell them, "But we all know that people now-a-days don't go to jail when they tell others about Jesus." That is simply not true.

There is a definite time and place for children to learn about persecution. In fact this will be introduced in the next chapter; however, preschool classrooms are not the place. There are plenty of Bible stories and biblical concepts, such as those mentioned in this chapter, preschool children should be learning without scaring them unduly.

Some Christian educators would not agree with this theory. For example, the story of Paul and Silas doesn't focus on them in prison, the theme is to be joyful in all circumstances. But most preschool children will not hear a word you say past, "Paul and Silas were in prison because they were telling people about Jesus." Of course more of the story *would* be told, but at that point the child might be preoccupied with thinking, "If I tell people about Jesus, will I go to prison?"

If your curriculum calls for you to tell a story about Paul in prison or Joseph being thrown into a pit by his brothers, I suggest you skip the lesson and focus on another area of your Faith Development Plan. Persecution is too frightening for a typical preschool child.

Preschool Learning Goals

By the time a two- or three-year-old child leaves his or her classroom at the Community Christian Church he or she will have:

- ✔ Reinforced and strengthened all ideas learned in the nursery and toddler area.
- ✔ Learned basic stories of the Bible such as Jesus' birth, Noah and the Ark, David and Goliath, and Adam and Eve.
- ✔ Learned of Jesus' miracles.
- ✔ Learned about heaven and begun to look forward to the hope of eternity there.
- ✔ Learned about evangelism and developed an enthusiasm for telling others about God.
- ✔ Learned the importance of giving and tithing.
- ✔ Realized the Bible is God's Word to us, and it is such an important book that we need to carry it with us and read it at home.
- ✔ Performed acts of service and learned that serving others makes God happy.
- ✔ Learned to pray in his own words and realized he can pray any time he desires, not just at meal and bedtimes.
- ✔ Learned that Jesus and the people of the Bible were real, not pretend.
- ✔ Begun viewing the world around them, specifically nature, animals, and the human body, as special gifts from God.
- ✔ Learned the books of the New Testament in order through song.
- ✔ Learned basic Bible verses.

In addition, by the time a four- or five-year-old child leaves his or her classroom at the Community Christian Church he or she will have:

✔ Reinforced and strengthened all concepts begun in the two- and three-year-old class.
✔ Learned more stories of New and Old Testament events and people.
✔ Learned the books of the Old Testament in order through song.
✔ Begun praying with petition, praise, and repentance.
✔ Learned longer Scripture passages such as John 3:16 or The Lord's Prayer.

Things a Parent Can Do to Reinforce What Is Taught in the Preschool Department (Family)

Parents have the strongest impact on their children during their preschool years. These children have not moved into the stage where they say, "I know everything, Mom. You don't know anything!" Preschool children are studiers. They carefully study their parents when mom and dad are not looking and frequently imitate what they learn.

In fact, I would ask you to think of a parent and thoughtfully consider their passion. Maybe you know of a father whose passion is NASCAR. Perhaps you know of a father whose passion is hunting. Maybe you know of a mother whose passion is country music. If you take a look at each of their children, you will most likely find a child with the same passion. Children learn from watching their parents. The same power of example works in spiritual commitment and lifestyle as well.

Here are some simple things parents of preschoolers can do to help reinforce the concepts and facts presented in church time:

✔ Set aside a special day to take your child for his first Bible. Show your enthusiasm as you allow him to help choose the Bible and maybe even a special bookmark. Once you get the Bible home, take time to look through it and read some of the stories, remarking what a special book it is. Remind your child to bring his/her Bible every Sunday to church. Make sure you are bringing your Bible to church each Sunday, too! Remember, children are imitators and they pick up on what is important to you. (If your church uses a special Bible such as *The Beginner's Bible*, try to encourage your child to choose this particular Bible so all the children have the same translation.)

✎ Set aside a special time each day to read the Bible with your child. If you know what your child learned in her church class time, read that story to help reinforce the lesson.

✎ Begin giving your child simple chores to perform at home. Set a predetermined amount your child will receive each week. Help your child learn the concept of saving, spending, and giving. (Purchasing "My Giving Bank" at a local Christian bookstore will help your child separate the money into different compartments.) Talk to your child about tithing, and make sure she is giving at least some money to the church each Sunday. Never prohibit a little one who wants to give more than 10% of their money "to Jesus."

✎ If someone close to you dies, take time to talk to your children about heaven. Talk about what you think heaven will be like, and ask them what they are looking forward to in heaven. Your enthusiasm toward heaven will show your child the hope we have as Christians.

✎ Use the church-provided prayer calendar to pray daily with your child. Take turns having your child pray and allowing your child to hear you pray. Encourage your children to pray in petition, praise, and repentance and to think of prayer as talking to their best friend. Avoid recited prayers and encourage them to pray from their heart.

✎ Make praying for your child a part of your daily faith journey. It is never too early to begin praying for his spiritual growth, his future career, or his future mate. Bathe your child in prayer and continue to lift specific requests to God on his behalf.

✎ Set aside at least one hour a month to participate in some act of service. This may be sharpening pencils, cleaning the bulletins out of the pews after church, pulling weeds in the church garden, or bringing flowers to shut-ins or those in the nursing home. If you make this a priority early in your children's lives, they will make it a priority when they are out of your nest.

✔ Make a point to use teachable moments with your children in the area of creation, the human body, and animals. God is a master designer and each of these areas shows His might and power. Children will gain an appreciation for all of these areas if they see your awe of His intricate design.

✔ Intentionally point out God's creation when walking with your child. If you see a beautiful animal at a zoo or around your house, marvel at how God made that animal so special. If your child hurts himself, take a few moments to point out how God made his body to heal. Once you begin pointing these concepts out to your child, you will quickly discover they will be pointing them out to you.

✔ Encourage your child to talk to others about Jesus. Children can learn evangelism at a very early age; however, it is almost certain they will not develop this habit unless they see it from their parents. Allow your child to hear you invite your neighbors to church. Include unsaved people in your daily prayer time. Take part in any church-sponsored evangelism projects. Take your child to a local homeless shelter and let her help you serve the people or pass out napkins.

✔ Work alongside your church teachers in helping your child learn the books of the Bible. Perhaps you will be learning this list with your child. Once she has learned the books of one testament, praise your child to friends and relatives, letting your child see that this was a special accomplishment. Continue repeating the books in order to aid in retention.

✔ Bring your child to church as regularly as possible. Many parents choose not to attend church simply due to the fact they are too tired. They will even tell their children, "We've had too big a weekend. We're tired and are just going to stay home today." The child will quickly learn that the parent does not stay home from work because they are too tired and will not allow their older siblings to stay home from school because they are tired. Thus, the child concludes school and jobs are important, but church is just for when you feel like it. If this is the lesson you are teaching your child in preschool, it will undoubtedly carry over in their later faith development.

✔ *Do not* talk adversely about the church or the teachers in front of your children. Speaking negatively about the church greatly restricts the impact it will have on their trust in the church and ultimately their faith development. If you are upset with something your child's teacher did on a given Sunday, make sure the child is out of earshot before discussing your concerns with the teacher. Be careful what you say at home.

Listen to this illustration: Mary's parents are not happy with the direction the church is taking. They make no attempt to hide how they feel from her at home. Each Sunday on the ride home from church, Mary's father tells her mother what he thought about the worship service, the special music, and the preaching; none of which is ever positive. One Sunday Mary's teacher told her mother that Mary was teasing another girl in the class about her "ugly dress." Mary's mother was extremely offended that the teacher scolded her for something "five-year-olds can't understand." Mother told Mary, "Your teacher was wrong for what she told you today. She shouldn't even be working with children!" Now, Mary doesn't know if she should listen to anything her teacher says.

➢ Live what you say. Don't allow your child to see the "Sunday Mom" and the "Home Mom." Don't allow your child to foster the idea that you act one way on Sunday and another way during the week. This will, without question, scar his faith development for years to come. The most detrimental thing to your child's faith development is inconsistency in your talk and your walk.

WARNING, WARNING, WARNING

A widely overused activity found in the preschool area of most churches is coloring. You can find a coloring page for just about any story you are covering in the Bible. If you decide to write your own curriculum, it will be tempting to use several coloring sheets. That's why I suggest sending a color sheet home in addition to their Bible as a "take home paper." This way the children who love to color may do so, and the others don't feel they have to complete the paper.

Coloring sheets are not bad; however, they are overused. Coloring usually requires a child to sit down for an extended period of time. I have observed Sunday school classrooms where two- and three-year-old children have been welcomed by one activity, a coloring sheet, every Sunday for a month. I have watched the children as they color, and most will scribble and look around the room with distracted curiosity.

Fight the temptation to use coloring sheets more than once a month in your preschool classrooms. If the curriculum calls for coloring sheets, try painting, gluing glitter, markers, or some other artistic flavor to help them fill those little pictures. If you need to offer children a coloring sheet, always give them the option of sitting or standing at the table while they work. Another tip: if you need to offer a coloring sheet, have the teacher parallel the child's work. Have one teacher sit with the children and color his or her own picture. Children will be more apt to take their time and will often choose the same colors as the teachers. Many times this stops the child who sits down, scribbles for thirty seconds, and hops up to play.

NOTES

1. Tracy, *Blues Clues*, 8.

2. William Chad Newsom, "The Greatest Story (Account) Ever Told," *Children's Ministry Magazine* (July/August 2003), http://cmmag.com/articles/detail.asp?ID=4861, 1.

3. Ibid.

4. Donna L. Alexander, Jan Kershner, Barbie Murphy, Lori Haynes Niles, and Bonnie Temple, *Service Projects Preschoolers Can Do* (Loveland, CO: Group Publishing, 2001).

5. Kenneth N. Taylor, *My First Bible* (Wheaton, IL: Tyndale House, 1989).

6. Joanne Marxhausen, *3 in 1* (Saint Louis, MO: Concordia Publishing House, 1973).

Chapter Seven

EVALUATING THE ARROWS:
EARLY ELEMENTARY
FIRST AND SECOND GRADE STUDENTS

*Where do you want your students to be by the time they graduate,
and how are you going to get them there?*

Nicole is seven years old and in the first grade. She has big blue eyes
and beautiful, long, straight, blonde hair, which her mom frequently puts
in French braids. Nicole is a typically thin seven-year-old girl. Nicole is
painfully shy and still sucks her thumb at bedtime. She is extremely com-
pliant, never cries when left in class, always obeys, and never causes a bit
of trouble. One Sunday school teacher remarked, "Nicole has been in my
class for an entire year, and I have never once heard her talk."

She is an only child whose parents are going through a very nasty
divorce. Nicole's parents share joint custody. Nicole's parents yell at each
other in front of her. Her parents work hard to manipulate her love and
affection due to selfishness and insecurities on their part. Nicole's mother
is dating a man who does not like children and Nicole can read that. She
does not feel safe when she is with her mother or her father. She is very
confused and cannot relate to anything she is being taught at church. She,
as typical seven-year-olds do, has many questions to ask. Most of the time
she keeps the questions to herself for fear of upsetting her mother or father.
One day, during prayer time, Nicole uncharacteristically raised her hand
and blurted out, "My mom says I don't have to go to my dad's house if I
don't want to." She smiled at her teachers, looking for some clue as to how
they felt about that statement.

Nicole seems very unhappy most of the time. She is a very bright girl.
She reads above grade level for her teacher at school. She can do math

on a second-grade level. She knows her address and her telephone number. She knows all the words to several of the country songs her mom plays in her SUV. She eats very little at meals and snacks and is content to play Barbies by herself for hours.

Nicole's teachers at church are wonderful. She has grown to love and admire both Miss Karen and Mr. Jim in the three short months she's been attending their class. They are always in the room when she arrives, and the centers for the day are all laid out for her and her classmates. They always have upbeat music playing in the background as she and her classmates work on their learning center activities. Most of the songs they play are those sung later in children's church.

Nicole always brings her Bible and her tithe money to church. This is something she has been taught since she was in preschool. She does not receive any candy or prize for bringing her Bible or her money; she simply does it because it is right.

Every Sunday Nicole and her classmates repeat their books of the Bible. Nicole particularly loves it when visitors come to her class for the first time. They always seem so impressed to hear the whole class repeat all the books of the Old and New Testament.

Although her face doesn't show it, Nicole feels a sense of warmth while she is at church. She feels safe there. Her teachers speak of heaven as a wonderfully peaceful place. They also tell her and the rest of her class exactly how they all can go to heaven. She loves to hear about that.

Her teachers challenge her and her classmates each week to invite others to church. One day, while on the playground at school, Nicole asked her teacher if she went to church. The teacher told Nicole a long story of how she used to go to church, but was very busy now. Nicole asked her teacher if she would like to come to her church. The teacher said "she would try." Nicole smiled from ear to ear the rest of the day.

After Sunday school, Nicole attends the "song time" in "big church" with her mother. She loves to hear the band and see the people clap and lift their hands to God. Sometimes she closes her eyes and lifts her hands to God, too. This is her favorite thing to do at church.

Early elementary children are fun-loving balls of energy who keep teachers on their toes. Unlike preschool children who typically nap once a day, early elementary-aged children can go and go and go until they hit the pillow at night. They have so much energy and so much excitement. The key to working with this age is channeling both.

Along with the excess energy, early elementary-aged children are full of questions. They have figured out there are many things they do not understand and that frustrates them. They want to know. A parent may become annoyed with the barrage of questions he or she receives from a child of this age. "Mom, why is that man standing there?" "Mom, what is that beeping noise outside?" "Dad, what does that mean when you say, 'Drop it?' I don't have anything to drop! Dad, why did you say that?" After several questions you may see a frustrated parent, but early elementary-aged children learn by asking questions. They have a strong desire to know of things they do not understand, religion included.

Early elementary-aged children learn by asking questions, with a strong desire to know of things they do not understand.

While first and second grade students are showing signs of growing up and maturing, at times they regress to preschool ways. This is very difficult for parents and teachers who must deal with their personality inconsistencies. They still have a hard time expressing themselves, which often results in anger, frustration, moodiness, or silence toward parents and teachers.

Early elementary-aged children are beginning to feel the influences of the outside world. Their parents "don't know everything." Now they are influenced by people like Britney Spears, what their friends say, and what they hear on television. They are beginning to formulate their own opinions on ethical and moral concepts. It is crucial at this age for parents and the church to step in and expect continued spiritual growth from these children and not shrug their shoulders with flippant or dismissive attitudes.

BUILDING ON EARLIER CONCEPTS

It is important to remember the arrows up and repetition keys at this time. Many of the concepts taught in the first and second grade classes are those previously introduced in the nursery, toddler, or preschool class. Now they are presented in more depth. We will briefly discuss previously introduced concepts and how to continue the development in these areas with first and second graders. We will then discuss some new areas to introduce in this age group.

STORY TIME

Although first and second grade students can sit for slightly longer periods of time than preschool children, honestly, it is not much longer. Children this age can easily sit through a two-hour movie, a theatrical presentation, or a slew of mindless cartoons on television, but subject a seven- or eight-year-old child to a sit-down, lecture-style lesson and their minds will begin racing after a very few minutes. Their muscles will be itching to run, jump, and play. We are dealing with children who are visually stimulated most of their day. We are working each week with kids who have watched several hours of television, played several hours of video and computer games, been at a school that teaches through interaction, and spent the rest of the week in organized sports or after-school activities. Trying to "teach these kids a lesson" and make them sit perfectly still for a Bible story with no excitement, visuals, or interaction is a difficult challenge for them. Not only will we be frustrated, but our students will be, too. It simply is not fair to them.

In the preschool section of this book, I presented the concept of a "master storyteller" or realistic drama presentations for children. The same concepts hold true for children in first and second grade. Conveying the Bible lesson through interactive, creative, enthusiastic storytellers are still the best way for children to hear and retain the lessons taught in their church class. Drama presentations are equally effective; however, drama presentations take more manpower and more time to script, costume, and rehearse. Most "master storytellers" can study a text of Scripture, decide on which visuals to use, and they are ready to go.

> **Do not let the title of "master storyteller" intimidate you. You can find several "master storytellers" at a church dinner. Just look around the room for the person at the table everyone is listening to and laughing at!**

If your curriculum is the same for first through fifth grade, allow classes to come together for story time to share the use of the "master storyteller" or drama presentation. If you minister in a smaller church, consider using the same storyteller or drama presentation for preschool through fifth grade. Again, this will be a welcome relief for a teacher who would merely need to sit with the children and make sure everyone is listening.

HEAVEN (Bible Knowledge and Feeling)

Having introduced and built an excitement for students about heaven in the preschool department, we have reached the time to teach the children further about this wonderful place. Set aside at least four weeks to study the subject of "heaven and how to get there." First and second grade is an age when many children raised in the church begin thinking about making a decision for Christ.

1) Allow them to look up Scriptures from Revelation describing what heaven will look like and provide markers and crayons for them to draw pictures of heaven based on what they have read.

2) Go through the plan of salvation and explain how they can live in heaven eternally by having a personal relationship with Jesus Christ and accepting Him as their Savior. An excellent workbook to study with all your students during this time is *Discovering Jesus*.[1] It is very easy to follow and teach.

3 Continue offering an annual "Heaven Night" and possibly include the seven- and eight-year-old children in the program. Scan your student's "heaven pictures" in class and make it into a PowerPoint presentation for the service. Include the child's name at the bottom of each slide.

TITHING (Bible Knowledge and Experience)

Following the Faith Development Plan, these children started giving in the form of a tithe when they were two years old. Continue encouraging parents to give their children some type of chores or jobs where they can earn money. It is important that the parents do not simply give the child the money for tithing each week. Remember, the key to a successful Faith Development Plan is looking at the child as a future adult. Even if the jobs and the compensation are small, the child will feel a sense of pride when the coins they put in the basket are something they worked for and earned.

Take at least four weeks to present lessons on tithing. Discuss the definition of the word "tithe." Take time to look at what the Bible says about tithing. Encourage the children to begin calling their "money for Jesus" a tithe instead. Allow the children to make lists of things in the church paid for by their tithe. Ask the financial secretary for a list of some expenditures for the church and show the children exactly how much it costs for electricity, water, and other items on a monthly basis.

A great lesson series for your students is *The ABC's of Handling Money God's Way*[2] by Howard and Bev Dayton. This series has a student workbook and a leader's guide. It teaches children God's design for money and introduces the concepts of stewardship and debt. Although the series is designed for twelve weeks, it can be modified for a shorter time frame or used in a Sunday or Wednesday night program.

PRAYER (Bible Knowledge, Feeling, and Experience)

At this point students have been learning about prayer for several years. In the preschool department they learned that praying to God was not just asking Him for something, but praising and asking forgiveness, too. Set aside two weeks in the early elementary section of your Faith Development Plan to present lessons on prayer, studying why we pray, how, and how often God wants us to pray. Children of seven and eight can now comprehend that God answers prayers in different ways, and it is time to introduce the idea that sometimes, just like their parents, God says, "Yes, No, and Not Yet." Studying "The Lord's Prayer" and the model it provides us, as well as memorizing this prayer, would fit perfectly into a two-week lesson series.

Along with the prayer calendar given to parents each month to help them lead their children in a daily prayer time, provide students with a prayer chart. Provide a space for things they would like to pray for and a place for answers. Create an area where they can write the things they have praised God for as well.

From time to time have different members of your congregation come in and tell of how God answered a particular prayer concern. This may be something recent or something that happened to them a long time ago. The children will enjoy having the guests in their class, and personal testimonies are applicable and easily retained.

EVANGELISM (Bible Knowledge and Experience)

You have already set the foundation for evangelism with students in preschool. You have encouraged them to feel comfortable sharing their faith in God with other people. Now it is time to introduce them to the "Great Commission" and the term "disciple." First and second grade students should memorize the "Great Commission" and study the events surrounding Jesus' command for us.

Seven- and eight-year-old children love to be challenged. They prove this by bringing in more money for the missionary at

Vacation Bible School if the youth minister will shave his head, or memorizing the books of the Bible if they can have a class party. They simply become driven when they are challenged. This is where channeling their excitement and energy is important.

One fall we decided to have a lock-in for our elementary-aged students. Two weeks before the lock-in I was walking into the children's church room and glanced at the sign-up list on the bulletin board. I noticed there were thirty-five children signed up for the event and all of them were our church kids. I went into the room and sat down for a heart-to-heart chat with the students. "I noticed on the sign-up list for the lock-in that all the kids who are coming go to our church. And that's great . . . but I want you to know that when we plan these events, we are not just planning them for you to come and have a good time. We can do that anytime. We plan these fun things so you will invite your friends. Sometimes it's hard to invite your friends to church if that friend has never been before. They may feel uncomfortable, but asking them to come to something fun at church is easy. And maybe if they come to something fun at church, they will see that church is a cool place and God is a great God and will want to start coming to church and become a Christian. So next week I want to see some different names on that list. Okay?"

That's all I had to say. Those kids took that as a *challenge*. They went home and started calling their friends, went to school and started inviting their classmates, and finally we ended up with seventy kids. Thirty-five of those seventy students did not attend our church and most of them didn't have a church home.

Present your students with a four-week study on the "Great Commission" and what it means to be a "disciple." When you present the "Great Commission" to your students, tell them it is a challenge. A challenge to not just be "any Christian," but a Christian who wants others to go to heaven, too. In addition, plan an afternoon mission trip twice a year for this age. This may be stocking food in a homeless shelter or cleaning the local Ronald McDonald house in your area to help those whose children are in the hospital. These "mini-mission trips" are going to set the stage for larger scale, longer, more intense mission trips as they grow physically and spiritually.

SERVICE (Bible Knowledge and Experience)

We are ready to place another layer on our service foundation. In the preschool years we began introducing students to very simple service projects they could complete with their parents. First and second grade students are now able to begin studying the Bible's definition of a servant. They can understand that Jesus was the perfect example of servanthood. Take one or two weeks in your Faith Development Plan for students to study the idea of servanthood.

Continue encouraging parents to choose a regular time of service with their children, ideally on a weekly or monthly basis. Ask parents to take pictures of their children performing different acts of service and place the pictures in visible places around the church. This will be a testimony to the rest of the church that the youth ministry, which includes the youth minister, parents, teachers, and students, view reaching out to others as a high priority.

In addition, begin scheduling three service projects a year for your first and second grade students. This will be a portion of your Faith Development Plan for their area. Schedule the projects a year in advance and space them out appropriately. Consider scheduling a service project in the fall to rake leaves and sweep sidewalks for the elderly people in your church. Another project may be around Christmastime, baking cookies, singing, and visiting with those in the nursing home. Perhaps another project could be offered in the summer for children to help pack clothes for people in third-world countries. Encourage parents to join in on these service projects and to make these times "teachable moments" for their children.

BIBLES ARE IMPORTANT (Bible Knowledge and Experience)

You have already stressed the importance of students carrying Bibles with them to church. This fact will be reinforced during the first and second grade years. Students should continue to use *The Beginner's Bible* during these years. Most children will be able to read all the stories in this Bible. Be sure to have several copies of this same Bible in the classroom for visitors and children who have forgotten their Bibles.

A common mistake many teachers fall into involves bribing children with candy if they bring their Bibles to church. Unfortunately this idea will backfire and ultimately hurt their students. Thom and Joani Schultz say, "Not only are rewards distracting and shortsighted, they may also actually kill interest in the very things we want learners to learn. How could this be? Everyone understands the nature of bribes. They're designed to lure us into something we wouldn't normally find that attractive. Your parents probably taught you this. 'Now, honey, if you'll eat your spinach, you can have dessert.' After hearing things like this for years, you've figured it out: spinach is yucky and dessert is good. Rewards are distractions because they devalue the real thing."

They go on to prove this very idea with research by Alfie Kohn, author of the book *Punished by Rewards*. "In one such study, schoolchildren were split into two groups. The first group was told that to draw with felt-tip pens they must first draw with crayons. The other group was told the reverse. Two weeks later researchers found that whichever activity had been the prerequisite for the other was now less appealing to the students. Half the class didn't want to draw with felt-tip markers, and half avoided the crayons. Whatever was required to earn the bribe was devalued." Thus, if the teacher requires children to bring their Bible in order to get candy, bringing your Bible must be distasteful.[3]

In our observation of this very concept with our students we noticed when they were given a bribe, they would bring their Bibles to class. When they moved to junior high or high school class and the bribes stopped, they stopped bringing their Bibles. Unfortunately, giving children candy for bringing their Bibles is not helping to achieve the goal we desire. If we ask a teacher why she gives children candy for bringing their Bibles, she might answer, "Because I'm helping them develop a habit that will hopefully last them a lifetime." However, this type of motivation does not help them develop a habit.

> Giving children candy for bringing their Bibles is not helping to achieve the goal we desire.

Bringing a Bible to church should simply be an expectation such as school children bringing their history, math, or science book to class on a daily basis.

BOOKS OF THE BIBLE (Bible Knowledge)

The Faith Development Plan in this book suggests teaching the books of the New Testament in the two's and three's class and the books of the Old Testament in the four's and five's class. At this point the first and second grade students should have a fairly firm grasp on the order and basic division of those books, New and Old Testament.

In the first and second grade class, it is time to begin teaching children the divisions within each of these testaments. Most Christian bookstores should have charts to aid in the teaching of these divisions. If not, check out the Rose Publishing website and ask for a catalog.

Continue taking some time at the beginning or end of class to review the Old and New Testament books. Print out the books of the Bible in large squares, laminate the sheets, and place small magnets or pieces of velcro on the back of each square. Provide students with a surface to stick either magnets or velcro and encourage them to place the books in order. This would be an excellent learning center idea for children who have arrived early to class.

SCIENCE AND ELEMENTARY STUDENTS (Bible Knowledge and Science)

Elementary students have started learning science in their school on a regular basis. Obviously they will not be taught science from a Christian point of view. Most likely they will begin learning of evolution. Unfortunately, many elementary teachers do not bother to present evolution as a "theory." They present it as the truth. Our children need to begin learning as young as seven and eight the truths of God's creation.

Ken Ham's Answers in Genesis is an educational organization dedicated to presenting the *truths* of God's creation. Their website, **www.answersingenesis.org**, offers a wide variety of quality teaching tools for children in the area of science, such as DVDs, books, and more. The presentation of any of these resources designed for children would be a great addition to your Faith Development Plan.

> **Video Usage: While organizing your Faith Development Plan for the older ages, you may come upon lessons which are better presented in video format. Some teachers simply don't feel qualified to teach Science to their students and will be more comfortable with an 'expert' teaching or presenting certain concepts in the lesson. As with the younger ages, videos should not be used simply as "filler" material or as a lazy substitute for careful lesson preparation.**

Answers in Genesis is working on a phenomenal creation museum in northern Kentucky, a short distance from Cincinnati. The museum is a family-oriented, interactive museum where people can walk through Noah's Ark, step into Noah's workshop, visit the Stargazers Room, The Bible Authority Room, or the SFX Theater. The six days of creation, representations of

Adam and Eve, large dinosaurs, and giant bugs are among many other exciting exhibits. If your church is within driving distance, this would be an excellent day trip for elementary children.

Moody Video has several videos geared for the elementary level that teach about the wonder and miracle of God's creation through nature, the human body, and animals. Although some "church teachers" may feel intimidated to teach science to their students, showing a video on the wonder of bees or the miracle of the solar system is something any of us could do. This may be a series to offer on Sunday or Wednesday nights.

If you have a science teacher in your church or know of a science teacher who is a Christian, ask him or her to come into the class and teach the children basic science experiments which demonstrate what a wonderful God we have. (The Christian service camp in our area has a week-long science camp in the summer, run by a wonderful Christian man who teaches science at a public high school.) If you have a weather expert or meteorologist in your congregation, you may want to bring him in to explain to your students about the weather. God has designed the world at an average temperature, not only for humans' survival, but for our comfort and pleasure.

There are many ways to present science to your elementary students. As mentioned in earlier chapters, the best way to do this is by getting your students outside and presenting God's creation with enthusiasm, excitement, and wonder, encouraging the sense of awe for all God has made.

One option is to offer a yearly family campout for your church. This may be such a special time that it will become a tradition in your church for years to come. Set aside a weekend in the fall to have an "all church campout." Organize nature hikes during the day and stargazing at night. Make it a fellowship time as well as a learning time for your students and families.

However you choose to build and strengthen the science leg under your student's faith table, I encourage you to devote a minimum of one month of lessons each year to dealing with God's creation. This may be one week on nature, one week on animals, one week on the human body, and one week for a wrap up. You may also want to offer a class on godly science in the form of an elective during Sunday or Wednesday night class time. Consider presenting these lessons in the summer months when students can get out and see what they are learning.

BIBLE STORIES (Bible Knowledge)

A majority of your Faith Development Plan should include the teaching of Bible stories. As with the preschool department you should go through *The Beginner's Bible* and determine which stories you want to reinforce from the preschool years and which stories you would like to introduce. You should also choose Bible stories to fill two years since these children will spend two years in this department. Decide which stories will be taught only one year and which stories you want repeated each year.

At this time I would still suggest leaving out stories of persecution. First and second grade students are still balancing their emotional development. Without oversimplifying it, first and second graders are just slightly older preschoolers. They are still exhibiting some of the same developmental characteristics as their younger siblings. Stories that tell of Paul and Silas going to jail because they told people about Jesus, John the Baptist's beheading, Stephen being stoned for preaching, Daniel being thrown into the lions' den, three men being thrown into a fiery furnace because they wouldn't bow to the idol, Joseph being thrown into a pit by his own brothers, are all stories of persecution. While none of us could honestly admit being spiritually and emotionally scarred by hearing these stories at such a young age, if they are told with biblical accuracy they can be frightening to small children and possibly detrimental to future evangelistic efforts.

MEMORY VERSES (Bible Knowledge)

Continue reviewing the key memory verses and passages learned in the preschool department. Decide which passages and verses you wish for your students to *know* by the time they leave this department and divide them up for one year. Since the children will be in this department for two years, they will have two years to master the verses you desire for them to use.

In determining key verses you would like the first and second grade children to learn, you may want to cover verses dealing with "the plan of salvation." For instance, you may want to start with Romans 3:23 while explaining to them that this is the first step anyone would have to take to become a Christian. They need to know that no matter how "good" they think they are, they are a sinner. This verse will not only teach them what *they* need to do to become a Christian, it will later help them to know how to lead someone else to Christ and how to back it up with Scripture, thus becoming an evangelism tool.

WORSHIP (Bible Knowledge, Feeling, and Experience)

Worship is such a beautiful way to communicate with God. Unfortunately, there are many adults in your congregation who do not understand the concept of worship. You may have long-standing members who come into the sanctuary each week asking, "What am I going to get out of this church today?" Imagine a church which intentionally teaches their members, beginning in preschool, about godly worship. Could this change the way worship is viewed for the entire congregation?

In the preschool level at our congregation, children participate in "song time" or "worship time" during each class session. Children learn to play their instruments and sing songs to God because they love Him and want to thank Him for all the wonderful things He has done. They hear the term "worship" over and over and associate it with something exciting.

Now you will take worship a step further. In your Faith Development Plan, set aside one or two weeks to talk about worship. It is important to begin teaching the children that worship is much more than what happens on Sunday morning. Study Scriptures that tell how people from the Old Testament worshiped and discuss different ways you have seen people worship. Teach the children sign language to a simple song and allow them to think of God on a throne in heaven as they lift their hands in praise to Him.

One of the most powerful ways for children to learn how to worship properly is by watching other adults worship. Some churches separate their children and adults for every aspect of church time. Some churches not only separate their children, they are in a totally separate facility than the adults and instead participate in "student worship" or "children's worship." **This is a serious mistake.** When children are not given the opportunity to worship with other adults, specifically their parents, they can only learn worship from their peers. Sometimes that is a negative situation if you have a very rowdy group of boys or an apathetic group of teenagers. These children need to see adults worshiping. They need to see their parents worshiping God and observe the importance of worship in an adult.

Fight the urge to separate your children during the entire church service. Allow children to participate in the opening worship time and encourage them to sit with their parents. Before the sermon, excuse the children to an age-appropriate Bible learning time. Most children this age will not receive anything in regard to faith development from an adult-directed sermon. At times teenagers even struggle to understand the meaning of a sermon. Once the children are in their "children's church" classroom, they can sing upbeat songs on their level to prepare for the morning lesson.

New Building Blocks for Early Elementary Age Students

History and Elementary Students (Bible Knowledge and History)

A new faith development step for the first and second grade students is the leg of history. As we mentioned at the beginning of this chapter, elementary-aged children have a lot of questions. This is also the age where they begin to wonder about some bigger questions:

- How did we get the Bible?
- The Bible is "God's Word," but the teacher said that Matthew wrote one book, Moses wrote another book, and Paul wrote a bunch of books. How can that be?
- Are the things in the Bible all true or just some of them?

Our job as Christian educators is to provide children with the answers to these questions before they begin formulating their own theories. Throughout my experience in youth ministry I have heard committed students discuss their theories of some issues regarding the Bible. "I believe the New Testament is true, but I think the Old Testament was made up. The God of the Old Testament was a mean God, and the God of the New Testament was a loving God. I don't believe God would have been that mean." Listening to such ideas of the Bible and its authenticity make me realize why these students are so far off base. We aren't teaching them any differently.

The best resource to help you in this area is found in the area of Christian homeschooling. Regardless of your view on homeschooling, the publishers do present history from a Christian perspective. One such book is called *History for Little Pilgrims*. This book is on a first-grade reading level and begins to present the world of history as "His" story. Publishers go to great lengths to provide colorful workbooks and reading material for students to learn "His" story. You may choose to use these books in a month-long series of lessons on Sunday morning, adding centers and interactive reinforcements for the story. You may also choose to provide these books for your parents to review with children at home. Most children in public, private, or home school must take time for "silent reading." This may be a perfect alternative to *Little House on the Prairie* or *Charlotte's Web* for part of the school year. You will find that the parents, to their delight and surprise, will learn more than the children.

Another idea Newsom gives in his *Children's Ministry Magazine* article is to begin using different terms in your classroom to reinforce the idea with children that the Bible is actual history. He says, "Could it be that the very terms we use to describe the Bible create a mythological distance between children and truth? Consider the difference in the terms used below to refer to a 'story-based faith' and historical factual events."[4]

The Bible Stories	*vs.*	*History Accounts*
Bible Characters		Historical figures
Bible storybook		History textbooks
Bible story time		History class time

GOD'S PLAN FOR THE FAMILY (Bible Knowledge and Family)

Another foundational addition to the Faith Development Plan for this age is the concept of God's plan for the family. We are constantly viewing these children as future adults: future fathers, future mothers, future spouses. We also keep in mind that each of our students is involved in this group called the "family," and he or she must learn what God expects of this group. God has spelled out His desires for each member of the family. What is the child's role? What is the mother's role? What is the father's role? What is God's desire for marriage? What is God's desire for the family? These are questions most children will not form at such a young age; however, it is important to show them God's intentions for the family, regardless of how dysfunctional their family may be.

> We are constantly viewing these children as future adults: future fathers, future mothers, future spouses.

Unfortunately, since learning about the family is not a "Bible story," children in the church typically do not learn about this concept. Although they may learn to obey their parents and that doing so is one of the ten commandments, the lessons often stop there. The plan for this age calls for a minimum of two weeks to teach about God's plan for the family.

DAILY DEVOTIONS AND BIBLE READING (Bible Knowledge, Feeling, and Experience)

In chapter three we listed four basic building blocks we want to lay in our student's spiritual development foundations. Daily devotion time with God or Bible reading is one of these. A thorough Faith Development Plan will include teaching this concept at least once each year. Consider teaching this concept at the *beginning* of each year in combination with prayer. In the New Year everyone is speaking of resolutions, and your students will hear much of this from their parents, teachers at school, and the media. Remembering that children this age love challenges, challenge them to begin the routine of daily devotional time and prayer. Take two weeks of your Faith Development Plan to teach your children about these two important spiritual disciplines.

Do not just stop at teaching them the importance of spending time with God each day. Provide them with resources to take home and begin daily devotional time. Too often in the church we instruct students, even adults, to do something—start evangelizing, begin devotions, have a daily prayer time, be a servant—but we don't provide them with the resources to encourage them to action. Picture a Sunday morning sermon where the preacher speaks on the importance of evangelizing. In the foyer there is a table set up with business cards with the church's name, address, phone number, and service times. These are to help the congregation invite someone to church. Picture a sermon where the preacher speaks on the need to begin daily devotions. In the foyer are tables stacked with various devotional books to help the people get started. Not only will this aid adults in simply retaining what the preacher said, it will move them to action.

If you desire your students to begin daily devotions, provide them with some type of resource to encourage them to get started. Some publishers make bookmarks with a different Scripture passage for each day of the week. Children can pick up a different bookmark each week and stick it in their Bible for devotions. Some churches provide homemade devotional material for their students each week. Other publishers have take-home papers that have Scriptures corresponding with the lessons to be read during the week. A quick visit to your local Christian bookstore will offer several options for your students in the area of devotional material. Purchase several copies from the store or at an on-line book page and provide them for your students to purchase.

A wonderful devotional for first and second grade students is John MacArthur's *A Faith to Grow On.*[5] Although the cover reads, "Important things you should know now that you believe," This book can also be instrumental prior to a child making a decision for Christ. The book covers such questions as, "Can we see God? How long has God been alive? Is there only one God? What happens when we sin? Can we hear God? Who wrote the Bible? Must we obey God all the time? Does God see everything we do?"[6] These are all typical questions raised by our inquisitive first and second grade students and Mr. MacArthur does an excellent job of using Scripture to support his answers.

This is another excellent time to have different members of the congregation come into class and give testimonies of how God has blessed them through their daily devotion time. Have them speak to the children of how it is not always easy to do, but they will be blessed. However you choose, make certain you convey to your students the importance of daily devotions in their lives and your life.

ETHICS (Bible Knowledge)

The last additional building block for this age is ethics. This word may seem a bit heavy for early elementary children, but seven- and eight-year-old children must begin learning to make right choices. Many public schools begin "Character Education" in the first grade. In fact some public school teachers are required to include "Character Education" modules in their lesson plans on a weekly or monthly basis. Subjects such as trustworthiness, respect, responsibility, fairness, caring, and citizenship are typically presented, repeated, and ingrained in children during their elementary, junior high, and senior high years. Please do not get me wrong. These programs are very good; however, they will not necessarily provide a biblical basis for making the right choices. We can take our cue from the public school system in this area and begin teaching our children biblical ethics beginning in first grade.

Josh McDowell has a wonderful ethics series for children of all ages. The study for first and second grade students is called *Truth Works.*[7] McDowell is an expert in Christian education and has done a tremendous amount of research with youth and ethics. This paperback book is one of many excellent resources useful for introducing godly ethics to your students. This may be a series you need to set aside for four weeks on a Sunday morning with your children. It may also be a series you want to use on a Sunday or Wednesday night.

One of the biggest mistakes Christian educators make in the area of ethics and children is the "what if" scenarios. Most children as young as preschool can give the right answers when questioned about ethical situations. The teacher asks the class, "If you get mad, should you hit someone?" The class yells in unison, "NO!" The early elementary teacher asks the class, "If you see an old person walking down the hall at church and he drops something, should you help him pick it up?" The class yells in unison, "YES!" The parent sits down with the child at night before bed to begin their nightly devotions. The devotion asks this question, "If you are at a friend's house and the family is watching a bad movie you know your mom, dad, and God would not want you to watch, what will you do?" The child thinks for a minute and says, "I should tell my friend's parents that I can't watch that movie." The parent smiles and pats their child on the head, confident their child would do just that.

Children are very smart. They know the right answers. For the most part they know the "right" thing to do, but when they are actually in that situation, things change. Now, none of us expect children to be perfect, and I'm sure we all can admit to making some really poor choices when we were younger. But I have spoken to frustrated Christian parents whose children have been raised in the church and *know* what is right, yet choose to do very wrong things. One elementary student who had been through a book on "What Would Jesus Do?" decided to surf the internet visiting all types of pornographic sites. Another parent said their child had been caught bullying children at school, and still another child had stolen a Game Boy from a child in his class. These parents were devastated to learn that their child had made such poor choices. These are the same children who had been through the church "what if" scenarios many times and had always answered correctly.

The best way for Christian parents and Christian educators to work together to present godly ethics to their children is by focusing on the consequences of their choices and considering the consequences of their choices before they act. Now I am not talking about parents saying, "If I ever find out that you have bullied another kid in your class, there will be consequences! I'm going to beat you!" (Although that always worked for me.) I am speaking of situational consequences. When a parent speaks to children about viewing inappropriate images on the internet, they could say, "God wants us to keep our minds free of these images. Not only would it disappoint us greatly if you chose to view those images, we believe those images are something you will never be able to erase from your mind. The images you see could affect how you think down the road, and it could make you want to look at more images and become addicted. If you decide to view inappropriate things on the internet, your computer privileges will be taken away until we think you are old enough to handle them." Perhaps the only one of those consequences that moved them to make the right choice was the punishment consequence. That is okay. It forced the child to consider the consequences before they chose.

Therefore we can take these church "what if" scenarios one step further. The teacher may ask, "If you get mad at someone, should you hit them?" The class will all say, "NO!" The teacher then asks, "Why not? I think you should hit them. Convince me I'm wrong." The children will begin to say things such as, "Well, I wouldn't want someone to hit me, and we're supposed to treat others the way we want to be treated." Another child may say, "I would probably get in trouble at school and at home." That is an honest answer, and it is a definite consequence for children to consider before they make a choice.

Make the teaching of godly ethics a priority throughout your youth ministry. Aside from the everyday relational situations they will find themselves in on a daily basis, children as young as seven and eight are faced with choices in music, television, computer sites, and video games. Hopefully Christian educators are taking time to train and encourage and support godly parents who will help their children make the right choices in these areas, but the church must work with the children also.

Early Elementary Learning Goals

By the time a seven- or eight-year-old child leaves his or her classroom at the Community Christian Church he or she will have:

- Reinforced and strengthened all concepts begun in the pre-school class.
- Learned what the Bible says about heaven and how he or she can get there and developed a further excitement for going there.
- Learned the definition of the word "tithe" and discovered what the Bible says about tithing in addition to being a faithful giver.
- Developed a routine of daily prayer and started to keep a prayer chart of how God is answering their prayers.
- Participated in a Bible study on the "Great Commission" and learned what it means to be a disciple of Jesus Christ while further being encouraged to share their faith.
- Participated in several service projects sponsored by the church and learned the biblical concept of servanthood.
- Developed the routine of bringing her Bible with her to church each week.
- Learned the divisions of the books of the Bible
- Started developing an appreciation for godly science and creation while studying the areas of nature, animals, and the human body.
- Reviewed and learned age-appropriate Bible stories that challenge their faith.
- Learned several Bible verses and passages including those used in the plan of salvation.
- Studied the biblical concept of worship.
- Participated in and observed worship with adults.
- Learned to view the Bible as a part of history and begun studying where the Bible came from.
- Studied the importance of the family in God's eyes and learned the design God has planned for each member of the family.
- Learned the importance of choices and consequences in regard to godly ethics.

Things a Parent Can Do to Reinforce What Is Taught in the Early Elementary Department (Family)

- Continue bringing your child to church each Sunday. Make church attendance as regular as school attendance.

- Set aside a time and place each day to begin helping your child with daily devotions and prayer time. This is a routine you want her to continue after she leaves your home.
- Continually bathe your child in prayer. Pray for his future spouse. Pray that God will help him to make wise choices at school. Pray for his salvation and his spiritual growth.
- Allow your child to join your family in the singing portion of your worship service even if your church does not provide this. Do whatever you can to make sure you sit together as a family. Your child needs to see the importance of praising God and worshiping.
- Continue encouraging your child to bring his or her Bible to church each week and back home for daily devotional time. Demonstrate the importance of this by bringing your Bible to church each week.
- While the teachers in your child's class are beginning to instill an appreciation for God's creation, take advantage of "teachable moments" and talk to your child about the wonders of God's world and His perfect design. Plan a family campout or a nature walk to reinforce this concept.
- Continue giving your child chores or different jobs to earn money for a tithe. Encourage your child to tithe on a regular basis as he is learning the same concept at church.
- Consider participating as a family in a servant evangelism project sponsored by your church.
- Continue to encourage your children to serve in some form with the church on a regular basis. Suggest projects such as visiting the elderly, pulling weeds on the church grounds, or making a meal for someone who has been in the hospital.
- Help your child's teacher by going over the books of the Bible at home.
- Help your child's teacher by doing his homework of memorizing Bible verses. View this in equal importance to his homework at school.
- Challenge your children to begin thinking of consequences before they make a choice. Begin discussing the importance of godly choices at home.
- When appropriate, talk with your child about the different roles in the family and God's design for those roles. Make it a point to model those roles in your home as God intended.
- *Do **not*** talk adversely about the church or the teachers in

front of your children. Speaking negatively about the church greatly restricts the impact it will have on her trust in the church and ultimately her faith development. If you are upset with something your child's teacher or other congregational authority figure did on a given Sunday, make sure the child is out of earshot before discussing your concerns with anyone else. Be careful what you say at home.

WARNING, WARNING, WARNING

Many Christian Educators fall into the trap of filling church time with student worksheets. Thom and Joani Schultz say, "We're referring to those Sunday school papers that dominate most brands of curriculum. From preschool through adult, they take the form of crossword puzzles, word scrambles, mazes, word searches, fill-in-the-blanks, and rebuses. The creators of this material believe they're adding interest to the Scriptures. But we contend they're adding confusion, wasting time, and blocking understanding." Here are some questions they encourage you to ask yourself when looking at one of these worksheets.

What is the value of this exercise?
Does this exercise illuminate and clarify the passage for the child?
Does it enhance understanding?
Is it the best possible use of time?
How will students grow closer to God as a result of this exercise?
What new insight is gained?

Unfortunately these worksheets do not clarify the Bible story, concept, or verse for the student. Group Publishing claims, "We've pledged we'll never include such exercises in the curriculum we create. Why? Because we know they do not help students understand and apply God's Word. In fact they can cloud and obscure understanding. Quite simply, they don't work. If they did, we'd all be using similar approaches in training situations elsewhere in life. We'd be using word puzzles to train computer operators. We'd be using mazes to train restaurant cooks. We'd be using crossword puzzles to train airline pilots. But these worksheets don't work."[8] Do not fall into the trap of using worksheets with your students unless it is absolutely necessary. Such worksheets may come packaged as learning tools but are really just time fillers, and ultimately a waste of your students' time.

NOTES

1. David Solomon, *Discovering Jesus* (From Creation Ltd., 2000). You can order this by calling 1-877-737-3893 or e-mail discoveringjesus@hotmail.com.

2. Howard and Bev Dayton, *The ABC's of Handling Money God's Way* (Chicago: Moody, 1998).

3. Thom and Joani Schultz, *The Dirt on Learning* (Loveland, CO: Group Publishing, 1999) 130-131. Quote from Alfie Kohn, *Punished by Rewards* (Boston: Houghton-Mifflin, 1993) 77.

4. Newsom, *Greatest Story*, 55.

5. John MacArthur, *A Faith to Grow On* (Nashville: Thomas Nelson, 2000).

6. Ibid.

7. Josh McDowell, *Truth Works* (Nashville: Broadman and Holman, 1995).

8. Schultz, *Dirt*, 33-35.

Chapter Eight

EVALUATING THE ARROWS:
LATE ELEMENTARY
THIRD THROUGH FIFTH GRADE

Where do you want your students to be by the time they graduate, and how are you going to get them there?

Kyle is ten years old, in the fourth grade, and an only child. He is a towhead blonde with big blue eyes that could melt your heart. He is a typically thin, wiry energetic boy on the low end of the height scale. He is much shorter than most of the girls in his class.

Kyle is very athletic and his parents make sure he participates in any sport that he would like to try. "We just want him to test all the sports and see which ones he wants to play. We want him to be well rounded." Unfortunately for them, Kyle hasn't been introduced to one sport in the city of Clarksville he doesn't like. He starts the fall with soccer, goes right into basketball during the winter months, and then into two different baseball leagues in the spring and summer. His parents have also sent him to football and tennis camp; however, the school requires children to choose between football or soccer and baseball or tennis.

He has learned that his father loves to spend time with him when sports are related. His father goes to all his games and insists on making sure he is placed on the best team, with the best players and the best coach. He has even put in a full-scale basketball court behind their house in the country with bleachers, lights, adjustable hoops, and a concession stand. Kyle's friends love to come to his house and play.

Kyle's parents are both senior high sponsors at their church. When they are not at sporting events, they are at the church. Both his parents are dedicated to helping build the youth program since the last youth minister left

*things in shambles. Kyle loves to go to church and help his parents
get things together for their Sunday school lessons. He loves to go to
all the senior high functions and really looks up to all the teens in the
group.*

*Wednesday nights are Kyle's favorite at church. His teacher is the
gym teacher at his school. Mr. Rose used to be a big basketball star
at Clarksville High School and is always giving Kyle tips on how to
be a better basketball player. He tries to come to several of Kyle's
games throughout the school year.*

*Kyle knows that Mr. Rose supports him in his Christian walk. About
two times a year he will take Kyle out for lunch and ask him how his
devotion and prayer time is going. He is always very positive in class
and never yells at the students. He is very good at getting all the students to participate in his funny activities such as "sword drill."*

*Kyle's Sunday school class supports a family in Haiti. The whole
class tithes extra money each week to send $40 each month to their
family. Everyone in the class takes turns writing to the Rejo family. Mr.
Rose also organizes servant evangelism projects for the students to
participate in. He always invites the student's families and has a pic-
nic after the work is done.*

Upper elementary students are typically showing increasing
signs of physical and social maturity. It is now very important to
be "cool" and both the boys and the girls are very cognizant of
who the "popular" people are in their youth groups and in the
school classes. They may say differently, but most of your students would give anything to be one of these "popular" kids. It
becomes more and more important to stress the idea of godly
choices to students in our ministries.

Nine- through eleven-year-old children are still very energetic, although they can sit still longer than their younger coun-
terparts. With this age you will see more mischievousness than in
younger years. One little boy's mind is working hard to figure
out how he can pull the little girl's hair in front of him without
the teacher seeing. Another child is throwing something out the
window if he or she thinks an adult isn't watch-
ing. This is all part of a child's process of testing the boundaries with those in authority,
whether it is teachers at school, teachers at
church, parents, grandparents, or child care-
givers. Setting expectations and consequences in and outside the
classroom is crucial with this age.

Setting expectations and
consequences in and
outside the classroom is
crucial with this age.

Upper elementary students are still very fun to teach. They remain at the age when they will try almost anything in a group; they have not quite moved into the stage of insecurities as often becomes common with the middle and high school years. With children in this age group the teacher may say, "Now that we've learned the Bible lesson, we are going to dress up in these clothes and have you act out the story for me." Most of the kids will be ecstatic.

On the other hand, there are always a handful of students in this age group who are painfully shy. They walk into the class-room with a frown on their face and, without speaking a word, make it clear to everyone in the classroom, "My parents made me come." It is important to make these children feel as comfortable as possible without crossing the line of catering to them. Dealing with children who don't want to participate can be frustrating for any teacher. While forcing a child to participate is not always the best route, insisting they sit with the rest of the group is not out of the question. If the activities and story time are engaging and interactive, your teachers will most likely find these children smiling in no time. Encourage them to participate and leave it at that. Many children love to be begged and pleaded with. Since the child enjoys this type of attention the teacher is in a no-win situation when the child refuses to participate and the teacher pleads more.

Toward the end of the upper elementary years, a very distinct difference can become obvious between the emotional ranges of boys and girls at the onset of puberty. Girls typically begin puberty during these years while boys typically begin a couple of years later. The changing of a girl's body shape, the imbalance of hormones, and the insecurities can all lead to emotions that are just hard to deal with—one minute she's crying, another minute laughing. One minute she's sassing her mother, the next minute hugging her and saying, "Mom, you're my best friend."

Typically, girls begin liking boys earlier than boys like girls. Many times girls will show their affection for boys in very odd ways, including grabbing their baseball hats and throwing them, telling them they hate them, hitting them, poking them, kicking them, and so on. At times this can surface as discipline problems in a classroom. Teachers must be aware of the underlying reason behind the teasing and tactfully ask the teaser to stop. It is common for some children to be so uncomfortable with such teasing that they simply will dread coming to any church function.

Boys will also pick on girls at this age, but for the most part they are simply trying to annoy their female classmates. This back and forth bantering between the sexes can be a frustration for any teacher dealing with this age in the classroom.

This age group will begin the third and early fourth grade years with the classic, "I'm not holding hands with a boy during prayer time." Toward the end of the fourth grade year and into the fifth grade year you will begin to hear, "He likes you" and "I like him, but don't tell anyone." You may even possibly see pairing off here and there. Unfortunately this innocent ritual can hinder what takes place in the classroom.

STORY TIME

The process by which an adult can tell of Bible events is beginning to change for late elementary students. Flannelgraph teaching is definitely a thing of the past. While the work of a "master storyteller" and drama presentation are still wonderful ways to present Bible stories, these methods can be used less often. Children in the third through fifth grade are now better able to more effectively read and more consistently comprehend stories from age-appropriate Bibles. In the late preschool and early elementary years we used *The Beginner's Bible*. With this age group you should move to something a little more challenging. *The Adventure Bible*[1] is an excellent resource for students of this age. As with the preschool years it is ideal for every child to have the same age-appropriate Bible. Encourage parents to purchase *The Adventure Bible* for their children or order several copies and allow parents to buy them directly from the church. It is also recommended to keep several copies of this Bible in the classroom for students who have forgotten their Bible or for visitors to use.

Aside from the "master storyteller," drama, and simple text reading to introduce the weekly Bible story, there is another way to present Bible stories to this age. Various members of your congregation can be recruited to tape the reading of the Bible story either straight from the Bible or paraphrased from a curriculum. Allow a few children at a time to listen to the story with headphones in a listening center. Another option is to purchase a set of dramatized Bible CDs that your children can listen to in a listening center. The key with this age is variety. They have moved out of the desire for routine. They want diversity.

HEAVEN (Bible Knowledge and Feeling)

Following the Faith Development Plan we have been working very hard to instill in our students an anticipation about going to heaven. In the first and second grade classes we began explaining to the students how they can live eternally in heaven. Late elementary is a crucial time for churched children. This is the time when the majority of your students are beginning to establish their core beliefs. George Barna's research indicates "that the probability of someone embracing Jesus as his or her Savior was 32 percent for those between the ages of 5 and 12; 4 percent for those in the 13- to 18-age range; and 6 percent for people 19 or older. In other words, if people do not embrace Jesus Christ as their Savior before they reach their teenage years, the chance of their doing so at all is slim. . . . In other words, by the age of 13, your spiritual identity is largely set in place."[2]

> The probability of someone embracing Jesus as Savior goes from 32% between the ages of 5 and 12 to 6% for people 19 or older.

Our desire as Christian educators is to aim our students at the target of spiritual maturity and discipleship. The obvious first step in this process is for the child to understand what it means to become a Christian and to make that decision for Jesus Christ. We realize through research such as that mentioned by George Barna that this age is very important and we must be very deliberate and clear on presenting our students with the message of hope for eternal life in heaven.

The proposed Faith Development Plan calls for a four-week lesson on "How to Get to Heaven" or "How to Become a Christian." This is something the students will have covered every year since they were in first grade and is not meant to be a "high-pressure" situation for students in need of making a decision for Christ. Our mission involves ensuring that our students understand how to become a Christian if they desire to make that decision.

An excellent study in this area is *Good as New!*[3] by D. Doug Gibson. This series includes a leader's guide and a student workbook and can be broken up into a four-week or eight-week series. It could also be simply used as a resource given to parents who want to work at home with their children.

Continue speaking of heaven with your students and continue offering the "heaven night" once a year. Allow your third through fifth grade students to participate in "heaven night" by writing and reciting a poem about heaven or simply handing out bulletins for the night.

TITHING (Bible Knowledge and Experience)

Tithing is one of the routines we have tried to develop with our students. There is a basket or church bank on the counter, and the students know that they are to bring in a tithe to place in this container. During the first and second grade year they learned what the word "tithe" means and more about stewardship and debt.

In the late elementary class children can begin learning more in-depth Bible stories of how to be cheerful givers and how God supplies all our needs. Howard and Bev Dayton have written a tremendous series for this age group entitled, *The Secret of Handling Money God's Way*. As with their series for first and second grade students, this series is designed for twelve weeks but can be modified to fit your program.

The proposed Faith Development Plan calls for a minimum of four weeks to study the idea of God's design for our money. In addition, children this age are in the position to begin giving to a specific person or organization on a regular basis. Allow children to choose a child to support from a third-world country as a class or on an individual basis. Encourage the children to write to their sponsored child. Many times these children will write the class back and tell them how their money is helping them, possibly in the area of clothes, education, food, or other needs for the family.

If the class has not given enough money in offering to make the commitment to the child they are sponsoring, be honest with the class and let them know the full situation. "The first of the month is coming and we only have $30 in our account to send to Petra. We made a commitment several months back to send her $40 each month. You all have done so wonderfully and we have seen how she has been blessed by your giving. But unless we have a bigger offering next week, we will not be able to send her the full amount to which we committed. Let's take time to pray for next week's offering. I know that God will help us provide for Petra." The worst thing you could do for that class is to slip in a ten-dollar bill of your own to make up for the deficit. Allow the children to step up to the plate and bring in the money needed. This is all part of maturing and faith development.

PRAYER (Bible Knowledge, Feeling, and Experience)

Daily prayer time with God is one of the four foundational building blocks we want our students to take with them after they leave our program. At this point you will have provided several resources to help your students and parents in developing this daily time with God. In preschool they were given a prayer calendar. In early elementary we added a prayer chart with the prayer calendar for children to write down what they had prayed about and documented how God had answered that prayer.

In the third through fifth grade classes we want to begin encouraging students to journal their prayer time with God. This may be once or twice a week, whenever they take the time to pray and write their thoughts to God. Journaling is dynamic, in part, because there is no right or wrong way to do it. Some children may choose to use one-word lists and some may write out their thoughts in paragraph form. Provide your students with either homemade journals or something available from a Christian bookstore. When helping a student journal, continue providing a prayer calendar for those who aren't sure where to start. Include some Scriptures or possibly some of your group's favorite worship song lyrics.

In addition, set aside a minimum of four weeks each year in your Faith Development Plan to study prayer. Several publishers have excellent canned curriculums on prayer, or you may write something on your own. This is a wonderful age to begin introducing the acrostic ACTS to help them with their prayer time— Adoration, Confession, Thanksgiving, and Supplication. Perhaps your lesson series can take one week on each of these areas.

Children this age can also begin to understand the concept of intercessory prayer. During your lessons in this area consider including the account of Moses and the battle with the Midianites in Exodus 17. Your late elementary students can learn to stand in the gap for those who cannot pray for themselves.

Continue asking various members of your congregation to come into the classroom and tell how God is working through their prayer life. Perhaps someone will tell of a time they were so low they could not pray for themselves. Perhaps someone else helped them and held their hands up to God for them. The power of testimony is totally underestimated in the church. Our students need to hear the struggles and the victories other

The power of testimony is totally underestimated in the church.

Christians have experienced in prayer. Don't be afraid to ask your students in private how their prayer life is going. This shows your students that you feel their prayer life away from the church is very important. If your students tell you they are not taking the time to pray at home, ask them what you can do to help them in this area.

EVANGELISM AND SERVICE (Bible Knowledge and Experience)

Late elementary students are ready to hit the road. They are at optimum age to begin participating in small scale "mission trips." They are even capable of raising money for such trips. If you have ever had one of these students come to you during Girl Scout cookie time or school fund-raising time, you know these kids can be extremely persuasive.

Two words typically sum up the experience of a mission trip: life changing. We have seen several of our students come back from mission trips with the mind-set, "When are we going back?" Third through fifth grade students are at a great age to begin experiencing firsthand the power of mission ministry. Providing students with an organized, short term, family mission trip can be a catalyst for their faith development.

> Third through fifth grade students are at a great age to begin experiencing firsthand the power of mission ministry.

To begin thinking of a mission trip suitable for this age, consider sending letters to several of the missions your church supports in the United States. Write a letter to these missions asking if they would be willing to have third through fifth grade students come and help them for two or three days in the summer or during spring break. Assure these missions that the children would come with plenty of adult chaperones, ideally an adult family member. Inform them of your desire for the children to see firsthand what it means to be a missionary, but also for them to do age-appropriate physical labor to help the organization. The proposed Faith Development Plan for this age lists a short-term mission trip every other year.

In addition the plan calls for a minimum four-week study on sharing your faith. Following the Faith Development Plan the first and second grade students have already studied and memorized the Great Commission. They have also done a study on what the Bible says about being a disciple. Now it is time to begin studying Jesus' calling of the disciples and the importance of the phrase "take up your cross." Taking up your cross and following was a definite theme Jesus was trying to get through to those who wanted to be His follower.

Unfortunately, no good "canned curriculum" will meet our specific students where they are in their own individual relationship with Christ. The Faith Development Plan concept is intended to help us increasingly personalize and specialize our specific teachings to our particular students. If you decide to write your own lessons or adapt previously developed material, remember, once the lessons are written they can be reused for several years in your Faith Development Plan rotation.

Lastly, provide two or three servant evangelism projects for your students each year. These projects can be multigenerational and family focused. Having three large servant evangelism projects including the entire congregation can magnify the impact of the project. If you are looking for ideas on what type of servant evangelism projects to implement, take time to read Steve Sjogren's book *Conspiracy of Kindness.*[4] Mr. Sjogren, founding pastor of Vineyard Community Church, is a national trainer in the area of servant evangelism and will help you understand how this type of evangelism can transform your church.

BIBLES ARE IMPORTANT (Bible Knowledge and Experience)

This is the last age we will include this step in our Faith Development Plan. After this point it will be well-established that Bibles are important through the lessons taught and the encouragement from teachers to bring Bibles on a weekly basis. Remember that this age has moved into a new, age-appropriate Bible, *The Adventure Bible.*

BOOKS OF THE BIBLE (Bible Knowledge)

Following the Faith Development Plan our two- and three-year-old children began learning the books of the New Testament, the four- and five-year-old children learned the books of the Old Testament, and the first and second grade students learned the divisions within the two Testaments. Third through fifth grade students are now ready for the ever-popular sword drill. Avoiding the winning and losing aspect of sword drills, it is important to keep in mind the goal of such an exercise: students are able to find a passage in the Bible without looking at the Table of Contents. Finding passages in the Bible or "sword drills" can be done as a group or between a teacher and individual. Taking five minutes at the beginning or end of class for this exercise quickly becomes a favorite for students this age who love competition.

Continue reviewing the books of the Bible in recitation with your students and continue reinforcing the divisions previously learned in the early elementary department while introducing the writers of each of these books. The progression of the Faith Development Plan allows for our arrows to become "studiers of the Word." To study the Word we must first know how to use it.

SCIENCE AND ELEMENTARY STUDENTS (Bible Knowledge and Science)

The late elementary portion of the proposed Faith Development Plan is the same as that of the early elementary, viewing God's world as a perfect design. Continue focusing on nature, animals, and the human body using the same resources stated in the early elementary portion in chapter seven.

BIBLE STORIES (Bible Knowledge)

As with the earlier areas of your Faith Development Plan, a minimum of half of the plan time and teaching will be taken up with specific stories or studies from the Bible. Third through fifth grade students are now at a point where teachers can introduce the historical accounts of persecution mentioned throughout the Bible. They can study the life of Paul, Job, Jonah, Stephen, John the Baptist, Daniel, and the whole story of Joseph while reinforcing the Bible accounts they learned in earlier years.

When introducing Bible accounts involving persecution, teach the children what the word "persecution" means and let them know that this is something that happens in many countries today. Consider bringing in a representative from a wonderful ministry called The Voice of the Martyrs. Visit their website at **www.persecution.com** and ask for a speaker to come and present age-appropriate material to your students.

MEMORY VERSES (Bible Knowledge)

Continue reviewing the key memory verses and passages learned in the early elementary department, while introducing new verses you feel are key for your students to lock in their hearts. Decide which passages and verses you wish for your students to *know* by the time they leave your department and divide them up for one year. Since the children will be in this department for three years, they will have three years to master the verses you desire for them to use.

WORSHIP (Bible Knowledge, Feeling, and Experience)

It is a blessing to see a third through fifth grade student singing choruses and worshiping. I have been humbled in children's worship to witness children worshiping with their voices and through sign language. It is very beautiful.

Children this age can begin participating in a variety of settings. We have allowed our children to sign up and serve as worship coordinator for a specific Sunday in children's church. (This worship time takes place after the children come from worship time with their parents.) We have formulated a worksheet which allows them to pick a number of fast songs and a number of slow songs. They have to have a list for the sound technician who is also an elementary-aged student. Special music is brought by the children. Offering and communion are passed by the children. We have even allowed the worship coordinators to design bulletins and appoint greeters at the door of the room. Our elementary-aged students absolutely love this format. Not only are they having fun and feeling a part of the worship time, they are learning how to lead worship. One of the keys for any worship coordinator is not simply picking the songs that "you like to sing." It includes helping the students ask themselves, "What songs will help the children in this class worship God best?" Taking the emphasis off "them" and putting it on "God" is an area of faith development which will stay with them forever.

This is also the age when students might begin attending worship concerts or concerts by contemporary Christian artists. The best worship experience I have ever had was not in a church service but at a Twila Paris concert. She led the whole audience to the throne of God, and it was absolutely phenomenal. Provide opportunities for your late elementary students, middle, and high school students and parents to attend at least one or two Christian concerts each year.

Continue keeping your upper elementary students in with the adults during the song service time. Strongly encourage your students to sit with their parents and encourage the parents to sit with their children. Many children this age like to sit in church with their friends. Family worship time, even if it is only fifteen minutes once a week during church service, is an important part of faith development.

Continue setting aside at least four weeks each year in your Faith Development Plan for the biblical study of worship. Third through fifth grade students are at a great age to begin studying Psalms and memorizing some of the key songs in this beautiful book.

HISTORY AND ELEMENTARY STUDENTS (Bible Knowledge and History)

Third through fifth grade students have been learning much about American history in the public school classroom. Unfortunately they are not learning it from a Christian perspective. American history is about our founding fathers and how they built this country on Christian principles. Often this becomes lost in a traditional educational setting. *The Light and the Glory for Children*[5] is an excellent book which introduces students to the principles on which our country was founded and how instrumental God was in the plan for this nation. Many of the great, early leaders of our country were not only devout Christians, but students of the Word. *Our American Heritage*[6] is an excellent, easy to read book about several key players in American history who were also followers of God. Many schools require students to read outside the classroom as part of their homework. Consider encouraging the parents of your students to read these or similar books with their children during this homework time. Often the parents will learn just as much as the children.

Public libraries all over the country have reading programs during the summer. Our local library has a summer reading program in which children can fill in a chart to show how much reading time they have accumulated during the summer months. If they reach a certain number of hours, they get to spin a wheel for a prize. The goal is to have enough hours to gain a ticket for admission to the summer reading program carnival in the middle of August. This program is so popular in our area, the sign up lists are three to four pages long before school has even let out.

Take this same concept and publicize a summer reading program for your church students. Instead of organizing your program where students can read "any book," compose a list of age-appropriate books on heroes of the faith or our founding fathers and work the program around these books. You may even decide to have a carnival at the end of the summer. Those who read a certain number of hours or a certain number of books could earn tickets to different stations such as face painting, duck pond, dunk tank, or others. This type of program can be offered for students of all ages in your ministry, including preschool. Children could earn tickets by having their parents or another adult read a specific book to them.

In addition, set aside four weeks each year in your Faith Development Plan to present your students with specific heroes of the Christian faith such as Martin Luther, Corrie Ten Boom, Billy Sunday, and Billy Graham. Many books have been written and videos produced on the lives of these heroes which show the important role they played in our history and the strength and courage they found in their relationships with God.

GOD'S PLAN FOR THE FAMILY (Bible Knowledge and Family)

In the early elementary department we introduced a new faith development step entitled "God's Plan for the Family." The children in our ministries come from such a wide variety of backgrounds. Many do not have a positive model of the family, let alone a godly one. When presenting a four-week study with her elementary girls' small group on God's plan for the family, one of our leaders devoted one whole lesson to God's plan for marriage. Several of the students in her group became squeamishly uneasy when she presented what the Bible says about marriage, the role of the husband, and the role of the wife. One girl said, "My parents are a team. Neither of my parents is in charge." This girl had been in the church since she was very little and has a fabulous set of parents. However, she saw her parents as a team. She did not know what was going on behind the scenes in the decisions of the house. Her dad *was* in charge.

Setting aside four weeks a year in your Faith Development Plan to focus on God's plan for the family is essential for children this age. The media portrays fathers as stupid and weak (and I am not just speaking of Homer Simpson and Al Bundy). If a child does not have a positive family model at home and watches even a small amount of television, their view of a father, mother, marriage, or parent-child relationships can be terribly skewed.

Group Publishing has a set of lessons in their Faith 4 Life series entitled *Family Matters*. These lessons can be used for late elementary, middle school, and high school as they present age-appropriate activities in each area. Use a series like this or formulate your own lessons on the family which will be used each year in your Faith Development Plan.

DAILY DEVOTIONS AND BIBLE READING (Bible Knowledge, Feeling, and Experience)

We still want to encourage our students to practice daily devotions and Bible reading at home on a regular basis. Enlisting parental help in this matter is key; however, I have had some parents tell me, "My child just does not like to read." I am a firm believer that everyone can love to read; we just have to find something they are interested in. If a parent is struggling with his child having their daily devotions, encourage that parent to try one of the following things.

Family devotions are a great way for parents to take the spiritual reins in their home. To support parents in their efforts to begin devotions as a family, choose a family devotion book you feel is the best for the parents of students in your ministry. Purchase several copies of these books and make them available to these parents for a donation. Include a commitment card with the devotional book and ask the parents to sign it. The card may read, "I, Steve Smith, commit to implementing daily devotions with my family for the next three months. I realize at times this will be a challenge for our busy family. . . ." Encourage parents to place this card in a visible place in the house such as the refrigerator or bathroom mirror. Keep a copy of the commitment cards for yourself and send out encouragement cards to the parents who have agreed to commit. "Steve, Just wanted to send you a quick note to let you know I am praying for you and your family as you strive to have daily devotions together. I know God will bless your family richly through the time you spend together. If there is anything I can do for you, please let me know." This will help your parents feel a sense of support and accountability in their efforts to raise godly children.

The second way to help parents who are frustrated with children unwilling to have daily devotions is by meeting with that child. Take this student out for a burger or a drink and ask him how his devotional life is coming. If he says, "Not good" or something similar, offer to take him over to your local Christian bookstore to choose a devotional he would enjoy. Such a trip would reveal to the student a variety of different devotional books that would fit his interests. Offer to purchase the book for the student to use and put back in the church library when he is finished. After the student has had a couple of weeks to begin his daily devotions, send him an encouragement card reminding him you are praying for him and are available if he needs you. This will show the student that it is not only important to his parents that he start daily devotions, but to you, too.

As with the early elementary age, set aside a four-week study on the importance of spending time with God through devotion and Bible reading. The proposed plan calls for presenting these lessons at the beginning of the year in conjunction with lessons on prayer.

ETHICS (Bible Knowledge)

At the beginning of this chapter we discussed how late elementary students are feeling the urge to be "popular." If you ask any of your students in this age group who the "popular kids" are in their school, they could name several. It is now becoming evident whether the individual students in your late elementary department are followers or leaders. Either role can be dangerous if they are not armed with the proper decision-making skills.

Students at this stage are also learning the art of compartmentalizing their lives. They have a different set of expectations, relationships, and circumstances at their school, their home, with their friends, in their free time, and at church. It is sometimes scary to observe children as young as third grade beginning to learn how to play the part in the different compartments that make up their lives. One Sunday school teacher presenting this idea to her students drew a box on the board. She sectioned off different areas of the box in different sizes and labeled them C for church, S for school, H for home, FT for free time, and F for friends. As the children stared at the different areas they nodded their heads. "Yes," they said. "That's what I do. I never thought of it that way."

Unfortunately, we can't be with our students 24/7. They need to make the right choices when they are away from their parents, teachers, and ministers. As mentioned in the early elementary section it is essential to continue presenting children with possible consequences to poor choices. This encourages them to think before they make a choice.

Josh McDowell has another excellent series geared specifically for this age group which you could implement on an annual basis in your Faith Development Plan. *Truth Works—Making Right Choices*[7] is an excellent resource to challenge your students to make godly choices.

In addition to studies such as this, invite members of the congregation to come and give testimonies to these children of a choice that was hard for them to make or a choice they made that was wrong and the consequences that followed. Again, the power of testimony is an underused tool in the church but an extremely effective teaching method.

SELF-IMAGE (Bible Knowledge, Feeling, and Science)

A new building block for third through fifth grade students is that of self-image or self-esteem. How our students view themselves ultimately determines everything they think, do, and say. This includes how they feel about God, church, and their faith. Unfortunately, as their bodies begin to change and hormones start to overact, many of your students will begin to feel very self-conscious about every aspect of their body and their personality. One girl in our ministry expressed her feelings, "I know I talk too much and I think everyone is like, 'Shut up! I wish she would stop talking.' But I just can't stop!" Children begin to feel that they are being judged on how they look, talk, and act. Truth be told, this feeling stems from the fact they themselves are beginning to judge others on the same areas.

> Children begin to feel that they are being judged on how they look, talk, and act, and they are beginning to judge others on the same areas.

A child with a poor self-image may never answer a question in your Sunday school class and may come across as painfully shy. Another child with a poor self-image may react by lashing out at other students in his class with anger. Still another may try to make up for poor self-esteem by constantly cutting down other children or making fun of them. Simply put, poor self-esteem inhibits the development of healthy self-esteem in your students.

In addition, your students' self-esteem is largely affected by the way other adults and peers treat them. This includes parents who constantly criticize and never build up their children, school teachers who degrade students in front of others, and children who bully or make fun of others to get a laugh from the crowd. We do not know how they are being treated, and we cannot control how our students are treated in every situation. However, we can train our students in positive self-image and how to respond to hurtful behavior.

Frank Peretti has developed a video curriculum series entitled *Wild and Wacky Bible Stories*. One of the lessons in this series is entitled "All about Self-Esteem."[8] Frank Peretti knows firsthand about the importance of self-esteem. He was ruthlessly teased as a child for a facial deformity. His series will be an excellent addition to your Faith Development Plan for the late elementary years and will help your students see how special and unique they are in the Father's eyes. They will learn how they have been made in God's image.

In addition, make sure to encourage and support students struggling with self-esteem as often as possible. Students with chronic acne or other appearance issues may not look us in the eye when we pass them in the hall, but they still need our love and attention. Make an effort to seek out these students and begin a conversation with them. This shows our students they are special, and we love and care for them regardless of how they look.

LATE ELEMENTARY LEARNING GOALS

By the time a third through fifth grade child leaves his classroom at the Community Christian Church he or she will have:

- ✔ Reinforced and strengthened all concepts begun in the early elementary department.
- ✔ Participated in a biblical study on "How to Get to Heaven," learning the steps to salvation.
- ✔ Had the opportunity to participate in the annual "Heaven Night" program.
- ✔ Started giving tithe money to a specific ministry on a regular basis.
- ✔ Studied how God wants him to handle his money.
- ✔ Learned the importance of keeping a prayer journal and tried to keep such a journal.
- ✔ Learned the biblical concept of intercessory prayer and its importance.
- ✔ Learned the acrostic ACTS and how to use it in his daily prayer time.
- ✔ Had the opportunity to participate in one of three servant evangelism projects sponsored by the church.
- ✔ Had the opportunity to participate in a short term mission trip.
- ✔ Begun to learn the importance of mission work.
- ✔ Received an age-appropriate Bible, *The Adventure Bible*, to bring to and from church each week.

- Begun using his knowledge of the books of the Bible to participate in sword drills.
- Learned the authors of the books of the Bible.
- Continued developing an appreciation for godly science and creation while studying the areas of nature, animals, and the human body.
- Reviewed and learned age-appropriate Bible stories that challenge his faith including those of persecution.
- Learned the definition of persecution and areas of the world which face persecution.
- Continued learning several Bible verses and passages including those used in the plan of salvation.
- Learned how to organize a simple worship service.
- Had the opportunity to attend at least one Christian worship concert.
- Participated in worship service with adults on a regular basis.
- Had the opportunity to participate in a church-sponsored summer reading program.
- Learned of the godly people and principles our nation was founded upon.
- Learned of various heroes of the Christian faith.
- Continued studying the importance of the family in God's eyes and learned the design God has planned for each member of the family.
- Continued the spiritual discipline of daily devotional time with God.
- Continued learning the importance of choices and consequences in regard to godly ethics.
- Studied the importance of a positive self-esteem.
- Learned how God made him special, unique, and in His image to counter low self-esteem.

Things a Parent Can Do to Reinforce What Is Taught in the Late Elementary Department (Family)

- Continue bringing your child to church each Sunday. Make church attendance as regular as school attendance.
- Set aside a time and place each day to begin helping your child with daily devotions and prayer time or begin imple-

menting family devotion time. This is a routine you want them to continue after they leave your home.

- ✓ Continually bathe your child in prayer. Pray for his future spouse. Pray that God will help him to make wise choices at school. Pray for his salvation and his spiritual growth.

- ✓ Allow your child to join your family in the singing portion of your worship service even if your church does not provide this. Do whatever you can to make sure you sit together as a family. Your child needs to see how important praising God and worshiping is to you.

- ✓ Continue encouraging your child to bring his or her Bible to church each week and back home for his daily devotional time. Show him the importance of this by bringing your Bible to church each week.

- ✓ Continue instilling an appreciation for God's creation, take advantage of "teachable moments" and talk to your children about the wonders of God's world and His perfect design.

- ✓ In addition to your child's weekly tithe, consider sponsoring a child from a third-world country as a family. Many organizations will send you your sponsored child's picture for your family to keep in a visible place. Make every effort to encourage your child to participate in any servant evangelism or short-term mission project offered by the church. Consider doing both these activities as a family.

- ✓ Continue to encourage your children to serve in some form with the church on a regular basis. Projects such as visiting the elderly, pulling weeds on the church grounds, or making a meal for someone who has been in the hospital.

- ✓ Help your child's teacher by going over the books of the Bible at home.

- ✓ Help your child's teacher by doing his homework of memorizing Bible verses. View this in equal importance to his homework at school.

- ✓ Continue challenging your children to begin thinking of consequences before they make a choice. If you see someone in your family or community who has made a poor choice and suffered consequences, point this out to your child. Likewise, if you have seen someone who has made a good choice and is being blessed, point this out to your child as well.

- ✓ Observe how your child behaves around his friends, at

home, at school if possible, and at church. Encourage your child to be consistent in his behavior and actions.

✔ Continue stressing the importance of God's design for the family. Make it a point to model those roles in your home as God intended.

✔ Praise your child as much as possible. Consciously avoid criticizing your child. Tell your child, "You are special." "I love you." "I don't know what I would do without you." "You are beautiful." "You can do it." "I think you did a great job." "Just do your best." "God has big plans for your life." Remember, your child's self-image is still in the developing stages at this point. He *needs* encouragement.

✔ *Do not* talk adversely about the church or the teachers in front of your children. Speaking negatively about the church greatly restricts the impact it will have on his trust in the church and ultimately his faith development. If you are upset with something your child's teacher did on a given Sunday, make sure the child is out of earshot before discussing your concerns with the teacher. Be careful what you say at home.

NOTES

1. *The Adventure Bible* (Grand Rapids: Zondervan, 2000).

2. Barna, *Transforming Children*, 34.

3. D. Doug Gibson, *Good as New!* (Joplin, MO: College Press, 2000).

4. Steve Sjogren, *Conspiracy of Kindness* (Ventura, CA: Regal Books, 2003).

5. Peter Marshall and David Manuel, *The Light and the Glory for Children* (Grand Rapids: Fleming H. Revell. 1992).

6. Naomi Sleeth, ed., *Our American Heritage* (Pensacola, FL: A Beka Book, 1997).

7. Josh McDowell, *Truth Works—Making Right Choices* (Nashville: Broadman and Holman, 1995).

8. Frank Peretti, *Wild & Wacky Bible Stories: All about Self Esteem*. Nashville: Thomas Nelson, 2004).

Chapter Nine

EVALUATING THE ARROWS:
MIDDLE SCHOOL

Where do you want your students to be by the time they graduate,
and how are you going to get them there?

Sydney is thirteen and in seventh grade. Sydney's parents have been divorced since she was two. Her father and mother, both of whom are remarried, agreed to attend the same church for Sydney and her sister Stephanie's sake. Sydney's mother remarried a man with two children, ages 16 and 14. Last year her mom and step-dad had a child together, Chad, who is now three months old. Sydney's father remarried a woman with three children; ages 11, 10, and 9. Sydney has one sister, one half-brother and five step-siblings.

Her father has joint custody of her and Stephanie, which means they spend every weekend, every Wednesday, and alternating holidays with dad. She has two beds, two dressers, two closets, two sets of clothes, and most importantly, two sets of rules. This has been her life since she was in preschool. She doesn't think anything about it, except when she spends the night at her friend Katie's house. Katie's parents are happily married and are very affectionate with each other in front of their kids. Seeing this makes Sydney slightly jealous.

Sydney's father is an insurance salesman and attends church solely for the business contacts. He does not have a personal relationship with Christ and believes that religion is for "those who can't think for themselves." He is a heavy drinker, smoker, and, when upset with Sydney, can throw around four-letter-words like a champ. Her father is a deacon (no one ever stopped to ask if he was a Christian) and an usher every Sunday morning.

Religion is never stressed at her father's house. Never a prayer. No encouragement or support whatsoever for her to grow spiritually or attend any church-related activities. At her father's house, Sydney has no restrictions on what she can wear, watch, say, or listen to.

Her mother's house is extremely different. Sydney's mother has very strict rules for what she can wear, watch, say, and listen to. Her mother prays with her before school each day and spends time with her in devotions on the nights she is there. Sydney's mother has a passion for her daughter to be a strong, mature Christian. Sydney loves her mother but is continually frustrated by all her "petty rules."

Deep down, Sydney is very indifferent toward spiritual matters. She sees her dad ushering on Sunday mornings and how he acts at home. During her stays with her father she thinks Christianity is a "Sunday thing." "You can act however you want during the week, but on Sundays you put on your best dress, smiling face and talk about 'God stuff.'" From what she can figure, this is what the rest of the church is doing, too. Despite her mother's efforts, Sydney has a distorted view of Christianity.

Sydney is slightly heavy for her age, for which she is severely self-conscious. She has extremely low self-esteem, and even though she is only slightly overweight, the boys in her class sometimes call her Sydney Pigney before making oinking sounds. No matter how many times her mother says, "Sydney, you're beautiful," she still thinks she is the most disgusting person ever to live. The smallest facial blemish can affect how she treats the world on a given day.

Her hormones are beginning to rage, and as a result she is extremely crazy about boys. She and her friends talk about which boys they like and spend a majority of their time e-mailing and instant messaging different boys from their class. She feels a great pressure to have a boyfriend, start wearing makeup, and start shaving her legs, all of which her mother forbids and her father couldn't care less about. When she is at her father's house, she spends hours on the computer instant messaging her friends and eating junk food.

Friends are very important to her, especially the need to have a "best friend." If she had her way, she would be with her friends all day, every day. If she finds out that one of her friends went to another of her friend's house without her, she is very jealous and upset, giving both girls the cold shoulder when she sees them again.

Her biggest "hate" is school; she loves the social aspect, but hates the class lectures and homework. Her "step-monster" (stepmother) is also high on her hate list. She idolizes her older sister and all her sister's friends and wants to be just like them. Unfortunately, they are not the best role models and are heavily into the partying scene at their high school.

Her mother is severely frustrated by her mood swings and is constantly "nagging" her about her "poor posture and body language." Sydney cries very easily and sometimes doesn't even know why.

Her small-group leader, Melanie, is a big encouragement to her. Melanie often takes Sydney out for a Coke and asks how things are going at home and spiritually. Sydney feels she can talk to Melanie and looks at her as a good friend.

Melanie has talked Sydney into going on a short-term mission trip with several other middle school students over spring break. Sydney and Melanie are very excited about it. Sydney is working on several prerequisites for the mission trip including: reading a book about sharing your faith, memorizing some verses on faith, and writing a devotion with Melanie which will be presented to the group one night during the trip. Sydney doesn't know it yet, but this trip is going to change her life and relationship with God.

Middle school students can be so much fun and so challenging, all in the same breath. They are some of the most passionate, overconfident, unpredictable students we will deal with from week to week. One Sunday they will come into class laughing, talking, and being generally goofy. The next week they will sit down in the back corner and not say one word. When we ask them how school is going they mutter, "Fine." Ask if anything is wrong, their answer? "No." More often than not, one word answers are the best they can do.

Sixth through eighth grade students are teetering on the edge of a happy-go-lucky "I'll do anything" attitude and "everything we do in class is lame" attitude. At times it is impossible to know which personality will show up. This makes lesson planning very frustrating for a middle school Sunday school teacher.

Many of our middle school students are smack dab in that wonderful phase of life called puberty. Their noses are too big for their faces, acne is out of control, and voices are starting to change. Excited boys will yell out in class, "Hey, you know what?" and the whole class will roar with laughter from the squeak. These students are getting hit hard by the puberty monster and it can be *very frustrating* for them. They need to shower more often, use deodorant, and deal with raging hormones. Girls may need to start shaving their legs (legs which are normally twice as long as those of the boys in the class). The middle school years can be summed up in one word: "change." It is vital to be sensitive to the insecurities students feel during these changing times, and to keep in mind that a student's view of himself has a direct influence on his faith development.

We also realize the *importance* of this age group and faith development. Recall the statistics from George Barna that "by the age of 13, your spiritual identity is largely set in place"?[1] These energetic, motivated, goofy, loving, rapidly changing souls are forming some crucial opinions regarding their faith which could remain with them throughout their life. Reinforcement of faith foundations laid in the nursery, toddler, preschool, and elementary years is crucial at this time, and it is also the right time to build on these foundations with new information and new challenges. And as with all the age groups we must be very intentional with the 1% of time we spend with our students.

HEAVEN (Bible Knowledge and Feeling)

Students who have participated in the Faith Development Plan from birth should now have a clear knowledge of heaven and how to get there, but we also need to remember that not all students will have had the benefit of growing up under the guidance of a Faith Development Plan. What about those students who begin attending your church in middle school? (For more information on this question, see question eight in chapter twelve.) This is why the proposed Faith Development Plan calls for presenting a four-week age-appropriate series on salvation each year. Group Publishing has a lesson series entitled *Becoming a Christian*[2] which would be a good fit for your middle school students. This material focuses on what it means to have a personal relationship with God. (This curriculum may need to be revised to fit your church doctrine.)

We will be adding another dimension to the heaven building block. Middle school students are now able to begin understanding the concept of grace in salvation. Set aside time for a four-week study on the book of Romans and the concept of grace Paul teaches. Romans tells of the difference between "law" and "grace" and the futility of trying to get to heaven by keeping the law. This is a key concept for middle school students who may begin experiencing feelings of extreme guilt when they simply cannot be good all the time. Grace is an essential concept in faith development yet is often not taught or discussed in a church setting. Grace is one of those words like redemption, sanctification, and justification, which are frequently used in the church but rarely explained. As Christian educators we owe it to our students to show them the importance of grace in our lives and where we would be without it.

Another concept is assurance of salvation. Sadly, many Christians have never been taught this principle. In one of our morning worship services we had three of our middle school girls come forward to accept Christ and be immersed. That evening, their small group leader decided to scrap the lesson and have the girls share why they came to make this important decision. She decided to teach on the concept of assurance of salvation and asked each of the nine girls in the group this question, "If you died tonight, would you go to heaven?" All three of the girls who had just accepted Christ that morning answered, "Only God knows." The small group leader asked them what unforgivable sin they had committed since that morning!

Many middle school students who have made a decision to accept Jesus Christ as their personal Lord and Savior do not know if they are going to heaven or hell from one day to the next. One day they are on the heaven side of the fence, and the next day they are unsure and may think they are standing on the hell side because they yelled at their parents before school. Some believe if they have committed a sin and die before they repent, they will go to hell. This is a seriously dangerous misconception. Remember, our goal for these students is for them to have a passionate, personal relationship with Jesus Christ and to eventually pass on their faith to others. If they are confused on this subject, how would they answer a potential convert?

Aim Training Ministries[3] has put together a four-week lesson series on grace and the book of Romans. This series is easily adapted for middle school students as well as high school. The proposed Faith Development Plan calls for a four-week study on grace to be presented annually in both the middle school and senior high departments.

We are also ready to begin a study on hell. Obviously we don't want to stress hell with our preschool or early elementary students. This can be very scary for them, especially if they have an unbeliever in their family. We did not study about hell in the late elementary program for one simple reason: we realize late elementary is the age many students make a decision for Jesus Christ. We do not want them to make this important decision out

> Many middle school students do not know if they are going to heaven or hell from one day to the next.

of fear. This "fire and brimstone" technique may influence a child to come to salvation from the wrong motives. While late elementary students should know the reality of hell, they do not need to study it. Set aside a simple one or two weeks in your middle school Faith Development Plan to do a biblical study on the place of hell. What does the Bible say hell is like? Who does the Bible say is going to hell? How could a good God allow anyone to go to hell? If I am bad, can I go to hell after I have accepted Christ? These are several of the questions to cover in this study.

TITHING (Bible Knowledge and Experience)

Middle school students are capable of diving deeper into the area of tithing and handling their money. Aside from the chores their parents have given them on a weekly basis, girls are now babysitting and boys are mowing lawns, doing paper routes, or even officiating little league baseball or soccer games. Some students have started savings accounts, and we have even seen middle school youth with checkbooks and ATM cards.

Middle school students can also begin learning the idea of tithing beyond money. They can learn the importance of giving God their talents and their time as well as their lives. These concepts spill over into the areas of service and salvation or heaven, so these are important concepts to middle school students.

In the area of talent offerings consider hosting a "Giving Thanks for our Talent Night" sometime around the Thanksgiving holiday. Like "Heaven Night," this can become an annual family event for your entire congregation. Encourage everyone in the church to come, regardless of age, to share the talents God has given them. One of your students may read some of her poetry. Another may play the flute at school and could play a solo or duet with piano accompaniment. Perhaps someone in your church has a gift for art. Have them paint, draw, or chalk a picture while someone else is singing a solo. Encourage everyone in the church to share the talents God has given them, not to be judged, graded, or gonged, but to praise God for what He has given us.

In addition, continue to set aside a four-week study on God's plan for money such as *Money Matters for Teens*.[4] This series teaches the concepts of budgeting and saving money for purchases rather than taking out a loan. It also teaches students how to keep a checkbook and has a special section on "How You Can Change the World with Your Money." Money is a powerful tool, and our students need to realize God's design for their finances, now and in the future.

PRAYER (Bible Knowledge, Feeling, and Experience)

Our students live in a hyper communication-driven world. Most of your students do not have any idea how much a postage stamp costs because they have never purchased one. Mailing a letter with a stamp will one day join such historical communication devices as smoke signals, carrier pigeons, horse-riding messengers, and switchboard operators. Most of your students have their own cell phones, not just for making and sending calls whenever they wish, but for text-messaging their friends. Most cellular companies provide free minutes on nights and weekends, so many students fill their time calling everyone they know. And what about instant messaging? As I sit and work on this chapter, I have three different students chatting with me on Yahoo! Instant Messenger while playing an internet game of checkers with another. Cell phones, instant messaging, e-mail, speed dial, call waiting, call forwarding—we really have no excuse for lack of communication. This is the world in which our students live and function on a daily basis. Their days are filled with communication, and they communicate with those with whom they have a personal relationship: friends, teachers, and parents.

Prayer must be taught in respect to communication with God. Communication is something our students understand, but sitting down without the television, MP3 player, computer, or cell phone and talking to God is a struggle. We must strive to encourage our students to communicate regularly with their Best Friend.

Middle school students are also ready to increase their understanding of the concept of listening to God. When they begin to relate their relationship with Jesus Christ to that of a friendship, they will see that this cannot be one-sided. If they had a friend who just talked and talked to them, asked them for favors, apologized for the things they did wrong toward them, praised them for how wonderful they were, and left, this would not be a relationship. A relationship is when both parties are communicating. A relationship is not one person giving and the other always receiving.

Encourage your students to set aside a specific time in their day, in a specific room or special place with no distractions. Have them talk to God in prayer for part of the time and listen to God the rest.

Many of your students have no idea what that means. One student timidly asked, "Can you actually hear a voice? What does that mean? How do you know when God has spoken to you?" These are legitimate questions and are not necessarily held only by children. Many adults in your congregation have never heard God speak to them and, sadder still, have never taken the time to listen to Him.

The Faith Development Plan for middle school students calls for a four-week study on prayer in conjunction with the study on devotion time and Bible reading. Various Christian education publishers have study series on prayer with emphasis on historical figures in the Bible who devoted themselves to communicating with God.

At several times in the Faith Development Plan we have suggested testimonies to help your students understand difficult concepts and hearing God's voice is one of these instrumental times. Invite members of your congregation to come and speak to your students about a time God spoke to them. Ask these adults to be very specific about how they relate this information to your students. Did they actually hear the voice out loud or was it something they just felt inside? God is speaking to your students. They need to be taught how to listen and understand this new form of communication. Through these times of sharing, your students will be able to draw on testimonies shared and relate them to their life. (Do not feel limited to having testimonies shared while studying a certain topic. If you hear how God laid something on someone's heart and you are studying grace, set aside the lesson for a few minutes prior and ask this person to share with your students.)

EVANGELISM AND SERVICE (Bible Knowledge and Experience)

Middle school is time to get serious with our students about evangelism. Like late elementary students, middle school students love to be challenged, keeping in mind these students know very well what is and isn't "cool" at school. Many of our Christian students who attend public schools have learned that they are in the minority. Don't expect it to be simple for students to share their faith with others. Presenting students with a four-week lesson on evangelism and ending it with, "Now go out and tell someone about God!" is simply not sufficient. Most of our students will walk out of the classroom thinking, "Yeah, right!" Asking our students to share their faith is an extremely difficult request. They can choose to walk out of our classroom with the attitude, "I am going to be bold and share my faith this week. I know I can do it," or they can walk out thinking, "They have told us this kind of thing for years, and no one really does it!" Unfortunately it is often the latter.

Asking a typical teenager with low self-esteem and high hopes for popularity to go to school and share their faith can induce paralyzing panic. It would be like challenging someone with a fear of heights, "Now go out there and look out that eighteenth story window." Your students fear rejection. They fear failure. As adults we can say, "Really, if you walk up to someone at school and share your faith, what is the worst thing that could happen?" In their eyes the worst thing that could happen is the student laughing at them, telling everyone else, and your student ending up eating lunch by themselves every day. *That's* the worst that could happen and, to be honest, that scenario is entirely feasible.

Tread lightly when you begin setting expectations for your students in the area of evangelism. Don't just get them on their bicycle for the first time and push them down the hill calling, "You'll be fine . . ." Be very sensitive to their insecurities while clearly communicating your expectations. Ask yourself this question, "Have my students ever personally witnessed someone else sharing their faith outside of the church building?" The odds are that they haven't. Most parents or other adults do not share their faith and, if they do, it is in a work situation where the students do not have the opportunity to learn.

Be very sensitive to their insecurities while clearly communicating your expectations.

Continue offering family servant evangelism projects sponsored by your church. Pair up your students with adults who will demonstrate how to share their faith. Present some type of biblical study and lesson series for a minimum of four weeks on your Faith Development Plan.

One of the ways to help your students share their faith is by providing them with "faith starters." A "faith starter" is something a student may wear or do that would prompt a question from a nonbeliever. One such "faith starter" is a bracelet with SYATP printed on the material. One of your students may be paying for their drink at a fast food restaurant when the cashier asks, "What's SYATP?" Your student now has an open opportunity to share their faith, and they didn't even start the conversation; they are simply answering a question. "SYATP stands for See You at the Pole. Once a year we meet around the flagpole at our school and pray for a bunch of different stuff. Would you be interested in coming to our church youth group? We do cool stuff like that all the time." Provide your students with these resources and encourage them to take advantage of questions raised by their "faith starters."

A middle school Faith Development Plan will typically run for three years, depending on how your public school system is set up. The proposed Faith Development Plan suggests offering a mission trip once every other year for this age group. The plan also calls for the same staggering of mission trips for your high school youth, so it is best to offer a week-long mission trip one year for middle school, the next for high school, the next for middle school and so on.

Consider putting some strict expectations on your students prior to and following the mission trip. Present these expectations up front before the students decide to sign up.

1) Require them to read a specific book on missions and write a one-page typed response.
2) Require them to present a devotion either individually or with one other person for the group during the mission trip.
3) Require them to submit their testimony to the mission trip leader answering this question, "How did I come to Christ?" For high school students, require them to share this testimony with the rest of the group.
4) Require them to attend a set amount of meetings prior to the mission trip.
5) Encourage them to bathe the mission trip in prayer several months prior to the trip.
6) Require them to attend a set amount of meetings after the mission trip.
7) Require them to write their own letter of support.
8) Require students to sign a pledge stating they will work hard on the trip, be respectful, and be a team player.

These may seem like strict goals for middle school students, but they are very attainable. Setting such goals for your group will also send an important message to our students: "This is not a vacation. This is serious." Of course with any mission trip our students can expect that mission trips will also include fun beyond belief while building relationships and growing in their faith development.

> **As with all mission trips offered in the Faith Development Plan, strongly encourage at least one parent to attend with their child. Both parent and child will be blessed and will grow from the experience.**

BOOKS OF THE BIBLE (Bible Knowledge)

Continue reinforcing the skills your students have been learning up to this point in the Faith Development Plan. One suggestion is to play review games such as Bible baseball every fifth Sunday with your students. At the end of each Bible lesson ask them to write a question for the review game during the next fifth Sunday. If the lesson was about grace, the question may be, "What book of the Bible did we study when we learned about grace, and who wrote it?" Have the students put their questions in a fish bowl or box in preparation for the next fifth Sunday review time.

To add to the fun of the review game you may throw in a question for a grand slam home run. "Name all the books of the New Testament." "Name all the books of the Old Testament." "Name the divisions of the Old Testament." "Who wrote the book of _____?" Some middle school students who love challenges will be led to learn the books of the Bible if they have not already done so, just to get that grand slam home run!

Your goal with the books of the Bible should be for all your students to know them in order, know the divisions, and know who wrote these books.

SCIENCE AND MIDDLE SCHOOL STUDENTS (Bible Knowledge and Science)

The three divisions of science we want to stress with students are: nature, animals, and the human body. As we mentioned at the beginning of this chapter, middle school students are in the period of "change." These students are now ready to begin learning about God's design for their body and reproduction. Many Christian educators shy away from any type of lesson on puberty or God's design for the body. There is no question about it; it is not the most comfortable thing to discuss with insecure teenagers. Some Christian educators simply do not feel it is their responsibility to teach students about such personal things. But teaching your students of God's perfect design for the human body, and how puberty fits into that design, is a distinct way of solidifying the science leg of their faith table.

Obviously, one of the topics in this area is sex education. When speaking with your middle school sponsors about this matter and its placement in the Faith Development Plan for this age, always keep two things in mind.

A) *Never* assume that your students know *anything* about sex education. Assume they know nothing. Most middle school students know more about sex than we knew in college. However, there are some students who have been sheltered from this information and don't know anything.

B) *Never* assume that it is okay with the students' parents to teach *anything* about sex education without their consent.

Obtaining consent from the parents is simply respectful. Most parents want to know what their child is learning about sex education, when, where, and from whom. Before launching into any lesson series on God's design for sex and the human body, consider holding a parents' meeting to inform them what will be discussed. Encourage parents to review the material you will be discussing and to follow up the series by asking their child questions at home following up what they learned in church.

Continue focusing on the areas of God's perfect design for animals. Two great web sites for studies in this area are **www. christianreality.com** and **www.moodyvideo.com**. One of the great videos they offer is *City of the Bees*. Bees are some of the most amazingly sophisticated insects. As with all animals, God has designed them for a specific function and created their bodies and minds to perform that function. Other videos follow the unbelievable journey of Pacific salmon who face tremendous obstacles to complete the circle of life God has designed for them.

In addition, continue spending some time presenting the miracle of nature. Again, Christian Reality and Moody Video have tremendous resources to help present the awesomeness of God's world to your students.

One of the issues you will see creeping in your student's public school science curriculum is the theory of evolution. At times it is not even presented as a theory. It is presented as fact. The presentation of evolution may not be as blatantly obvious as some adults may think. My son's public school history book began the year introducing students to what the world was like millions of years ago. Many adults do not realize that this is evolutionary teaching and is not a biblical view. Set aside a minimum of two weeks in your middle school Faith Development Plan to help your middle school students see the difference between God's creation of the world and the theory of evolution. The very best resources in this area come from **www.answersingenesis.com** and the thorough research of Ken Ham. Answers in Genesis has several resources available in the form of books and videos for you to use with your students.

When presenting the faith table spoken of in chapter two and the need for godly science to be taught in the church, I once had a friend ask me if I honestly believed a typical church teacher was qualified to teach science to students. This was my answer. "I know many adults who teach the Bible to students on a weekly basis that are not 'qualified' to do so. Many of these teachers do not have a clear understanding of the Bible or its teaching. They are simply a warm, willing body with a heart for children.

But maybe you are thinking the same thing, "I don't know anything about God's design for bees or for the Pacific salmon." The fact is, you don't have to know about all these areas. That is what these resources are for. All you need to do is set aside some church teaching time to present these videos or similar materials to your students. You and your teachers will be learning right alongside the students for the first one or two years. I didn't know anything about God's perfect design for nature, animals, and the human body until I started teaching my own children.

If you have teachers who are truly reluctant to present any of the information in regard to science, simply show the videos as an extra activity for your students. Make one Friday night every month a movie night. Use a projection unit in the sanctuary or a television with VCR to show the movies. Offer popcorn and drinks and follow up the movie with discussion.

BIBLE STORIES (Bible Knowledge)

Your students can now study a large portion of Scripture over an extended period of time. Prior to middle school your students had been focusing on one Bible account or biblical concept each week. These students can now handle a one-month series on the book of Matthew or a one-month set of lessons on Paul's prison epistles.

We must remember to stretch our students. The biggest mistake we can make is to underestimate what they can learn. These teenagers are past learning simple concepts such as "God made the world" and "Jesus loves me very much." They are ready for meat, and your Faith Development Plan for this age should reflect that fact. Middle school sponsors can make a list of which books of the Bible or biblical figures they would like to cover over the three years the students are in their program. After they have made this list, decide which they feel should be repeated each year or every other year. After the list has been compiled, begin filling in your middle school plan with the biblical accounts, figures, and books you would like for them to study before they leave the middle school program.

> We must remember to stretch our students. The biggest mistake we can make is to underestimate what they can learn.

It is also time for these students to switch from an elementary-age-targeted Bible to something more developmentally appropriate. There are several choices in the area of teen Bibles. Take the time to surf the internet or make a trip to your local Christian bookstore to choose a Bible you feel is appropriate for this age. While it is not as important for all your middle or high school students to have the same Bible as the previous years, you will want to choose the best Bible to keep in your classrooms. Provide several extra Bibles for each of your youth classrooms. Make sure the students understand these are only to be used for visitors or if someone accidentally forgets his or her Bible. They should be bringing their Bibles to church with them each week.

MEMORY VERSES (Bible Knowledge)

Oftentimes memory work is limited to the younger grades in a church youth ministry. Middle school youth need to continue reviewing the passages they have learned to this point and continue working on new verses. Choose verses that relate to the concepts taught in the Faith Development Plan. Include the memorization of these verses in your fifth Sunday Bible baseball review game.

WORSHIP (Bible Knowledge, Feeling, and Experience)

A common trend in larger churches is the separation of youth and adults for worship time. As mentioned in previous chapters there is a time and a place for youth to worship in their own group. The Sunday morning worship service is not one of those times. Consider your church programs.

There is a time and a place for youth to worship in their own group. The Sunday morning worship service is not one of those times.

From the time a family walks into the building until the time they leave, how long are they together? Many times families don't even come in the door together and, if they do, Mom takes Johnny to his class in the preschool wing, Dad makes sure Susie gets to her elementary class, and Jimmy knows his way to the garage where the senior high students meet. Once the children are all in their classes, Mom and Dad go to theirs. After the family members are finished in their respective classes, Mom and Dad go to the praise service, Johnny stays in his preschool class, Susie goes to junior church, and Jimmy either goes to youth church in another part of the building or sits with his friends in the adult assembly. Church is over, Mr. Smith tries to gather his family to make it to Pizza Hut before the lunchtime crowds hit, and the family was never together that morning. Christian educators be warned: this is not God's design for the spiritual growth of the family.

If we can fight this separation at any time, it should be during the time of worship. Encourage your leadership to see the importance of the family sitting together during the worship service. After the singing time is finished, children can be excused to participate in age-appropriate teaching time. This family worship time may only be fifteen minutes, but it is something. It is a start.

In addition to your middle school youth participating in the adult service, allow times for them to worship on their own "turf." Consider forming a praise team or praise band with your middle school or senior high youth. Most youth groups include student members who play instruments. A youth praise team or praise band is an excellent, hands-on way to teach our students about worship.

Continue setting aside at least four weeks in your middle school Faith Development Plan to study the concept of worship and God's desire for us to worship Him. If you have someone in your church who could teach your students basic sign language, offer an extra class teaching the signs to several praise choruses. This will especially be popular with the girls in your group.

Make sure you are taking every opportunity to involve your students in corporate worship with other teens. If you know of a youth rally or a conference where a praise band will be playing, load your students in the church van and go. Most students love music and love to sing praise songs to God. Some of your "too cool" guys may just go and listen, but that's okay. You may be surprised to hear their parents come up to you later and say, "I know Justin just sat at the youth rally last week and didn't sing. But he has been singing those songs all week at home. He was even singing them at the top of his voice in the shower this week!"

Lastly, consider investing in a youth music library for your students. If budget allows, purchase worship music of different genres and make it available for your students to sign out for a period of time. If you notice a student is becoming interested in a certain artist or group, a certain musical genre, or a specific recording, put a bug in their parent's ear about ideas for a Christmas or birthday present.

HISTORY AND MIDDLE SCHOOL STUDENTS (Bible Knowledge and History)

Where did the Bible come from? How were the specific books we read in our Bible chosen? What archaeological evidence supports the accuracy of the Bible? What other than the Bible supports the idea that Jesus Christ ever lived? How will we respond to questions such as, "My teacher told me that Moses wrote the first five books of the Bible, but he wasn't even alive during some of that time? How could he write about things that he didn't even know about?"

These are all legitimate questions that begin creeping in the minds of our students. And often they are too intimidated to ask. As with many other areas in the Faith Development Plan our students deserve explanations when it comes to the evidences for believing in the reliability of Scripture. If we do not present the facts of history to our students, they will come up with their own theories, and those will most likely be incorrect.

> Our students deserve explanations when it comes to the evidences for believing in the reliability of Scripture.

Fortunately, there are a few resources available to help you present this information to your students. Among others, Rose Publishing[5] has a few resources that will help answer some of your students' toughest questions. Two resources are in the form of pamphlets. *Archaeology & Bible Old Testament* and *Archaeology & Bible New Testament* offer 50 archaeological finds for each testament that "support the veracity" of the Bible. In addition they have a PowerPoint CD-ROM and pamphlet on "How We

Got the Bible." All of these items from Rose Publishing are excellent and worth the investment.

Our young teens also need to begin learning the history of the church and/or denomination heritage. Many of their friends may attend the Catholic Church, the Lutheran Church, the Presbyterian church, the Church of God, the Church of Christ, or the Christian Missionary Alliance. The differences between denominations can be confusing to a normal adult. Imagine how a middle school student must feel.

Many churches are now offering 101, 201, 301, and 401 classes for their members. A 101 class may be a basic class which shares the beliefs of your church. Consider taking the information presented in the adult 101 class and modifying it for your middle school students. Turn this into a four-week class for your students to teach them what your church believes.

Also teach them the history of other denominations and show them how your church differs from those of different names. Rose Publishing also has a "Denomination Comparison" chart which will help students understand the different views held by various churches.

GOD'S PLAN FOR THE FAMILY (Bible Knowledge and Family)

Divorce is not a foreign word to your students. Many of the students in your ministry either come from a split home or know of someone close to them who does. We do not have to look at the divorce statistics to show its prevalence, we can simply look at our churches. Remembering that many of our thirteen-year-old middle school students could realistically be married in five years, we must be diligent to teach them of God's design for marriage. We must teach them how God feels about divorce.

Christian educators tend to shy away from teaching on the dangers of divorce with their students, mainly because they do not want to offend their students or parents. You may teach a lesson and say, "God hates divorce. It is his desire for the man and woman to stay together in marriage for life." And you may cringe anticipating the question the student in the second row, waving his arm, is going to ask. "My mom and dad are divorced. So did they sin? Can they still go to heaven?" It is very hard to teach a concept such as divorce when your students' parents are modeling the very sin you are speaking of. This should not stop you from teaching the biblical view of marriage. Constantly view your students as future adults—arrows which need to be aimed at the target.

DAILY DEVOTIONS AND BIBLE READING (Bible Knowledge, Feeling, and Experience)

Persuading middle school students to spend time in daily devotions is not an easy feat. These students want a devotional book that is cool, relevant, easy to read, and fun. The creative people at Thomas Nelson have come up with two exceptional devotion books for middle school and high school students.

Revolve[6] is a complete New Testament presented in the New Century Version, specifically designed for girls. This New Testament Bible and devotional looks like a magazine. It is presented in magazine form with several pictures of teens and church activities. This devotional is jam-packed with prayer calendars, Bible studies, questions and answers, hints on how to share your faith, suggestions on how to "get along with your mom," and a section for girls to hear how guys feel about the same issues they are facing.

Its counterpart is *Refuel*,[7] a complete New Testament in the same version targeted just for the male audience. This resource has music reviews, practical ways to live our faith, and articles about girls, cash, and cars; all things our teenage guys love to talk about.

While the outside of these devotionals look suspiciously like something you would see while waiting in line at the checkout counter, the content is not watered down in the least. Your teenage students will love these two devotionals and will not be afraid to carry them to school as they do not look "religious."

Constantly be on the lookout for up-to-date, applicable, challenging devotion books for your students and continue challenging them as well. Hold your students accountable to a regular time of devotion and prayer with God. Encourage them to set aside a specific time and place to spend a moment with God and to make this arrangement nonnegotiable.

The biggest devotional obstacle to overcome with your middle school and high school students is busyness. If your youth group is in the norm, your students are involved in sports, music, drama, band, choir, and dance. You may even have to battle sharing your students with a host of parachurch organizations such as Youth for Christ, Fellowship of Christian Athletes, and Young Life. Sometimes we feel as if we are competing for our students' time, and it is our mission to accept that challenge.

The biggest devotional obstacle is busyness.

Here is an e-mail sent to a youth minister. It may sound familiar to you.

Dear Kevin,

I need your help with something. You were talking in youth group last night about how important it is for us to do daily devotions. My problem is my schedule. I get up every morning at 6:30 so that I can make the bus by 7:15. I don't get off the bus from school until 3:00 every day. On Mondays, Wednesdays and Fridays I go straight to soccer practice for two hours. On Tuesdays and Thursdays I have conditioning for track. On Saturday I have softball practice, soccer games and piano lessons. Most Sundays I have soccer games. My question is, when can I do my devotions? By the time I get home from practice, do my homework and take a shower, its time for bed. I've tried doing my devotions at night, but I keep falling asleep because I'm so tired. Let me know what you think. Sara (Personal E-Mail)

Sara is not alone. Many of the students in your youth group struggle with finding time for regular devotions. Their lives are just so . . . busy. Continually encourage your students to set aside time on a regular basis for time in the Word with God. Some of your students may find daily devotions impossible, but three times a week is perfect. Along with presenting your students with different resources to continue regular devotion time outside of church, continue offering a four-week study on the armor of God. When studying these passages, clearly let your students know that Satan does not want them to have regular devotions. Satan does not want them to pray, period. Satan's desire is for them to be lukewarm Christians. At the end of your study on the armor of God, print out the verses on a 3×5 card and ask the students to hang the card in a visible place in their home. We encourage our students to hang their cards on the bathroom mirror. Urge your students to commit each day to putting on their spiritual armor and reading these verses to prepare for the day. Putting on our armor every morning is a sure way to let Satan's arrows bounce right off us with the Holy Spirit's protection.

ETHICS (Bible Knowledge)

WWJD may have become a bit overused. The phrase, "What would Jesus do?" has become so cliché that many of our students don't even contemplate its meaning. Most Christian educators know that the phrase was started by a group of students in Holland, Michigan, who had just finished reading the book *In*

His Steps by Charles Sheldon which was originally written in 1896. Many years later, Mr. Sheldon's great-grandson rewrote this book for more modern times. The title is simply *What Would Jesus Do?*[8] It is an excellent book that challenges readers to ask themselves that very question.

We decided to take our cue from Oprah and offer the study of this book in an official book club format during the summer months in lieu of small groups. While studying the book, we also studied the life of Christ and His encounters with various people. We realized, "We can't truly answer the question 'What would Jesus do?' until we actually know Jesus." We spent several group times together discussing His personality, His boldness, His love for fun, and other characteristics. At that point we were ready to ask ourselves, challenge ourselves, to question what Jesus would do in our place. At the end of the book club we wrote those things down and circled which of those would be the hardest to follow through with, which of the items on our list would push us most out of our comfort zones. The students were very open and transparent.

Take the time to study the life of Christ in relation to ethics and the WWJD question. Living your life ethically from the standpoint of this continuous question is very eye opening. The combination of this "life question" and the idea of consequences can greatly influence the ethical choices of our students.

Another useful resource for our middle school students is *Right Choices.*[9] As with the other biblical studies in ethics by Josh McDowell, it is simply the best. It's a dynamic study which can be offered in a small group or on Wednesday nights instead of the traditional Sunday school time. It's a wonderful resource to add to your middle school Faith Development Plan.

Media: The power of the media is a major issue your middle and high school students have to deal with. Music videos have become pornographic. The internet can be used to access a cesspool of filth. Movie ratings have become a joke. Video games have become obsessively violent, and music has just become negative and hateful. And then there is the television. Most of us would be hard pressed to find even one sitcom that has any form of biblical ethics, not to mention the rash of trashy reality shows. The media is a strong influence on our students, and most of them can choose to listen to or watch whatever they want.

Please do not take this sitting down. As Christian educators we should do everything in our power to counter this influence

As Christian educators we should do everything in our power to encourage our students to make wise decisions in their listening and viewing choices.

and encourage our students to make wise decisions in their listening and viewing choices. True Lies,[10] a ministry founded by Phil Chalmers, is an excellent tool for Christian educators. Chalmers and his speaking team travel all over the country presenting seminars in churches and secular settings educating youth and parents to the dangers of the media. The True Lies website also has some helpful resources such as research on the effects of media on today's youth. The site also has several positive Christian alternatives to the various genres of secular music.

Another resource in this area is the Focus on the Family website at **www.family.org**. If your students or parents are questioning a certain music group or movie, they can read reviews of what they are about to see or hear and judge for themselves. This is also a tremendous resource to check periodically and keep up to date on what your students are taking in on a daily basis.

Relationships: Maybe you've heard it said, "If you want to know what your students are like when you are not around, look at their friends." This phrase is the absolute truth. Your students hate the phrase, but here it is—peer pressure. They will tell you over and over that peer pressure is not a big deal, but in most cases it is not the truth. No one wants to be lame. Everyone wants to be accepted, and middle school and high school students make highly uncharacteristic, sometimes self-destructive, choices because of this. If a student has friends who are all smokers, chances are that student smokes. The choices your students make in the area of friends are absolutely crucial to the choices they make in everyday life.

In the area of godly ethics it is essential to present your students with the tools to choose friends wisely. Middle school ministry is an excellent time for a Bible study on the friendships such as David and Jonathan or Jesus and His disciples. Study the importance of being equally yoked. Sometimes your students will try to persuade you that they are different and unaffected by peer pressure. "I know I don't hang around with good kids. But I hang around them because I want to be a good influence on them. I'm not like them. Really, I'm not." This is an opportune time to explain the concept of an equal yoke. If this student and his friend were to put on a yoke, would they be moving toward the same target? If they are moving toward the target of spiritual maturity and their friend is moving in a different direction, then the relationship cannot work.

We are speaking here of the area of "best friends" or "best buddies," not casual acquaintances. Realizing that God calls us to be "in the world, not of it," we do not want to convey to our students a separatist attitude, yet the person who is the closest to them should be of the same belief. If not, the yoke will break, one student will slow the other down, or one student will lead the other down the wrong path.

> **If you ever come across a yoke in an antique store or auction, buy it. Hang it in your youth room as a reminder of the yoke concept in friendships and in marriage.**

SELF-IMAGE (Bible Knowledge, Feeling, and Science)

Self-image was a new building block in the late elementary years and is also a branch of ethics. We will see our students make poor choices simply due to their low self-esteem. They want to be accepted. They want to fit in. They are very insecure.

In their Faith 4 Life series Group Publishing has a study on self-image for middle school students called *Finding Your Identity*.[11] This study presents self-image from God's eyes.

As in the late elementary program, continue building your student's self-image whenever possible. Often, adults do not realize the power of their words with teenagers. One mention to a student such as, "Alyssa, I love your hair! Did you get it cut?" That one simple conversation can boost a student's self-confidence tremendously.

While filling a permanent substitute teaching position for seventh grade Language Arts, I quickly realized the importance of my words. Some children had such confidence and some had none. One girl in the class, Cassandra, absolutely loved to write and had even ventured into entering her writing in contests. One day I asked her how she became so passionate about writing. Without hesitation she said, "One day I turned in a paper and Mrs. Kees told me that I was a great writer and had a lot of potential." And that started this student on a path and a passion. How long did it take for that teacher to mention those words? Maybe ten seconds. They were words of encouragement and praise and many of our students never hear such things at home or

Take the time to verbally encourage your students as often as possible.

with their friends. Take the time to verbally encourage your students as often as possible.

SMALL GROUPS (Bible Knowledge and Experience)

The last area in the middle school department is small groups. While some excellent curriculum is written for elementary small groups the proposed Faith Development Plan implements it in middle school.

At the beginning of each school year, have a meeting with the parents of your students. Offer this meeting more than once to allow all parents to attend. At these meetings, spell out the expectations for your students. Stress regular church attendance, personal Bible study, prayer at home, and evangelism as your four foundational blocks. In addition, stress the potential value of their child's involvement in small groups. Small groups allow students to dive deeper into faith in a gender-specific small group setting. It allows them a high degree of accountability with a spiritually mature adult. It also allows them the accountability of other peer believers.

Offer gender specific small groups or discipleship groups for all ages, middle school through high school. Run these groups through the school year allowing a break for the summer months. No matter how much the students pressure you, especially the girls, do not offer the small groups during the summer months. Offer a book club or a different format, but allow the groups a break during the summer months. Taking a break during the summer will bring students back to small groups refreshed and ready to grow.

It is very important to require your students involved in a small group to sign some type of small group covenant. This covenant should cover the following:

† attendance—"Look at this small group as a sports team. We are working together for a common goal. You would not miss a basketball practice or game, and I am asking that you make every effort not to miss this group time. When you are not here, it affects how the group interacts"

† confidentiality—nothing said in this small group is repeated outside the group

† respect—when someone is talking, you need to listen and respect what they are saying

† participation—the students should promise to open up

and participate in the small group in order for the group to attain its goal of growing closer to each other and God.

Once you set these expectations, follow through with them.

MIDDLE SCHOOL LEARNING GOALS

By the time a middle school student leaves his or her classroom at the Community Christian Church he or she will have:

- ✓ Reinforced and strengthened all concepts begun in the late elementary department.
- ✓ Learned the concept and importance of grace.
- ✓ Learned the concept and importance of assurance of salvation.
- ✓ Participated in a Bible study on the place of hell.
- ✓ Studied the plan of salvation in relation to his/her life.
- ✓ Learned the concept of tithing not only money, but time and talent.
- ✓ Had the opportunity to participate in a "Giving Thanks Talent Night."
- ✓ Studied the concept of listening to God during prayer.
- ✓ Been challenged to share his/her faith in Christ with an unbeliever.
- ✓ Had the opportunity to participate in at least one week-long mission trip.
- ✓ Had the opportunity to participate in one of several servant evangelism projects.
- ✓ Participated in a Bible study on the importance of evangelism.
- ✓ Learned the truth of God's creation and the faults in the theory of evolution.
- ✓ Studied in depth different animals and God's perfect design for them.
- ✓ Studied God's design for the human body and human sexuality.
- ✓ Been challenged and stretched in his/her Bible knowledge while studying whole books of the Bible and large passages.
- ✓ Been encouraged to participate in adult or family worship.
- ✓ Had the opportunity to attend church-sponsored youth praise services with his/her peers.
- ✓ Had the opportunity to participate in a worship service through singing or playing instruments.

- Studied God's desire for us to worship Him.
- Studied God's design for marriage and the biblical view on divorce.
- Studied archaeological evidence which supports the Bible.
- Studied the history of our denomination and what sets us apart from other denominations.
- Studied the answers to questions on how the Bible was written and compiled.
- Studied the armor of God and how this affects our daily devotion and prayer time.
- Participated in a study of the book *What Would Jesus Do?*
- Studied the life of Christ and related His interactions with various people to ethical choices.
- Learned the importance of godly choices in regard to media intake.
- Studied the importance of choosing friends wisely.
- Studied the importance of a godly self-image and how to maintain a healthy self-esteem.
- Had the opportunity to participate in a faith-building small group.

THINGS A PARENT CAN DO TO REINFORCE WHAT IS TAUGHT IN THE MIDDLE SCHOOL DEPARTMENT (FAMILY)

- Continue bringing your children to church each Sunday. Make church attendance as regular as school attendance.
- Set aside a time and place each day to begin helping your child with daily devotions and prayer time and continue having a family devotion time. This is a routine you want them to continue after they leave your home.
- Cotinually bathe your child in prayer. Pray for your child's future spouse. Pray that God will help him/her to make wise choices at school. Pray for your child's salvation and their spiritual growth.
- Allow your child to join your family in the singing portion of your worship service even if your church does not provide this. Do whatever you can to make sure you sit together as a family. Your child needs to see the effect praising God and worshiping has on you.

✔ Continue encouraging your children to bring their Bibles to church each week and back home for their daily devotional time. Show them the importance of this by bringing your Bible to church each week.

✔ Continue instilling an appreciation for God's creation, take advantage of "teachable moments," and talk to your children about the wonders of God's world and His perfect design.

✔ If your child has not made a decision to accept Jesus Christ as her personal Lord and Savior, take the time to speak to her about making that decision.

✔ In addition to your children's weekly tithe, encourage them to tithe their time and talents.

✔ Continue to encourage your children to participate in church-sponsored mission trips and servant evangelism projects.

✔ Help your child's teacher by going over the books of the Bible at home.

✔ Help your child's teacher by working with them in doing their homework of memorizing Bible verses. View this as of equal importance to their homework at school.

✔ Strongly encourage your child to choose friends with their same interests. Intensely watch your child's friends and make sure you are comfortable with the influence they have on your child.

✔ Insist that your children make godly choices in their media intake. Do not allow music or movies with profanity or sex as a theme. Monitor your children's video games and do not allow them to play anything that is not rated on their age level. In addition, monitor their television intake. Do not allow your children to sway your decisions in this area with the statement, "But everyone is watching it!" Children using this "line" are playing on your emotions. The truth is, not everyone is doing what your children say they are doing.

✔ Observe how your child behaves around her friends, at home, at school if possible, and at church. Encourage your child to be consistent in her behavior and actions.

✔ Continue stressing the importance of God's design for the family. Make it a point to model those roles in your home as God intended.

✔ Praise your child as much as possible. Consciously avoid criticizing your child. Tell your child, "You are special." "I love you." "I don't know what I would do without you." "You are beautiful." "You can do it." "I think you did a great job." "Just do your best." "God has big plans for your life." Remember, your child's self-image is still in the developing stages at this point. She *needs* encouragement.

✔ Strongly encourage your child to be involved in a church-sponsored small group.

✔ Whenever possible, take your child to a Christian concert and make a conscious effort to play positive, uplifting music in your home.

✔ *Never* talk adversely about the church, its leadership, or teachers in front of your child. Derogatory remarks about the church greatly restrict the impact the church can have on your child and ultimately his faith development. If *you* are upset with something that is or has been taking place at your church, make sure your child is out of earshot before discussing your concerns. Doing so could be detrimental to their faith development. Be careful what you say at home.

NOTES

1. Barna, *Transforming Children*, 34.

2. *Faith 4 Life: Becoming a Christian* (Loveland, CO: Group Publishing, 2002).

3. www.aimtrainingministries.com.

4. Larry Burkett and Todd Temple, *Money Matters for Teens* (Chicago: Moody, 1998).

5. www.rosepublishing.net.

6. *Revolve* (Nashville: Thomas Nelson, 2003).

7. *Refuel* (Nashville: Thomas Nelson, 2003).

8. Garrett W. Sheldon, *What Would Jesus Do?* (Nashville: Broadman and Holman, 1993).

9. Josh McDowell, *Right Choices* (Nashville: Broadman and Holman, 1995).

10. www.truelies.org.

11. Debbie Gowensmith, *Faith 4 Life: Finding Your Identity* (Loveland, CO: Group Publishing, 2002).

Chapter Ten

EVALUATING THE ARROWS: HIGH SCHOOL

Where do you want your students to be by the time they graduate, and how are you going to get them there?

Sam is an eighteen-year-old in his senior year of high school. He is the youngest of six children. Sam is somewhat shy around people he does not know; however, his parents say he never stops talking at home. He is very confident (but not overly so) and well mannered and will eventually be voted "Nicest Guy" in his graduating class. He starts defensive line on the varsity football team and hopes to get a scholarship to the University of Alabama. He is six feet tall, 200 pounds, and very meticulous about his body. He lifts weights every day after school, will not drink soft drinks, eat sweets, consume alcohol or drugs, or smoke cigarettes. He thinks of his body as a machine and strives to keep it running smoothly. He has recently grown a goatee. In all physical respects, he is a man.

He receives average grades. He could do better but doesn't feel the need to bring his books home. He does not see the importance in most of the things he learns at school because, he figures, he's not getting an academic scholarship.

Sam has a girlfriend, Jessie, whom he has been dating since his sophomore year. Prior to dating Jessie, Sam had several good friends he had hung out with since elementary school. After Jessie came along, it was all about her; no time for friends. Sam and Jessie are very serious and are, in fact, sexually active. Sam loves Jessie very much and believes with all his heart he will marry her after he graduates from college. He has never confided in anyone about the status of his relationship with Jessie. He would never think of

disrespecting Jessie by bragging to his football buddies about his rela-
tionship. Jessie is a very beautiful girl, and while Sam is generally very
laid back, he gets jealous when Jessie speaks to other guys.

During his high school years Sam has slowly lost interest in religion.
He has attended church since he was three days old, and his parents
tell him repeatedly, "You should never miss a Sunday in church." He
knows all the Bible stories from Sunday school: Adam and Eve, Jonah,
Noah, Esther, Peter and Paul. He knows all the books of the Bible and
was captain of his Bible Bowl team in junior high. But Sam has come
to believe the church is full of hypocrites. He knows most of the church
people personally and observes the way some of them behave out-
side of the church building—in an un-Christian manner. He has had a
few spiritual highs during his high school years. He attended a large
conference two summers in a row, the first summer rededicating his
life and the second summer committing his life to Christian service.
After the conference was over, he forgot why he ever made those
decisions. He once told Jessie, "Those things just get kids all stirred up
until they would say or do anything."

However many times he has been spiritually stirred, he has never
felt any guilt about his physical relationship with Jessie. "If two peo-
ple are in love and know they are going to get married, it can't be
wrong to 'make love.'" He believes the rules in the Bible were made
for Bible times, not for the times we live in now.

Between sports, Jessie, and his part-time job driving the delivery
truck for the local florist, he doesn't have much time for church activi-
ties. Sam was very close to his youth minister who left when he was
a sophomore. He had a great deal of respect for Chris and the two
were best friends. The new youth minister is, according to Sam, "sub-
standard." Sam has the "I'm outta here" mentality with church these
days. He attends as infrequently as possible. When he goes to col-
lege, he has no intentions of attending church. He only does so now
to appease his parents.

His parents, while adamant about church attendance, only view
church as a "good thing." They feel the Bible and its teachings simply
"help develop children of good morals." While both are professing
Christians, neither have a personal relationship with Jesus Christ. They
have no expectations for either of their children spiritually and are
happy with "whatever they learn in church."

→

Each age group considered thus far in the book has unique
attitudes and attributes, and high school is no exception. These
students are a totally different breed. As the time creeps closer
and closer for them to leave the nest, these "late teens" are devel-

oping a strong desire for independence. (This desire seems exaggerated when they get their driver's license.) In general they are becoming more satisfied with who and where they are in life. Some will even give off an attitude of defiance or challenge, "This is who I am. Take it or leave it!" But others are struggling to move out of the "poor self-image" stage of middle school. (Unfortunately many people never make it out of this stage either.)

> **A Faith Development Plan can help people become spiritual adults as they become physical adults.**

High school students are also becoming more independent in their thinking. You may hear frustrated parents sigh, "I don't know where she came up with that idea! She didn't get it from us." They are beginning to consider everything they have learned since preschool and are forming their own opinions. While this does not mean they can't be molded, it does mean we must be more intentional in our efforts to shape them into godly young adults.

As these students steadily move from lowly freshmen to all-important seniors, you may see them become frustrated or at times nervous. Students are bombarded with two pivotal questions, "So, have you decided on a college?" or "So, have you decided what you're going to do after you graduate?" These are very weighty decisions, and as time ticks by, students are keenly aware of the potential effects of their choices. Students will often not admit it, but they need guidance in this area. Ideally such guidance comes from their parents, but some parents have a different theory on this issue. "It's his life. He can go wherever he wants. I can't tell him what to do." Guiding a child in his or her postgraduate plans is not the same as forcing. Remember, within a few short years, these students will go from rules, regulations, and expectations to freedom and choices galore. If they have not reached it already, our arrows are moving closer to the target of spiritual maturity and discipleship. We have four more years to plant that tip securely into the target.

The countdown is on with this group. Of all the age levels, high school is the most crucial. The word "intentional" cannot be stressed enough in relation to programming and ministry plans. We must be highly intentional in our curriculum selections for this age and constantly view our students as future adults.

As you review this chapter, you might note that some of the sections are shorter. These topics have been presented and constantly reinforced for the last several years. Remembering the repetition key introduced in chapter three, we realize that at some point in our Faith Development Plan our students need to move from the point of learning a concept to expectancy. For example, we have mentioned tithing in most developmental areas throughout the plan. During the high school years we will still reinforce the concept of tithing, but not as strongly. This concept has moved into an area of expectancy. It is still on the Faith Development Plan for two reasons. 1) Tithing still needs to be reinforced so the students remember why it is important. 2) Students will come into our programs who don't have any knowledge of tithing or it's importance. They need to know this information, too.

Some areas mentioned in this chapter will be proposed as possible electives. If you are interested in learning more on how to provide electives to your students, see question nine in chapter twelve. This will give details on how to organize and implement electives with your students.

One of the biggest struggles you will encounter with this age is busyness. Some have jobs. Many are involved in sports, bands, choirs, and other outside activities all of which come after one or two hours of homework a night. (They have to sleep and eat in there sometime, too.) Some are involved in parachurch organizations such as Young Life, Fellowship of Christian Athletes, or Youth for Christ. On top of this, most have an insatiable desire for social activities and, in some cases, that includes a romantic relationship. At times it seems we are fighting a losing battle with our programming. Most of your students are overscheduled. You might as well give up trying to fight it. Do not try to counter this by providing excessive programming on the youth ministry end in an attempt to make them "choose which is more important." Doing so can produce frustrated teenagers who feel they simply can't keep up. Try to strike a balance for your students. You must provide several opportunities for them to grow spiritually. It is a crucial age. Just remember where your students stand in many areas of their lives and program accordingly.

Do not try to counter busyness and overscheduling by providing excessive programming on the youth ministry end.

HEAVEN (Bible Knowledge and Feeling)

We know our mission. We want to shoot our student arrows at the targeted goal. That goal is spiritual maturity and discipleship, but we can't hit that mark unless the students have taken the initial step of accepting Christ as their personal Lord and Savior. It is common for a student to reach high school age without having made a decision for Christ. Statistically we realize they are becoming harder to reach on this issue. Remember, they are forming opinions that could stay with them for several years. If they come to view Christianity as a farce or a joke, this is where they will stay for some time.

Continue offering a four-week series on salvation each year. Changing the curriculum slightly will help reinforce the idea while preventing boredom in your students. You may offer one salvation series every other year and another series the opposite years. Remembering our target for these students, allow your mature seniors to teach the salvation lessons to the rest of the group.

High school students now can begin to realize the importance of submission in salvation. *They* are no longer in control. They submit their lives, their problems, their hurts, their fears, their joys, their decisions to God. This concept can especially appeal to frustrated students as they are considering their future. To let an almighty God be in control sounds better to them than risking it all on the bright ideas of a know-nothing teen. Submission can be a separate four-week study for this group.

> High school students now can begin to realize the importance of submitting their lives, their problems, their hurts, their fears, their joys, their decisions to God.

Another four-week series should be taught on "How to Lead Someone to Christ." If these students are to achieve the goal of discipleship and spiritual maturity, they must be taught *how* to do this. The plan of salvation should be memorized as well as the Scriptures behind each point in the plan. Allow students to role-play how they would interact with someone who wanted to accept Christ. This class may be offered as an elective.

TITHING (Bible Knowledge and Experience)

Many of our high school students now have part-time jobs. Some are saving to buy cars. Others are actually paying for their own car or insurance. Most are saving for college. Money is holding more and more significance to them whether they like it or not.

When these teens graduate from our ministry, ideally they will want to be givers in every sense of the word. As with the middle school plan, this includes their time, talents, and money. We want students to see a need and do their best to meet it. Consider offering three separate electives in these areas each year. The elective on giving of your time can speak of the importance of service. The elective on talents can also branch into determining spiritual gifts. The elective on money can deal with tithing and money managing. Offer these same three electives in the fall and spring to provide students with an opportunity to attend more than one class.

PRAYER (Bible Knowledge, Feeling, and Experience)

Your students who have a relationship with God should desire to communicate with Him. In addition to presenting a four-week study on prayer and its importance, provide your students with special times of prayer. Group Publishing has a resource *Prayer Path: A Christ Centered Labyrinth Experience*, which actually comes in a can and has the plan and extras to organize a prayer path for your students to take. Various stations encourage the students to pray for different areas of their lives and those around the world. You could create something like this on your own.

Incorporate prayer in everything you do with your students. If you are on a mission trip and find yourself in a hard situation, ask the students to stop and pray. You never want them to think that prayer is confined to certain times of the day such as meals, bedtime, and devotional time. One of our ministries in the church was struggling due to members with divisive attitudes. These people were beginning to cause division and strife. Without going into detail about the problems, I asked my high school small group to pray with me.

If you are on a mission trip and find yourself in a hard situation, ask the students to stop and pray.

We literally paced the aisles of the sanctuary praying at each pew. At times one student would sit in a pew and pray for the person who would sit there the following Sunday. Several took the lead and went to the musical-instrument area, sitting on the piano bench, the keyboard bench, the drum bench, and praise team chairs, praying for everyone involved. Almost every one of the teens, at some point, went to the pulpit and prayed for the minister. It was an extremely moving experience, so peaceful and quiet. Take time to incorporate prayer in all you do with your high school youth.

EVANGELISM AND SERVICE (Bible Knowledge and Experience)

As mentioned in the evangelism area of the middle school chapter, evangelism is hard for most teenage students. As our high school students become more comfortable with themselves and who they are, we need to continue to encourage our students to make evangelism a natural way of life for them.

We must conquer the idea that "not everyone is cut out to share their faith. I think telling others about God is great for some people, but I'm just not comfortable with that." Unfortunately, this attitude is also shared by many adults. The Great Commission does not list any exemptions. It does not say, "Go and make disciples of every nation, but if you are not comfortable with that, don't worry about it." It is a command for all of us, just as any other command in the Bible should be regarded to include everyone unless specified otherwise.

The amazing thing about evangelism is, once we take the first step to become bold with our faith, sharing it becomes easier and easier. It is like stepping out on the stage in front of a large audience and singing a solo for the first time. It is frightening, but each time a person steps out on that stage and sings, it gets easier and easier. Take the time to encourage your students to step out on that stage and "sing out" their faith. When they finally take that first step, make sure you praise them for their boldness and allow them to share their testimony with the rest of the students, if they feel comfortable doing so.

The proposed Faith Development Plan for this age group calls for a four-week lesson series on evangelism each year. It also calls for two or three different servant evangelism projects throughout the year and a week-long mission trip, out of the country, every other year.

BOOKS OF THE BIBLE (Bible Knowledge)

If we fail to continue reinforcing the books of the Bible we've ingrained in our students, they will forget them. Every fifth Sunday we can review, playing some type of review game like Bible Jeopardy with our students. At the end of each Bible lesson ask students to write a question for the review game during the next fifth Sunday review game. If the lessons have been about forgiveness, they may write, "What Old Testament figure did we study during the lesson on forgiveness? Why would he have a hard time forgiving?" The first answer would be "Joseph" and the second, "because of the terrible things his brothers did to him." Have the students put their questions in a fish bowl or box in preparation for the next fifth Sunday review time.

To add to the fun of the review game you may throw in a question for "Final Jeopardy," like "Name all the books of the New Testament." "Name all the books of the Old Testament." "Name the divisions of the Old Testament." "Who wrote the book of _____?" Some students who love challenges will be led to learn the books of the Bible, if they have not already done so, just to get that "Final Jeopardy" answer!

Your goal with the books of the Bible should be for all your students to know them in order, know the divisions, and know who wrote each book.

Science and High School Students (Bible Knowledge and Science)

Creation vs. evolution issues are often big struggles for our students. If they attend public school, they are taught so-called "facts" about the world, such as how many million years old the earth "really" is. We must present the truth of creation and the biblical support behind it. We must also show our students the problems with the evolution model and several simple facts to refute evolutionary claims. Your goal should be for the students in your ministry to understand why they believe in creation and why they don't believe in evolution. Your students should learn the importance of evolution as a "theory." When their teachers speak of the world millions of years ago, your students should be able to say in their minds, "This is *their theory*. I do not believe in evolution."

Answers in Genesis has developed curriculums for this very purpose. Ken Ham has developed a curriculum called the "Creation Mini-Series." This set contains six DVDs and covers very important issues for your students. 1) Genesis: The Key to Reclaiming the Culture; 2) Where Did God Come From? Defending Creation in a Scientific Age; 3) The Six Days of Creation: A Young Earth Is Not the Issue; 4) The Bible Explains Dinosaurs: The Real History of Dinosaurs; 5) Only One Race: The Scientific and Biblical Case against Racism; 6) Why Won't They Listen? The Power of Creation Evangelism.[1] This, or any other resource from Answers in Genesis, would be an excellent series to present to your students who must know where they stand in respect to evolutionary theory.

In addition, continue searching for curriculum which stresses the perfect design of God in the areas of nature, the human body, and animals. Visit the Christian Reality web site at **http://www.christianreality.com/category/vsmoody.htm** and consider purchasing some of their videos on this topic. This web site has several excellent resources for your students to see God as the Almighty Designer of the world.

MEMORY VERSES (Bible Knowledge)

Often memory work is limited to the younger grades in a church youth ministry. High school youth need to continue reviewing the passages they have learned to this point and continue learning new verses. Choose verses that relate to the concepts taught in the Faith Development Plan. Include the memorization of these verses in your fifth Sunday review game.

HISTORY AND COMPARATIVE RELIGIONS AND HIGH SCHOOL STUDENTS (Bible Knowledge and History)

The wide variety of religious beliefs like Mormonism, Jehovah's Witnesses, New Age beliefs, Satanism, Islam, and Kabbalah can be confusing to high school students as well as adults. However, your high school students are at an age where they can learn about the different beliefs of today's most common cults. Set aside a minimum of four weeks in your Faith Development Plan to study different cults and their beliefs. Explain the differences between what they believe and what we believe, and how Christianity offers the best answers. The Christian Reality web site has several wonderful resources to teach your students about the various cults. Group Publishing has a curriculum series entitled *Searching for the Truth*.[2] This series includes Hinduism, Buddhism, New Age, Judaism, and Islam. It also has a student booklet for your teens to work on in class, in a small group, or on their own.

Consider bringing in a cult member to speak to your students during one class session. If you are focusing on Jehovah's Witnesses one week, ask your sponsors if they know of any Jehovah's Witnesses who would be willing to speak to the class. Assure the speaker the students will be respectful and will not try to convert him or her during his or her time in the class. Allow the students to ask the speaker respectful questions and, after the speaker leaves, question the students on what they heard. At the end of class take time to dive into the Bible and see what it has to say about the false belief presented.

As the time creeps closer for these students to leave home, it becomes crucial to ensure they will know how to choose a new church home. Continue teaching your students the history and beliefs of other denominations and what makes their beliefs different from yours. (Don't even assume your students know what the word "denomination" means.) Consider taking your students to different churches after you have discussed their beliefs. For example, after studying about the Catholic church, offer to take your students to a mass during the week. Seeing the church firsthand will help them better retain the information you have presented.

While teaching students denominational beliefs and history, present them with biblical answers on each portion of your worship service. For example, "We take communion each week because . . ." "We sing each week because . . ." "We baptize by immersion because . . ."

As technology increases, we are able to learn more and more about the past. Archaeologists continue to uncover buried cities, ruins, and artifacts which affirm the words written in the Old and New Testaments. The strength of the history leg of your student's faith table lies in the presentation of this information.

Most of us "normal people" simply do not know the latest findings in biblical archaeology. As with the science leg we do not have to be "scholars" to present this information. You are not less of a youth minister to say, "I'm learning about the history and science legs as I go." The first two or three years you teach this information you will learn as you go.

The Biblical Archaeology Society[3] has a bimonthly magazine detailing many of the latest finds supporting the Bible's teachings. Sharing this information with your students can help solidify their faith. In addition, their web site has several resources to consider sharing with your students. The Discovery Channel frequently airs special programming on biblical history. Their web site, **www.discovery.com**, offers many of these programs available on DVD and videotape. As with any resource you consider using in your youth ministry, always carefully review every piece before presenting it to your students. (While reviewing a missions video to present at VBS, I ran to the kitchen to grab a drink. When I later presented the video—on the 20×20 big screen in front of our two and three-year-old children—I saw what I missed during my preview: clips of severely malnourished, naked African children receiving shots in their bottoms!) Never feel you have to present an entire resource in DVD or videotape form. Your students may benefit from small portions as a part of the study.

Continue asking yourself, "How can I strengthen my student's history leg?" "What do I want them to know about the history of the church, the history of the Bible, the history of our denomination and others before they graduate?" Remember to consider the best interests of your students. While teaching this information may make you feel uncomfortable at first, keep in mind your target for the students and your passion to get them there.

> "What do I want them to know about the history of the church, the history of the Bible, the history of our denomination and others before they graduate?"

GOD'S PLAN FOR THE FAMILY (Bible Knowledge and Family)

Speaking to youth about love, sex, and dating can be uncomfortable for them and for us, but do not forget the reasons you teach these things. These teenagers are questioning many things they have been taught over the past sixteen years. How those questions are answered can affect their view on the family. Teens are looking for answers to questions like:

1) Is premarital intercourse really wrong? Or was that just for the Bible times?
2) What does the Bible say about same-sex marriage?
3) How does God feel about homosexuality?
4) What does the Bible say about infidelity?

The media plays such an astronomically large role in how our students view subjects such as homosexuality and premarital sex. Movies, television, music, and video games typically do not support the biblical standards of abstinence, heterosexuality, and marital fidelity. The more our students view images on television and in the movies, such as teens having several sexual encounters before marriage, the more they will be tempted to accept these practices as the norm. One Wednesday night before their elective started, three girls were talking to each other, "I truly believe we are the only three virgins in our high school." Their exasperation over their virginity is yet another sign that purity is no longer the norm and therefore that much more difficult for our students to maintain.

Realizing that your high school students could realistically be husbands and wives or mothers and fathers soon after they graduate, the question must be asked: "What do you want your students to know about the family? What do you want them to take with them into a marriage? How can you make sure these students have godly family principles instilled in their lives before they graduate?" Obviously, this is no easy task.

Several elective lesson series could be helpful in this area. Each of these topics has an impact on the family:

1) A four-week lesson series on contemporary issues such as abortion, homosexuality, premarital sex, and pornography.
2) A four-week series just for girls. How to be a woman of integrity.
3) A four-week guys-only series. How to be a man of integrity.
4) A four-week series on God's design for marriage.

Considering some of the student scenarios presented at the beginning of each chapter throughout this book we are reminded of the sad state of many church families. Regardless of how dysfunctional a student's home may be, they still have a chance to lead a healthy family life in the future if they are taught biblical principles.

DAILY DEVOTIONS AND BIBLE READING (Bible Knowledge, Feeling, and Experience)

Persuading "too busy" teens to commit to daily devotional time is very difficult. However, avoid lowering your expectations for your students in this area simply because of the motto "you're only young once." When they graduate, their lives will not slow down. Most will attend college and spend a good deal of time attending classes, studying, and socializing. Making time for a devotional life now increases the chance of a devotional life later. Here are some suggestions to help your high school students:

1) Continually provide quality, up-to-date, age-appropriate devotional resources. Make them available for your students for a small donation.
2) Encourage your students in the area of daily devotion

time. Be bold and ask them, "How is your devotional life?" Some students just need to be held accountable.

3) Continually train your parents to encourage their children to practice daily devotions at home. As Christian educators with a 1% time constraint, we can only do so much.

4) Use the power of testimony with your students by bringing in adults who testify how God revealed himself through daily devotions. Begin a t-tag game (as mentioned in chapter two) which allows students to encourage and minister to each other. Give everyone a specific devotional area for the week and ask the "tagged" person to tell how that helped them.

Ethics (Bible Knowledge)

Absolute vs. Relative Truth

While taking a class on ethics at our local college I had a quick lesson on the thoughts and minds of a typical "late teen." This particular class had thirty students—with 98% of the students in their late teens and 2% of . . . the rest of us. During one class session the professor, an ordained Quaker minister, broke the students up into groups of four. He mentioned a topic and we discussed it. The first topic was simply, "Bill and Monica." Our group of older men and women discussed our thoughts. It came time for the groups to share their thoughts with the class and a group of four young men began, "We feel that any guy in Bill Clinton's position would have done the same thing. And any guy who says any different is lying." I was a little shocked and looked at the professor to set these guys straight. He said nothing. The groups that followed echoed the feelings of the first group—"Anyone in Bill Clinton's position would have done the same thing." The professor never guided the students to think about what they were saying or to look at it from a different perspective (perhaps, "What about Hillary?").

This is the world of relative truth, the world in which your students live. If they are attending a secular university, they will be assaulted with moral relativism. Relative truth states, "What is okay for you is okay for you," no matter how twisted or immoral it may be. So, their best friend is a homosexual? Not to worry, homosexuality is what is right for them, so it is okay. Your married next-door neighbors are involved in wife swapping? Big deal! If they are consenting adults, it is fine.

Clear and thorough presentations of godly ethics are crucial to your Faith Development Plan. They need to know homosexuality is not okay. Wife swapping is not okay. Abortion is not okay. Infidelity and premarital intercourse are not okay. Why? Because as Christians we believe in absolute truth and the lifestyle prescribed to us in the Scriptures.

In the World, Not of It

Another ethical principle your high school students need to learn is how to be "In the World, Not of It." Growing up in Bowling Green I was definitely "in the world." Going to Bible college was a wonderful change. Taking a break from the worldly ways of a college town to bask in the "safeness" of the hill called Cincinnati Bible College was soothing. After two years at the Bible college I went home to work for the summer. I remember having a sick feeling in my stomach for the first two weeks. None of the BGSU summer school students were wearing WWJD T-shirts. They were not praying before class. The student body was not involved in discipleship groups, and they didn't send each other encouragement notes with warm fuzzies through the campus mail. These students were cussing, drinking, partying, and, in my eyes, disgusting. I didn't even want to be near them.

Your town may look a lot like Mayberry—no crime, no drunkeness, no homosexuality, and no partner swapping. You may feel very safe, but Jesus did not call us into a life of "safeness." In fact, we do not find one verse in the Bible where we are commanded, "Go out there and be safe." On the contrary, Jesus asks that we drop everything, take up our cross, and follow Him. He calls us to be just like Him, "in the world, not of it." Jesus didn't hang out with the Pharisees and the Sadducees or in the "safeness" of the Temple. He hung out with women, he touched lepers, he ate lunch with tax collectors and even called one of them to be his disciple. He went to parties and, on one occasion, spoke to the demon possessed. There was nothing "safe" about his ministry.

Only strong, spiritually mature Christians can successfully be "in the world, not of it." It takes a person who can go to a rough public high school or a state university known for its crazy parties and maintain her Christianity. It takes a person who can stand up for what he believes and still be respected by those around him.

Lindsay, was one of our strongest students in her late high school years. We were so sad to see her leave. When she arrived at college, she met her new roommate. Shortly into the school year, her roommate sat Lindsay down and told her she had something very important to tell her. After a long preface as to *why* she was revealing this information, her roommate told Lindsay that she was a homosexual. Lindsay went into a tailspin. This was not what she had anticipated. She listened to the advice of many different people from church. Unfortunately, the majority told her this, "You have to get out of that room. No matter what you do, get another roommate." She experienced a lot of anxiety and frustration, and questioned the right course of action.

One night while I was working on this book, she sent me an instant message and we discussed her situation at length. I told her, "Lindsay, this is what your parents and the church have been working toward for the past eighteen years. We have worked our hardest to make you spiritually mature so you would be ready to be set free into the world. This *is* the world. Unfortunately, it doesn't look like the high school youth group or your Christian friends. The world is full of sinners, and this is where you have been set free. You have to stay strong and remember the things you have been taught. You have to draw on that and figure out the right thing to do."

Fortunately, she decided to stay with her roommate. She is learning day by day how to handle the various topics which arise in the room and she has chosen to narrow down the counsel she seeks to help her with her struggles. She is a survivor. She is living "in the world" but not succumbing to it. She is right where God wants her; attending church regularly, reading her Bible daily, communicating with God in prayer, leading a small group of sixth grade girls, and talking to her roommate about her faith in God.

The proposed high school Faith Development Plan calls for three four-week studies on ethics each year. One of these sessions will be relative vs. absolute truth. One of the many resources available on this topic is Focus on the Family's video and book, *My Truth, Your Truth, Whose Truth?* The other series can be "in the world, not of it." It might be necessary to search thoroughly and carefully for suitable curriculum available on this topic. This is an area you may have to develop yourself. The last series will be on the media. (See the middle school plan for details on ethics and the media.)

Self-Image (Bible Knowledge, Feeling, and Science)

Many of your late teen students are still struggling with the idea of a poor self-image. If a boy in your youth group feels poorly about himself, he may find a group of friends that make him feel good, even if this group is making poor choices. If a girl in your youth group feels ugly or fat, she may enter into a serious relationship with a boy who makes her feel beautiful even if that means giving in to his sexual desires. Whether your students admit it or not, self-image plays into many of the decisions they make.

One of the areas to watch for in the area of low self-esteem is suicidal tendency. The late teen years can be extremely difficult, and some teens choose not to deal with them at all. Many students will talk about suicide simply to get attention. Never take these threats lightly. If a student ever even suggests he or she is thinking of suicide, immediately inform his or her parents and encourage them to get help for their child. To learn the warning signs of suicide and how to react to a student who mentions suicide, go to the suicidology web site at **www.suicidology.org**.

Continue offering a four-week lesson on self-image and add a four-week elective on "Talking to a Friend Who Is Suicidal." Remember to encourage and build up your students as much as possible. Note their strengths and accomplishments as much as possible, even if it seems small. Your praise may mean more to them than anything else.

Your late teen students' self-images are apparent in how they talk, walk, and dress. The dress issue seems to be a recurring obstacle with Christian young women. Short skirts, short shorts, low-cut shirts, and tight, revealing sweaters have all been around for a while. Unfortunately, if your church is like ours, the mothers are as guilty as the girls. We struggle to teach our girls the "proper" way to dress when their mothers' outfits are inappropriate, too. Our female students may not have a problem with this type of dress. "Don't be a prude. This isn't the 1940s. This is the way girls dress." What they do not realize is the effect their dress can have on visually stimulated men and boys. Males are more likely to struggle with lustful thoughts when they see women wearing short skirts and revealing "excess" skin. We are trying to teach our boys to be men of integrity. To be quite honest, it can be a distraction for them during a worship service or youth group lesson. Consider offering a workshop, just for girls, teach them they can look their best and maintain personal purity at the same time. This lesson could include teaching from Romans 14 about the girls' responsibility to their Christian brothers not to cause them to stumble.

SMALL GROUPS (Bible Knowledge and Experience)

Our goal should be for every student in our high school ministry to be involved in a small group of some kind. Small groups offer a chance for our students to share in a close-knit setting, receive encouragement from their peers, and accept accountability from one adult. Groups should be gender specific and not exceed twelve students. Consider offering several different small groups on various nights of the week to accommodate your students' busy schedules.

Make students' parents aware of your goal in this area. Offer a parent meeting each year to discuss your goals for the year, emphasizing the importance small groups play in faith development. Parents may initially need to push their children to attend small groups, but eventually most students will develop bonds with their group and their leader, and they will grow spiritually.

OCCUPATIONS AND FUTURES (Bible Knowledge)

High school students are busy planning for the future. There are so many options available for them. Does God want me to take a specific route? How should I pray? What should I choose? They could go to a secular college out of state, a secular college in state, a junior college in town, a Christian college in state, sit out a year, enlist in the military, get married, audition for Big Brother or Survivor, get a job that does not require a college education, live in their parents' basement and watch soap operas all day, or enter a convent. (Don't laugh, it happens!) These are just a few of the many options your students have for their future, and it can be very frustrating for them to choose.

Many school districts allow students up to five days for visits to prospective college campuses. It is important for them to experience a range of campuses from Christian colleges to state universities. Encourage your students and their parents to consider a Christian college visit. Offer to take the student on a visit if the parents are unable to do so. Some youth ministers have chosen to use spring break as a time to pack up the church van and head out to different Christian colleges.

The proposed high school Faith Development Plan calls for a minimum four-week lesson series on occupations and college choices. Be creative and ask recruiters from several different colleges to come in and talk to your students. Ask previous youth group members to come "home" and talk to the students about their college decisions. Allow the high school students to ask these college students questions about their choices. Why did you choose a Bible college? Are you glad you chose to go to a state university? What is the hardest thing about going to college out of state? Do you feel God called you to sit out one year before you went to college? Do you regret the decision you made to go into the military? Is it hard to be a Christian on a state university campus? These questions and the answers will help your students make the best choice for their future.

LEADERSHIP (Bible Knowledge)

Many of your students are natural leaders. You know who they are. If you gave your entire youth group these instructions, "I am leaving for twenty minutes. I need you to clean the youth room. The list of items needing cleaned is on the board. Have fun." Who would be the first to say, "All right! Jake, you sweep the floors, Lydia, you wipe off the chairs . . .?" Who would take the initiative?

Even if it is hard to imagine now, some of the students in our ministries will be in leadership positions after they leave our program. Some will be supervisors. Some will be bosses, CEOs, husbands and fathers, military officers, business owners, and yes, even youth ministers. Our desire is be for them to be godly leaders, full of integrity.

The Bible gives us several wonderful examples of leadership, including Moses, Joshua, Nehemiah, Jesus, and Paul. Offer a leadership elective once each year for your high school students. Study the characteristics of these leaders and what it means to be a godly leader.

HIGH SCHOOL LEARNING GOALS

By the time a high school student leaves his or her classroom at the Community Christian Church he or she will have:

✔ Reinforced and strengthened all concepts begun in the middle school department.
✔ Learned the importance of submission in their Christian walk.

- Been encouraged to make a decision for Christ if (s)he has not already done so.
- Learned how to lead a person to Christ.
- Learned the importance of tithing money, time, and talents.
- Had the opportunity to participate in a prayer walk.
- Learned further of the Great Commission and how it applies to him/her.
- Learned the facts about creation and scriptural proof to support it.
- Learned the theory of evolution and how to refute it.
- Learned of different cults, their beliefs and how they differ from Christianity.
- Learned of archaeological evidence which supports the Bible's authenticity.
- Learned what the Bible says about contemporary issues such as abortion, homosexuality, premarital sex, and pornography.
- Studied God's specific design for marriage.
- (Girls) Learned how to become a woman of integrity.
- (Boys) Learned how to become a man of integrity.
- Learned the importance of and the difference between relative and absolute truth.
- Learned the importance of being "in the world, not of it."
- Studied self-image from God's eyes.
- Studied the danger signs of suicide and how to deal with a suicidal friend.
- Learned the importance of being a godly leader.
- Had the opportunity to participate in small groups.
- Had the opportunity to participate in several servant evangelism projects.
- Had the opportunity to attend summer church camp.
- Had the opportunity to participate in Heaven Night and Giving Thanks Talent Night.
- Had the opportunity to participate in at least two different mission trips out of the country.

Things a Parent Can Do to Reinforce What Is Taught in the High School Department (Family)

- Continue bringing your child to church each Sunday. Make church attendance as regular as school attendance.
- Set aside a time and place each day to begin helping your children with daily devotions and prayer time. This is a routine you want them to continue after they leave your home.
- Continually bathe your children in prayer. Pray for their future spouses. Pray that God will help them to make wise choices at school. Pray for their salvation and their spiritual growth.
- Encourage your child to join your family in the singing portion of your worship service even if your church does not provide this. Do whatever you can to make sure you sit together as a family. Your child needs to see the effect praising God and worshiping has on you.
- Continue encouraging your child to bring his or her Bible to church each week and back home for his/her daily devotional time. Show him/her the importance of this by bringing your Bible to church each week.
- Continue instilling an appreciation for God's creation, including nature, animals, and the human body.
- If your child has not made a decision to accept Jesus Christ as his/her personal Lord and Savior, take the time to speak to him/her about making that decision.
- In addition to your child's weekly tithe, encourage him/her to tithe his/her time and talents.
- Continue to encourage your children to participate in church-sponsored mission trips and servant evangelism projects.
- Encourage your child to memorize specific Bible verses.
- Strongly encourage your child to choose friends with similar interests. Intensely watch your child's friends and make sure you are comfortable with the influence they have on your child.
- Insist that your children make godly choices in their media intake. Do not allow music or movies with profanity or sex as a theme. Monitor your children's video games and do not allow them to play anything that is not rated on their age level. In addition, monitor their television intake. Do not

allow your children to sway your decisions in this area with the statement, "But everyone is watching it!" Children using this "line" are playing on your emotions. The truth is, not everyone is watching or doing what your children say they are doing.

✦ Observe how your child behaves around his/her friends, at home, at school if possible, and at church. Encourage your child to be consistent in her behavior and actions.

✦ Continue stressing the importance of God's design for the family. Make it a point to model those roles in your home as God intended.

✦ Praise your child as much as possible. Consciously avoid criticizing your child. Tell your child, "You are special." "I love you." "I don't know what I would do without you." "You are beautiful." "You can do it." "I think you did a great job." "Just do your best." "God has big plans for your life." Remember, your child's self-image is still in the developing stages at this point. Your child *needs* encouragement.

✦ Strongly encourage your child to be involved in a church-sponsored small group.

✦ Whenever possible, take your child to a Christian concert and make a conscious effort to play positive, uplifting music in your home.

✦ *Never* talk adversely about the church, its leadership or teachers in front of your child. Derogatory remarks about the church greatly restrict the positive impact it can have on your child and ultimately his faith development. If *you* are upset with something that is or has been taking place at your church, make sure your child is out of earshot before discussing your concerns. Doing so could be detrimental to his faith development. Be careful what you say at home.

NOTES

1. Ken Ham, *Creation Mini-Series* (Answers in Genesis, 2002).
2. *Searching for the Truth* (Loveland, CO: Group Publishing, 2002).
3. www.bib-arch.org.

Chapter Eleven

DRAWING THE BOW: DEVELOPING AND PRESENTING THE PLAN

Where do you want your students to be by the time they graduate, and how are you going to get them there?

STEP ONE

Answer This Question: Do You Believe in the Importance of Organizing a Faith Development Plan?

This may sound like a silly question. Why would you take the time to put together a Faith Development Plan if you didn't believe in its importance? The truth is, Christian educators make that kind of mistake all too often. They read a book on a new ministry methodology, become half-heartedly inspired and vow to make changes in their ministry because they know what they have been doing isn't working. Let me ask a few questions:

> Do you want your students to become true, passionate disciples of Christ?

1) Do you want your students to become true, passionate disciples of Christ, true in the sense they will someday be mature enough to reproduce themselves spiritually?
2) Do you agree with Mike Yaconelli's statement, "If we want to see young people have a faith that lasts, then we have to completely change the way we do youth ministry in America?"
3) Do you believe setting goals is important?
4) Do you believe the best way to reach a goal is to have an intentional plan on how to reach that goal?

5) Do you have the energy, passion, and desire to develop a plan of action for faith development in your students?

If you answered "yes" to all these questions, you are ready to go. If you answered "no" or wavered with some of these questions, I have three suggestions: 1) Go back and read the first two chapters in this book again. 2) Take three hours from your schedule to read George Barna's *Transforming Children into Spiritual Champions.* 3) Meet with another Christian educator who has read this book and discuss your concerns with developing a Faith Development Plan. If you are still not sold on the process, don't do it.

Step Two

Answer This Question: Is Your Church Leadership behind You in This Endeavor?

Having the confidence that your church leadership is behind you is crucial for any change you are making, or will potentially make, in your ministry. When I speak of leadership, I am referring to your ministry staff, elders, board or whoever approves leadership decisions for your church. The reason behind this question is fourfold:

1) The leadership of your church deserves to know you are serious about developing and raising up spiritually mature disciples of Jesus Christ in your ministry. Make it clear to them that this is the overriding goal of your ministry.

2) The leadership must know you have an intentional plan of action on how to aim your students toward the goal of spiritual maturity.

3) The leadership needs to know how you are spending a majority of your work week time. (The organization and implementation of a Faith Development Plan will not only take your passion for the goal, but also your time and energy.)

4) The leadership should be familiar enough with the basics of a Faith Development Plan to be able to field any questions from congregational members, specifically parents and sponsors.

The key member of leadership who must remain 100% behind your work in developing a Faith Development Plan is your senior minister. You and your senior minister must be on the same page in the belief that faith development, beginning and ending with evangelism, is of utmost importance for your church, not only for the youth but for adults as well. Experience has taught me that the senior minister's support, or lack of it, can determine the success of a program.

In addition, if you are in a multistaff situation where you share Christian education responsibilities with another staff person, you must ensure this person is ready to partner with you to move ahead with a Faith Development Plan.

Step Three

Answer This Question: Are Your Sponsors behind You?

A simple way to help your youth teachers or sponsors understand the basics of a Faith Development Plan is to have them read the first few chapters of this book. Ask them to sacrifice an hour or two of their time to become aware of the ministry strategy you're recommending. Allowing them to read these chapters will encourage your teachers and sponsors with the challenges in youth ministry today and your specific proposal for how to change it.

Some of your teachers and sponsors are not readers or will simply tell you they do not have the time to read anything. (Don't you love people like this?) For these people you may want to schedule a meeting and present them with the information on a downloadable PowerPoint presentation available at **www.collegepress.com**. This is a visually stimulating way to present the information.

At this point in the process it is not necessary for you to present an entire, completed Faith Development Plan to your teachers and sponsors. What you are conveying to your sponsors is the *need* for a plan. Remember, you are not going to organize and implement this Faith Development Plan on your own. It is important to obtain the input of your sponsors throughout the planning stages. I am a collaborative planner. I can plan a mediocre event or come up with a semi-creative plan on my own, but when I am teamed up with my volunteers, the results are often much more dynamic and fun.

If your sponsors are not behind you, it may be necessary to take additional time to determine the reason for their apprehensiveness about setting these goals for the ministry. Be patient; sometimes we must have patience as we wait for the Holy Spirit to do His work.

Step Four

Pray

Throughout the entire organizational process with your Faith Development Plan seek God's guidance. Daily bathe your ministry, your sponsors and teachers, your students and their parents, and your potential plan in prayer. Ask your leadership and sponsors to do the same. Pray for patience for everyone involved and pray that you do not lose the passion and conviction to implement such a plan in your ministry.

I cannot say enough about the importance of prayer throughout the process of organizing and implementing your Faith Development Plan. Throughout the entire process you should crave God's guidance. Remember, you are just as responsible for "rightly dividing the Word of Truth" (2 Tim 2:15) as a senior minister would be in delivering a message from the pulpit. A Faith Development Plan is not simply about filling in Bible study topics on a chart. It is intentionally setting out to aim your students at the target of discipleship. Pray that the Holy Spirit would guide you every step of the way.

Step Five

Evaluate Your Students

As I mentioned in the beginning of this book, evaluation is at times painful but necessary. The actual process of organizing a Faith Development Plan begins and ends with evaluation. The initial evaluation can be done in one or a combination of the following ways.

ADMINISTER A BASIC BIBLE KNOWLEDGE TEST TO YOUR STUDENTS

Administering a basic Bible knowledge test allows you to see which areas of the Faith Development Plan may need more emphasis than others. It allows you to know the students' needs, deficiencies, or strengths in different areas. This test can be given to students of any age who are able to read. Begin with your high school students. Take a two-week time slot to ensure you are including as many students as possible. Bribe them with candy bars or food for taking the test if you have to! Assure the students that all tests will be anonymous, so no one is to put their name on the paper. Students will only be asked their physical age, their spiritual age, and their gender. (Some of the kids will groan and complain, "You'll know who it is if I put that stuff down." If they do not want to list this information, they do not have to; it is more important that you obtain the test information.) See Appendix C for an example of the types of questions you might include.

Based on the results, you could begin to see what areas need to be covered in your plan. For example, if most of the students did not answer the questions correctly in the "other religions" section, you will know that a series on "cults and other religions" is needed. If a majority of your students answered, "Only God knows" on the question about heaven, you will know that a series on "The Assurance of Salvation" needs to be in your plan. Take the time to make percentages out of the final test answers and keep those. We will be using them in the next step.

OBSERVATION

A second evaluation method is observation. Evaluation by observation is simply stepping back from your ministry, your students, and your programs and compiling your thoughts. Put yourself in this scenario: You are about ready to hire an intern from a local Christian college to come work with you for the summer. The intern inquires, "So tell me a little bit about the kids in your youth group." What would you say to this person? Take some time to either write or type out your response. Maybe it would sound something like this: "For the most part our youth group is really great. We just graduated a large group of seniors that were all really active. We have a very strong group of sophomores that are so on fire for God. Well, actually it is a strong group of sophomore girls. It seems that we struggle with keeping our guys involved as they get older. Part of that is due to job-related time constraints, but others don't come by choice and the parents simply don't insist on attendance. In general they are not as deep or committed as our girls. Our freshman class has a good mix of guys and girls; however, none of these kids seem to be very deep spiritually. They are pretty regular at Sunday school and the fun things, but when it comes to small groups, Bible Studies, or service projects, they are less interested in participating."

This short but concise written observation of one church's high school youth group is "evaluation by observation." With this method of evaluation you must be as detailed as possible;

generalities will not help you at this point. Honesty is very important. You will only be hurting yourself and your students without it. After you have written an observation for your high school students, continue on through each of your age groups until you have reached preschool. When you are finished, keep your observations for use later in the planning stages.

An additional step to the observation evaluation method involves your youth sponsors or teachers. Ask this group to give you a written observation of the age group from which they teach, specifically describing the students in their church class. (This is different from the observation of youth culture in general. "I think high school students in today's world are very self-centered and overstimulated.") Ask them to give you an observation which is specific to the children in their class.

STUDENT INTERVIEWS

The last evaluation method is the student interview. If you have been a youth or children's minister for long, you know the most effective way to motivate students: food. One suggestion for this observation method involves offering to take a few students out for ice cream, a Coke, or a meal. Take time to ask how they feel about the education they are receiving at your church. The reasoning behind this method is simple: sometimes you do not see the needs. Chances are many of the comments you will hear are things you have already figured out on your own. But between those comments you will find a different set of eyes, a unique perspective on their spiritual development. You may be surprised to hear they are growing more than you thought or struggling more than you ever imagined. Ideally you would meet with students individually. This will prevent scenarios like this from occurring:

You take four of your middle school boys out for ice cream. One of the questions you ask is this, "So, what are some things that you struggle with in youth group?" One boy speaks up, "Well, since you asked, I think our Sunday school teachers are lame. All they talk about are their kids, and I'm like, 'Hey, Kathy Lee, we've heard enough about your kids!'" Inevitably the other students will chime in with "Yeah! That's crazy!" "Oh, I hate it when they do that!" The other boys will give you these reactions *even if they have never had that thought cross their mind, ever.* What you have now is three boys who will take a very new, negative view of their Sunday school class which they never had before your meeting.

Ideally, you will interview four or five students from each of the age groups, keeping a good cross section of students such as different genders, a variety of social groups, and ethnic groups if possible.

Here are some lead-in questions:

- ✔ What are some things that you really enjoy about youth group?
- ✔ What are some things that you dislike?
- ✔ Do you feel that you are growing in your relationship with God through youth group?
- ✔ If so, in what ways?
- ✔ Do you feel comfortable inviting your friends to youth group?
- ✔ If no, why not?
- ✔ How is your prayer life?
- ✔ Have you seen any answers to prayer lately?
- ✔ How is your devotional life?
- ✔ What devotional book are you using right now?
- ✔ What could we do differently in youth group to help you grow spiritually?
- ✔ Which class at church do you feel helps you grow the most: Sunday school, Sunday night, or Wednesday night?
- ✔ Have you ever been on a mission trip?
- ✔ If no, would you be interested in going on a mission trip this summer?

Looking at the first two questions may make you shudder or desire to skip to something else; however, the answers to these questions may give you deep insight into the future direction your Faith Development Plan should take. A high school student may say, "I hate Sunday school. The teacher is a good guy and all, but he is so boring . . . he just stands up there and lectures. I've seen his teaching book and know there are all these cool things we could be doing. To tell you the truth, I don't even think he likes kids!" Now this comment is very important to your Faith Development Plan. If the other kids in the high school Sunday school class feel the same way about their experience during that time, they will not be growing, and that slot of time (which is factored into our mere 1%) is a waste of potential faith development time. You may see the need to step back and do some teacher training before you implement your Faith Development Plan.

Above all else remember that the purpose of these evaluation methods is to determine how you can help your students grow spiritually. We have actually had boys in our youth group tell us the reason they do not attend church on a certain night is due to this important fact, "There are no hot girls there." Unfortunately, this is not something you can control. If, during your interview, things move in this direction, try to redirect the conversation.

An additional step to the student interview evaluation method is to include the sponsors or teachers. Take time to interview your teachers and ask them very pointed questions about their view on the faith development of their students. Make sure they are aware that this is not an evaluation of their effectiveness as a teacher. This is an evaluation of the youth ministry as a whole. Here are some questions you may want to ask:

- Do you feel the current curriculum we are using is helping your students to grow spiritually?
- Do you believe that the students are retaining the information taught in this curriculum?
- What do you think the youth ministry could do, specifically for your students, that would help them grow spiritually?
- Tell me about one student in your class you have seen grow spiritually in the past year?
- What has the church done to help that child grow?
- Is there an area of the youth ministry you feel is not effective in helping the students grow?

Step Six

Compile Your Information

After you have evaluated your students and the current effectiveness of the youth ministry in your church, take some time to organize your information. "Grade" the Bible knowledge tests showing the percentage of students who answered each question. For example, on the question regarding assurance of salvation you might list your results like this.

30. If I died today, I would go to heaven.
❏ Absolutely (15%—30/200) ❏ No way   (5%—10/200)
❏ I hope so (45%—90/200) ❏ Only God knows (35%—70/200)

If you want to be more detailed, you can break the numbers down by physical age, spiritual age, or gender. Or better yet, find an accountant in your church who loves to work with numbers and make charts!

Take significant portions from your interviews and observations and put them together. Include some quotes that make strong points including submissions by the students, sponsors, and yourself.

After you have compiled and taken a serious look at all this information, write a conclusion. "After looking at this evaluation I have concluded that we are very effective in the elementary Sunday school department, but lacking in all other areas of the elementary ministry." "After looking at this evaluation I have concluded that we need a stronger ministry to our high school boys. We are losing them during their sophomore year and must find ways to prevent this from happening. We have to be more intentional with that specific group to help them spiritually."

You Are Armed

You are convinced of the need for a Faith Development Plan in your ministry. Your leadership agrees with the idea that you need a Faith Development Plan in your ministry and they are behind you 110%. Your sponsors are on board and ready to move forward to assist you in organizing and implementing a Faith Development Plan. You have evaluated the students in your ministry and the current effectiveness of Christian education presently offered to your students. You are now ready to move onto the next step.

Step Seven

Faith Development Plan Item Determination

Step seven involves determining what specific items you will place on your Faith Development Plan. This is a crucial point when you meet with your sponsors to begin the actual organization of your plan. It is imperative that you do serious planning before you meet with your sponsors. Here is why.

When the whole idea of a "mission statement" became popular, youth ministers across the country began the process of designing such a statement for their ministry. Rule number one in developing a mission statement is for the participants to feel ownership. With this in mind youth ministers met with their sponsors and said, "We have to come up with a mission statement. What would you like to include in the mission statement for our youth ministry?" Pause, silence, silence, more silence. Joe Smith say, "Well, we should have something about the Bible and God in it." And so it went, several, long drawn out meetings between youth minister and sponsors to determine a mission statement for their ministry. Finally, one youth minister got smart. He went into a sponsor meeting and said, "We have to come up with a mission statement. I want all of your input on the exact wording of this statement. I have come up with an idea to start with and you can tell me what you think." He proceeds in presenting his idea for a potential mission statement. One sponsor says he thinks they should add this, everyone agrees. Another sponsor comments about changing a couple phrases here and there. And after an hour, BOOM! this group has a mission statement.

The seriously wrong choice in organizing your plan is to come into a sponsors meeting and say, "Well, here are the evaluations we have compiled over the last couple months. Now it's time to start putting the plan together. What would you like to see in our Faith Development Plan?" Most likely you will hear silence, silence and more silence, followed by one sponsor finally saying, "Well, we should do something on sex. These kids need more education on sex." You will end up frustrated and wish you had never started the process.

The right approach at this stage is to spend some time in preparation, reflecting on the things you would like to see in your Faith Development Plan and present these ideas to your sponsors and teachers. Here are some items to consider. If you need help determining what age would be appropriate to introduce a certain topic, refer to the section in this book on that age level.

Mission Trips—At what age do you want to start encouraging mission trips? How often do you want to schedule mission trips, and where are you planning to go in the next four years?

Service Projects—At what age do you want to start encouraging service projects? How often do you want to schedule service projects, and what are some projects you would like to see your students accomplish?

Retreats—At what age do you want to start offering retreats? How often do you want to schedule retreats, and what type of retreats would you like to offer your students?

Camps—At what age do you want to start encouraging your students to attend camp? How often do you want to encourage your students to attend camps, and what camps do you want them to attend?

Conventions—At what age do you want to start taking your students to conventions? How often do you want to offer a weekend convention to your students, and what conventions do you want them to attend?

Small Groups—At what age do you want to start offering small groups for your students? Do you want to strongly encourage all of your students to be involved in small groups, or do you only want the students who feel passionately about small groups to participate?

Evangelism Opportunities—At what age do you want to start encouraging your students to share their faith? Where would you like to see your students as far as sharing their faith? How are you going to build your faith development plan so they will grow in this area? (One possibility is to combine your service projects and your evangelism and provide servant evangelism projects.)

Worship and Music—How are you going to introduce worship and music with each age group? Do you plan to encourage your students to participate in the adult worship service? If so, how are you going to facilitate this? Are you planning to bring in any worship bands or concerts and, if so, how many? Are you planning to have a youth choir, and, if so, will it meet for one semester or two? Does your youth choir develop your student's faith? If not, what could you do differently to make it a faith growing opportunity?

Leadership—At what age do you want to start offering leadership classes and opportunities for your students? How do you want to promote leadership skills in your students? By what age or school year do you want to see them leading and how?

The Basics—What basic Bible facts do you want your students to know? You want them to know the books of the Bible, the twelve apostles, certain Bible verses, and other basics. At what age do you want to introduce these basics, and what exactly do you want your students to know by the time they leave that age group?

Devotions—At what age do you want to begin encouraging

your students to commit to daily devotional reading? How are you going to encourage your students in this respect?

Other items to consider include:

- ✦ Which of your programs is the most heavily attended?
- ✦ What is the purpose of each of your programs (i.e., Sunday school is for Bible study, Sunday night small groups, Wednesday night is more evangelistically oriented, etc.)?
- ✦ Do you need to consider teacher training before you begin your Faith Development Plan?
- ✦ What were the problem areas you identified in your evaluation? (I.e., although they were frequent attenders in their late middle school and early high school years, you are losing your guys as they move toward their senior year. Are you having trouble with your students becoming too cliquish, not wanting to include "outsiders"?) How are you going to program differently to correct these problem areas?

You also need to consider possible topics you would like to cover during your programs while constantly keeping in mind the Faith Development questions, "What do I want my students to know by the time they graduate?" and "How am I going to get them there?"

This is the information you must bring to the meeting with your sponsors or teachers. This initial meeting should take approximately two hours if you are adequately prepared with the items mentioned in this step. Showing up at the meeting with a blank slate for your sponsors and teachers to work with will make for a much longer, more frustrating meeting. Offer to put all the information discussed during the meeting into a proposed, rough draft, Faith Development Plan for your sponsors and teachers to approve at your next organizational meeting.

STEP EIGHT

Filling in Your Plan

You are getting close! Armed with the elements of your plan, you are now ready to organize and put them into a formal plan. Your plan will last the number of years you have students in your group. For example, your high school plan will be four years if they are in that group from ninth to twelfth grade. Your middle school plan will last three years if that group includes sixth through eighth grade. Your upper elementary plan will last three years if that group includes third through fifth grade. Your lower elementary plan will be two years if that group consists of first and second grade. Your preschool plan will last four years if that group includes two through five-year-old children. Your nursery and toddler plans can either be together or separate. When meeting with your sponsors, discuss which topics you feel justified in repeating.

> **We feel the spiritual disciplines are a great way to start off each new year, challenging students to daily prayer and devotion time as they are making their New Year's resolutions. We feel that love, sex, and dating is an important enough topic to repeat every year. Adding it during February, the love month, could also set the stage for a special Valentine's Banquet.**

Any items that cannot fit into calendar format can be printed in paragraph form and attached to the plan. For example, the desire to have every one of your students participating in small groups is not a calendar item. This is something you will want to type out and include on the bottom or back of your plan.

STEP NINE

Proposing Your Faith Development Plan

After you have completed your Faith Development Plan, you are ready to present it to your sponsors and teachers. Meet with each group individually and be ready to make some adjustments. There may be some problems you did not notice on the plan—items that may conflict with your students. One of your sponsors may see that you are proposing to offer a mission trip at the same time the church is celebrating its fiftieth anniversary. (You totally forgot, but love your sponsor for remembering.)

As with any meeting you conduct involving teachers or sponsors, you should send out meeting agendas ahead of time. This is a courtesy to the volunteers who work with youth. It allows them the opportunity to see what will be discussed and perhaps formulate some ideas to prevent long awkward pauses that are bound to surface in meetings where agendas have not been given out prior to the meeting. This meeting is no exception. It is imperative you not only send out your meeting agenda, but the plan itself for the sponsors and teachers to look over. Ideally, every participant will have looked over the plan prior to the meeting.

> May I suggest providing teachers and sponsors with a three-ring binder with a clear pocketed front? Print out the name of your church, the ministry in which they serve, and that volunteer's name on a sheet of paper (e.g., High School Youth Ministry, Community Christian Church, Lisa Barker). Put the title page in the clear pocket front of the three-ring binder and include pens, highlighters, and blank monthly calendars for notes and brainstorming. Before each meeting send your sponsors and teachers the meeting agenda (three-hole punched) to be placed in their binder and brought to the meeting. Always have extra agendas available at the meeting for those who accidentally leave theirs at home.

Do not leave the meeting until you are confident all your teachers are in favor of the plan for their age group. Do not go into the meeting anticipating that the teachers will accept your proposed plan without the need for some revisions. Remember, you do not want this to be *your* Faith Development Plan. The intention is for this plan to stay in place at your church with or without you at the helm. What a wonderful present for a minister who succeeds you to find a well-thought-out plan, mapped out for him to continue.

STEP TEN

Presenting Your Faith Development Plan

PRESENTING THE PLAN TO YOUR TEACHERS

This meeting is so crucially important, I suggest you offer it more than once so all teachers have a chance to hear the information. Some teachers have made it a point to be at every meeting about the plan up to this point and some have not. Some will take the attitude, "Whatever you (the youth minister) decide about this plan is fine with me. I don't really care what you do.

You're the expert." However, this meeting is different and should be mandatory for all teachers to attend.

The most important aspect of this meeting is for each teacher in each age group to know three important pieces of information: what the children will learn and will know before they come into their class, what the children will learn and need to know while they are in their class, and what the children will be learning in the next class. It is imperative that teachers know this information and have it in the back of their minds through all the lessons they teach. They need to realize there is a level of expectation for what takes place in their classroom and they need to know what their students will need to know before they leave their class.

For example, the Faith Development Plan for your church may state the four and five-year-old group will learn the books of the Bible during their time in that department. It is crucial that the first and second grade teachers know that the students coming into their department will know their books of the Bible and then use that knowledge through repetition in future lessons.

Presenting the Plan to Your Parents

This meeting is also crucial. The parents of your students need to know that you have an intentionally laid out plan for their children's spiritual development. They also need to understand the information their children will be learning in church so they can reinforce this in the home.

If their child is in the first or second grade, he or she will be learning about the importance of tithing. This is the perfect age for parents to begin assigning weekly chores where children will receive regularly set allowance money. This is the concept of church and home working in tandem with the common goal of producing spiritually mature disciples of Christ.

Prepare yourself for many different reactions. One parent might shrug his shoulders and say, "That's great, whatever you think is best. Looks good to me." Another parent may ask several questions and show a great deal of interest in the plan. Yet another parent may lean over to their spouse and say, "This seems like such a waste of the youth minister's time. What was wrong with the way we were doing things before?"

Remember, for some parents this is the first time they have even heard the term "Faith Development Plan." You may choose to take some time to describe your convictions and the need for such a plan prior to presenting the plan itself. Reuse some of the information previously presented in the initial meeting with your sponsors and teachers. Try to recall how you convinced them of the importance of a formal Faith Development Plan and use this same information with the parents.

Remember, for some parents this is the first time they have even heard the term "Faith Development Plan."

Perhaps you can use some of the evaluation material, citing specific scores on the Bible knowledge test or comments from the student interviews. Some of this information may shock the parents and help them realize it is time to do things differently.

STEP ELEVEN

Gathering Curriculum

This step is the most tedious and time consuming. Now is the time to look through your Faith Development Plan and determine what curriculum you have, will need to create, or need to purchase.

The key to gathering curriculum is starting several months in advance. If you plan to start your Faith Development Plan in August, which is suggested, you need to begin gathering curriculum no later than March of the same year. Devote each month of developing curriculum to one month of the Faith Development Plan. For example, the month of March will be devoted to accumulating curriculum, or writing lesson plans, for August. In April you will devote yourself to accumulating curriculum, or writing lesson plans, for September. With this method you will begin your Faith Development Plan with six months of material in place. Some of the study topics have several different options in "canned curriculum." If you decide to use this type of curriculum you will be able to get a jump on the next month and could possibly have eight or nine months of curriculum planned out before you start the plan.

This is also the time to get your teachers and sponsors involved in the preparation process. Ask your teachers and sponsors if they have any curriculum at home for the topics you will be studying. Ask them if they know of any available curriculum on the topics you will be studying and to keep an eye out for those topics for which you are having trouble finding curriculum.

Now is a great time to teach your sponsors and teachers how

to write a lesson plan. Whether they use the "Hook, Book, Look, and Took" method, the "Head, Hands, and Heart" method, or something else, teachers can learn to write lesson plans. Writing lesson plans is something to incorporate into your monthly teacher's meetings or have a workshop leader come right to your church and include it in the teacher training.

The goal? Have all your curriculum for the age group and rotate it after the students leave that area. If your high school plan includes freshmen through seniors you will have a four-year plan that will continue to loop until you decide to add, delete, or change a topic or the month in which it is taught.

Step Twelve

Evaluation

Evaluating Your Faith Development Program

No, this is not a mistake. I have listed evaluation twice on purpose. Evaluation is essential in every aspect of ministry, but sometimes not handled properly or thoroughly. I have seen leadership, senior ministers, youth ministers, and children's ministers evaluate programs too quickly after implementation. We may see that our program is not growing as we thought it would and decide to pull that program and try something else. The truth is, sometimes programs need time for people to catch on and see the vision we see. The Holy Spirit does not have a time limit. Give Him a chance to help the program grow. Take several steps in the right direction, giving the program some time, and then look back and determine its effectiveness, make adjustments and improvements, and keep it and your students growing.

In your planning stages, decide in conjunction with your leadership, sponsors, teachers, and parents how long you want to wait until you evaluate this ministry approach. "I would like to organize and implement a Faith Development Plan for the youth and children's ministry at our church. After one year I will sit down with several sponsors, teachers, and parents to evaluate its effectiveness."

After your predetermined waiting time, you might evaluate your Faith Development Plan and observe that the middle school and high school areas of your plan are going well; however, the preschool teachers are not happy with the plan in their area. Maybe you are not happy with the disproportionate amount of time you are spending on Bible knowledge and see more of a need for science and history. Or maybe you had broken your Sunday school topics into one for every month, and you are finding this is just not enough time to spend on one topic. Whatever the case may be, you can adjust your plan accordingly.

A big mistake would be taking the time to organize and implement a Faith Development Plan and then sitting back, wiping your brow, and saying, "Whew! Glad that's over. I'm going to go park my car in front of the church (to make it look like I'm there working), pull a George Castanza, and go play some serious golf!" While completing the organization of your Faith Development Plan is an accomplishment, you must view it as your prize sports car. It needs to be tuned every 3,000 miles and you know better than to just park it under a tree for days on end.

EVALUATING YOUR STUDENTS

If you have not read George Barna's book, *Transforming Children into Spiritual Champions*, you must. The seventh chapter in this book is entitled, "Better Performance through Evaluation." In this chapter he speaks of the necessity of evaluating students. He starts the chapter by asking the readers to put themselves in this scenario: You have moved to a new area you have chosen specifically because of its reputation for fine schools. This is important to you because you want the best for your nine-year-old daughter. Everything seems to go well the first semester and you are excited to have that first parent-teacher conference to see how your little one is doing.

> You get to the classroom and meet the young, bright-eyed instructor. You inquire as to your child's progress. "Oh, she's doing just great," beams the teacher.
>
> "What is her grade-point average so far?" you ask, hoping to get a more definitive sense of just how "great" things are going.
>
> "Oh, we don't actually have any grades. But she's doing very well," comes the confident reply.
>
> "But you must have some test scores to look at." The teacher keeps smiling but nods from side to side, dismissing the idea. "Some evaluation of in-class exercises?" You receive another dissenting nod. "Notes assessing her class participation or math skills?" Wrong again.
>
> "How is it that you know she's doing so well if there are no tests, no papers, no grades, no written evaluation, and no apparent measurements of any kind?" you ask, incredulous that four

months have passed with seemingly no effort by the instructor to objectively gauge you daughter's progress.

"Oh, well, I can tell that she's doing well," the teacher begins. "You see, she comes to class every day. She almost always has her textbook with her . . . I have a sense that she is rather bright and she seems to pay attention most of the time. You should be proud of her—she is polite, she keeps her desk clean and organized, and the other students like her. And believe me," the educator says with her biggest smile yet, "all semester long I have worked very hard to teach the necessary math principles to the best of my ability."[1]

Barna goes on to say that as a parent you would be "incensed" at the fact this teacher had not been evaluating your child for an entire semester. Now, let's take this out of the cognitive area and move it to the spiritual. How are your students doing spiritually? Have they grown spiritually in the last year, two years, or five years? One children's pastor frustratingly shares, "In my 27 years of ministering to children and their families, I have never once had a parent come up to me and ask how their child is progressing spiritually. Every weekend I get parent after parent chasing me down to ask about their kids. But what they want to know is whether or not their child showed up to class, whether their child had his or her Bible and whether their child was well behaved during the class. Nobody seems to care very much about how the child is doing spiritually, as if merely showing up two or three times a month precludes having to even ask the question."[2]

But how, you may ask, am I supposed to assess where my students are spiritually? Tests, quizzes, oral exams, or assigned papers I grade? I would like to suggest several different ways to evaluate your students.

The first is offering to meet with the parents of your students once a year to evaluate their spiritual progress. (The actual word "evaluate" holds somewhat of a negative connotation so we will use the word "assess.") This meeting could consist of the parents, the child (optional), one of the child's church teachers or sponsors, and yourself. Please notice I used the word "offering." Making an assessment meeting mandatory is not a road you want to take in this culture. Parents do not like to be "told" what to do with their children. "Optional" is the key word with this type of evaluation or assessment method. You offer these annual meetings with any of the students in your ministry from elementary to high school.

Some of the questions you may want to ask the parents are:

1) How does your child seem to be doing at home?
2) How is your child doing in school?
3) Are you satisfied with the friends your child has chosen?
4) How do you think your child is doing spiritually?
5) Do you know if your child has a regular prayer life?
6) Does your child have a daily or weekly devotional time?
7) How does your child view church? (Do you have to push him or her to go?)
8) Is there anything you think the youth ministry or children's ministry at this church could do to better help your child develop spiritually?

Next, take some time to share your perception on how the child is doing spiritually and allow the teacher or sponsor to do the same. It is very important to keep in mind this fact: Parenting is hard work. It is very hard for parents to hear negative remarks about their children. To be honest, many parents are actually trying to do what is best for their children. Always try to focus on the positive or at least begin with some positives; however, speak the truth in love. "Joey is extremely respectful to me and the teachers. He is never a problem in class, he always participates in the activities, and he is really such a joy to have in the youth ministry. But, I have noticed that he made a decision to be saved last year and, to be perfectly honest, seems to be just going through the motions. He just doesn't seem to enjoy his time here at church or desire to build relationships with any of the other kids." At this point you will most likely see some head nodding from the parents. If these issues are real, it's likely they see them, too. The parents may go on to tell you that things haven't been going well in the home. Perhaps their marriage is struggling and there has been talk of a trial separation. Joey has probably heard more than he should and this has affected the way he acts at church and in his spiritual life.

If the parents answered "no" to the questions of prayer life and devotions, discuss how you and the parents can work together to help the student in this area. Maybe the answer is simply for the family to begin nightly devotions together until Joey seems to want to do them on his own. Make notes on your meeting and create a file for Joey. Encourage the parents to schedule another meeting with you whenever they feel necessary, but no later than one year from that date.

Many parents will inevitably decline your invitation to meet with them for such an evaluation; however, there may come a time when they bring their child to your office with a problem. "We found out Annie is sexually active. What do we do?" "Jason has been making poor choices in the friends department, and we are really worried about him." "Brandon is starting to talk about suicide. What do we do?" These parents are coming to you for help. This would be a great time to bring up a meeting. You may say, "Here is the number of a good friend of mine that can help you with counseling for Annie. And, I know you didn't take me up on the invitation to meet with you about Annie's spiritual progress, but I would love to sit down with you and talk. We don't want to simply fix her immediate need. We want to see her growing a solid foundation in Christ.

Another method of evaluation involves getting into your student's schools. In some ministries this is simple, because only one school is represented. Other ministries involve students from a number of schools and school systems. The students in our ministries come from seven different school districts including a number of students who are homeschooled. Some children's and youth ministers have asked their church leadership permission to go on their school's substitute teacher list one day a week. This is a great way to get into the schools, see your students on "their turf," and earn a little extra money, too.

I had the privilege to work as a substitute teacher for eight different school districts one full school year. I learned many practical lessons that year, most of which are not appropriate to speak of in this book. One substitute assignment found me teaching language arts every day to seventh grade students. When parent–teacher conferences came around, I distinctly remember thinking, "How hard can this be?" The parents could pick which teachers they would like to meet with, and everyone met as a group. The first conference consisted of a mother, the math, history, science teacher, and myself. We all took turns telling this woman how her daughter was doing in our classes, which wasn't well. (Hence the conference.) Her daughter's problems were not merely scholastic, she had a bad attitude that was getting her into a lot of trouble. After we had all taken our turns sharing our test results and struggles, the mother hung her head and started to cry. "I don't know what's gotten into her. She's always been such a good girl. We've gone to church ever since she was little. She doesn't act like this at church."

I remember trying to hold my jaw up for fear it would fall on the ground. I was thinking to myself, "This girl that caused trouble in my class every day, who had to be threatened with detention because she wouldn't get a piece of paper out for a spelling test, who rolled her eyes at almost everything I said, this girl went to . . . church! You've got to be kidding me."

One of the classes I taught had a familiar name on the class roster. It was a boy from our youth group, and I could tell he was uncomfortable with my presence. The other boys in the class, throwing paper airplanes, kept asking him (by yelling across the room), "Hey, Brandon, what's up with you today?" After several other such incidents, I came away from that class with this mental note, "Brandon, the sweet angel at church, is most likely not a sweet angel at school."

Your students may be able to fool you on Sunday morning and Wednesday night, but seeing them in school will open your eyes to the person student. If they are fooling you in church and school, send them to Hollywood, because they must be great actors.

Another option for getting into your student's schools is volunteering to monitor playgrounds during recess. One youth minister told me he volunteered to teach kindergarten gym once a week and absolutely loved it. When his elementary students saw him in the halls, they would high-five him, smile, and go out of their way to greet him. Some schools will let ministers come in and have lunch with the students. This always seems popular with male and female elementary students, female middle students, and senior high girls (especially if the girls think their youth minister is hot!).

And of course, there is the sports and music route into the schools. I don't know of one game I've attended where a student has not thoroughly appreciated my presence. Most kids are so excited to have their youth minister attending, it seems they try a little harder just to impress him or her. On the other hand, I have been very disappointed at times to watch a student's game and see horrible disrespect toward coaches, officials, and parents in the stands. (I have been equally disgusted to see students perform in school musicals and community theater where the lyrics and message are anything but godly.)

The last way to assess your students is by simple observation. Here are some questions that can help you assess your students in this manner:

1) Is this student regular in his/her attendance at church?
2) In class, does this student participate?
3) Do you see any signs of this student's spiritual growth (i.e., baptism, inviting others to church, asking deep questions, developing relationships with others in the group, attending a Bible study outside of church, practicing daily devotions at home, leaning toward attending Bible college, participating in service projects and mission trips)?
4) Do you see eventual leadership possibilities in this student? If not, what does he or she need to do to get there?
5) Do you see evidence of this student's faith outside of church activities (with parents, girlfriends or boyfriends, friends, in sports or other extracurricular activities)?
6) Does this student appear to desire a deeper faith?

These are just some of the many questions you can ask yourself and record about the students in your ministry. Perhaps you can think of other questions that would pertain specifically to the culture in which you minister? These questions may apply to your kids and not others.

Regardless of how you choose to assess your students, you must do it. If you minister in a large church, you may not have the time to assess students individually. You may need to use the observation method and assess the group as a whole. Do what it takes to determine how your students are progressing spiritually. It takes the guesswork out of your ministry. Many of us have had those bad days in ministry when we lay our heads on our desks asking ourselves, "Why do I do this? I don't even know if I am making a difference in these kid's lives!" You may not be aware of this, but some of your teachers and sponsors ask themselves the same questions.

Take the time to consider how and when you are going to assess or evaluate your students. If possible, discuss this with your church leaders, teachers, and youth sponsors. List this as one of your ministry goals and keep it in front of you.

After you have organized and implemented your Faith Development Plan, keep it in front of you at all times. This has now become the road map to your goal. Continually pray that the Holy Spirit will work through this plan to produce spiritually mature disciples of Christ in your students.

Where do you want your students to be by the time they graduate? And how are you going to get them there? Will you choose to form an intentional plan of action for your students? Will you choose to aim your arrows at the target of spiritual maturity and commit to investing your time and energy into forming a Faith Development Plan for your ministry?

Andy Stanley says, "So, like me, you have probably come to the end of a stretch of ministry and wondered, 'What did they learn?' You know what they heard. But what did they take away? Sure, they will remember the events and the people who were 'there for them.' But did they walk away with the tools and the truths they will need to survive and thrive in the world beyond high school? . . . Once the room is full . . . let's make sure the content we throw at them sticks. Let's make it memorable. Let's make it transformational. And let's keep coming back to a handful of concepts over and over until our students dream them in their sleep."[3]

Let's "change the way we do youth ministry" and choose to begin a Faith Development Plan. Let's utilize the 1% time slot we have with our students. Let's expect nothing less from our graduated seniors than true discipleship and fight with all our might to keep them from becoming a twenty-something statistic. How about ruining Satan's day and aiming for nothing less than spiritual maturity in our students? Choose to organize a Faith Development Plan, stand back, and watch the blessings flow.

NOTES

1. George Barna, *Transforming Children*, 122.
2. Ibid., 124.
3. Stanley and Hall, *Seven Checkpoints*, xvi-xvii.

Chapter Twelve

QUESTIONS AND ANSWERS

Q1 *Our church is very small. Our attendance runs 100 on a good Sunday. We have a very small youth program. Do you really think a Faith Development Plan would benefit a church our size?*

Absolutely! The wonderful thing about a Faith Development Plan is that you tailor it to the needs of your church. Look through the information in chapters four through ten of this book and determine which areas you believe should be covered in your plan. Despite the fact your church is small, your students are still arrows and still need to be aimed at the target of spiritual maturity.

Q2 *I am a children's minister and believe fully in the concept of a Faith Development Plan. But our youth minister doesn't seem to be as convicted as I am. Is it possible for our children's ministry to have a plan and not our middle school or high school?*

The answer is yes and no. Having a goal in mind for your children's ministry is essential. You have to decide where you want your students to be after they leave your ministry. The success of the combined ministries depends on the youth minister's goals for the students once they leave your program and begin his. Does he have a plan of action and a specific target for these students? He may not call it a Faith Development Plan, but if he has a plan of action and his target is graduating youth from his program who are passionate, sold-out believers in Jesus Christ who will share their faith, then that is a plan.

Q3 *Realistically, how long do you believe it would take to organize, develop, and implement a Faith Development Plan in an average-sized church?*

Generally, I believe you could organize, develop, and implement a Faith Development Plan in six months at the most. I believe it can be done, and done well, in less. If you delegate much of the initial planning to your age-appropriate youth sponsors and guide them through the process, the organizational stages should not take that long.

Q4 *This seems like a lot of work. My plate is already full with my ministry. I just don't know when I would have the time to put together such a plan. What do you suggest?*

The organizational stages of the Faith Development Plan are time and energy consuming. They are an investment. You must remember, once your plan is up and running, it can, in some ways, run itself. After each department has run through one cycle, your teachers should have it down. Once the teachers of four- and five-year-olds have gone through their two-year cycle, they will simply do the same thing for the next two years, making minor adjustments as needed.

Set aside a small amount of time each day or each week to look at your plan and make some decisions. Look at the proposed plan in this book and see how you can draw from it.

Beginning a Faith Development Plan is an investment. But you, your teachers, your students, and their parents will reap the eternal rewards.

Q5 *I have some differing opinions about the items you listed in your proposed plan. I think preschool children can learn of persecution stories and benefit from them. I also think small groups should be offered for elementary students. What should I do?*

Remember that a proposed plan is just that, a proposed plan. The information shared in chapters four through ten are simply a guide. You may want to shift an area such as "heaven" up to your elementary group. You may want to delete an area or add something you feel was not mentioned. This is the beauty of tailoring your program to fit the needs of your students and your church.

Q6 *I am a children's minister. Our church is experiencing severe financial difficulty at this time. I am afraid if I propose such a plan, the leadership will question the expense of the resources. If they ask, what should I tell them?*

I imagine your church is already purchasing curriculum for the children's or youth ministry. Take some time to crunch your numbers and find out what you spend on curriculum in a year. Ask several of your parents what they do with their child's take-home papers during the week. Many of your parents will admit throwing them away. Your leadership needs to hear this information. The money you are spending on curriculum is being thrown in the trash. Perhaps changes can be made which increase the spiritual *and* financial efficiency of the youth program.

Writing your own curriculum is not so much an investment in money as it is time. Take the money you would have spent on curriculum and buy several resource books on Bible crafts, snacks that correspond with Bible lessons, and Bible learning centers. Choose three centers which correspond with the lesson, one craft, one snack, several songs, and your Bible story. The expense in that lesson would be materials for crafts and snack items, both of which could be donated by congregation members.

Remember, regardless of a church size or financial situation you must have a goal for your students. Where do you want your students to be by the time they leave your program, and how are you going to get them there?

Q7 *When I have completed the Faith Development Plan for my ministry, what exactly do I need to present to my teachers?*

You need to share three essential pieces of information:

1) What the children learned in the previous department. (What will these students know coming into your class? What should you reinforce? What should you expect from them?)
2) What the children will learn in their department. (Share the goals such as those mentioned at the end of chapters four through ten. By the time a child leaves your department they will have learned . . .)
3) What the children will learn in the next department. (What will the students be taught in their next class?)

Q8 *Your plan seems to assume that a child will be born and graduate in the same church. This seems atypical. What about the student who begins attending our church in high school?*

Glad you asked! This is the biggest question with any type of Faith Development Plan. There is no easy answer. Some students who enter your program midstream may not benefit from the full efforts of your plan. I think we could both agree that children learn quickly. If the rest of the class knows something and one person doesn't, they make it a point to figure it out. When I moved to another school in the middle of my fourth-grade year, I was surprised to hear of something called long division. Unfortunately the whole class knew about it. Within a week I had the concept mastered—not because I was exceptionally smart, but because I knew that it was important and needed to be learned.

I believe that most of the students entering your ministry at any point will benefit from a Faith Development Plan. It is not accurate to say that no student who enters your program midstream will benefit from the full effects of your plan. You may have a student who goes through this program from nursery to graduation and never makes a decision for Christ, and you may have a student who begins attending your church his junior year of high school who ends up in full-time ministry. That student who did not make a decision for Christ prior to leaving your program may decide to surrender his life in college.

Remember to make your fifth Sundays a time of review. Play games and reinforce concepts and lessons taught during the last month, year, or two years. Most children are naturally competitive and will be challenged to remember something if their team is counting on them!

Q9 *In your proposed Faith Development Plan you plan most lessons in four-week increments. Could you schedule some studies for longer or shorter? In some age levels you do not list anything for Wednesday nights during the summer months. What should we do during those months if we do have a Wednesday night program? And you do not have anything listed for Sunday nights. What is your suggestion for that time slot?*

You are correct. The proposed Faith Development Plan does schedule most lessons in four-week time slots. Of course you can run a lesson series for a longer or shorter period of time. Remember to tailor the plan to *meet the needs of your church and aid your students in reaching your faith development goals*. You may choose to offer a twelve-week Wednesday night series on God's design for money. Great! You may choose to only study evangelism for two weeks instead of four. Great! Remember, this is just a proposed plan.

The Wednesday night time slot is not listed on the proposed plan simply because most churches do not have Wednesday night programs during the summer months. If your church does have a Wednesday night program, you may consider offering some of the other Wednesday night topics for longer than four weeks to stretch out the curriculum.

Note the months are staggered with a Bible study in Sunday school one month and a topical lesson series the next. Each year you offer the study you can flipflop the material so as to share with all your students. Some of your students will only come to Sunday school. Deciding to present all Bible studies during Sunday school and all topical studies on Sunday night would unbalance your faith table.

The Sunday night time slot is not filled because many churches offer their kids choir rehearsals and small group Bible studies on Sunday nights. If you are looking for something to fill that slot, choose small groups for your middle and high school students and consider offering a children's choir too. These are additional faith development areas to plug into your plan.

Consider offering four-week electives for your students on Wednesday nights. We have titled our Wednesday evening program for middle and high school students CSI: Wilmington. The CSI stands for "choosing something interesting." We want the students to be able to choose the area they would like to study. You may offer three different electives and open it up to middle and high school students. Some electives may only be open to boys and others only to girls. You may even choose to open up some electives to your adults.

There are several benefits to this type of programming. 1) It is much easier to get adults in your church to commit to a four-week time slot than a nine-month slot. We have found that almost anyone will agree to teach a four-week study. 2) You can choose adults from your congregation to teach in the area they are gifted. One gentleman who works at a bank taught a class on God's design for your money. One woman who was fluent in sign language taught a class on "Worship and Sign Language." Another woman who is an expert in PowerPoint, taught a class on how to program and run this audio-visual tool. Since we use this program in our worship service, this would train students in an area of service to the church. 3) The students love to be able to make choices.

We have learned to offer several electives twice, once in the fall and once in the spring, just in case a student is torn between attending two electives. We try to assure them, "The elective you miss will be offered again in the spring." Since beginning this program we have had a boost in our Wednesday night attendance.

Q10 *The "Proposed Faith Development Plan" is very repetitious. Is there a reason for this? When we organize our plan, do we need to repeat lessons as often as you suggest?*

Absolutely not. As mentioned in the earlier stages of this book, repetition is key in faith development. However, if you feel your students would benefit from a greater variety of lessons and only wish to teach a particular topic once every other year, that is fine. You may organize your plan however you wish. When offering lessons from year to year, especially in a three-year plan such as late elementary and middle school, make sure to slightly mix up your lesson material. The students may enjoy a little variety in the presentation.

Also consider allowing your students in fifth grade, eighth grade, and twelfth grade to help present the lesson with the teacher. This will greatly aid in their retention of the material.

Q11 *Our curriculum has a "Scope and Sequence" clearly mapped out. What is the need for a Faith Development Plan if we already have this plan in place?*

The answer is found in chapter two of this book. Reread this chapter which discusses the importance of strong legs under your student's faith table. Typically curriculum publishers only focus on the Bible Knowledge leg of your student's faith table. They will not cover things such as history, science, and the family. The beauty of a Faith Development Plan is that *you choose* what your students need to learn. You plug in the lessons on the calendar and decide what they will take in to reach the specific long-term goals you have set for your students. Remember, chapters four through ten of this book are there to guide you in making the decisions on what areas to cover with your students. You may choose all, some, or none of these areas. They are there to guide you in the organization of your own plan.

Q12 *In looking at your "Proposed Faith Development Plan" it seems very light in the Bible study category. With so many topical studies, do you feel students will get enough Bible Knowledge?*

Emphatically, yes! Each of the topical studies listed is based on biblical principles and biblical content. For example, the study on persecution will be based on the stoning of Stephen found in Acts 7. The study on missions will include the life of Paul. A study on leadership will be based on the lives of Moses and Jesus. The study on history will stem from the study of David's Psalms. The heaven and hell series will bring a study of the book of Revelation. Each of the topical studies is foundationally based and presented from a biblical standpoint. The students will be getting the Bible Knowledge but in a very practical way.

Appendix A

CURRICULUM AND THE PRESCHOOLERS

Choosing the right curriculum is absolutely essential for all your classes beginning at this age. Unfortunately, choosing curriculum is a difficult and grueling task for most children's and youth ministers. Next to recruitment it may seem to be the biggest frustration for Christian educators. Some of the best material available for children is only designed for one hour a morning, while most churches have their children at least two hours, if not three.

Unfortunately, there is no quick and simple answer for the area of curriculum. "Try XYZ curriculum and you, your teachers, your parents, and your students will be happy and well fed." After reviewing more curriculums than I care to, I suggest one not-so-simple answer: write your own curriculum.

Writing your own curriculum ensures you are meeting the needs of the children in your church. I compare such a task to building a house. It may take a year of hard work, but it will pay off in the end with a comfortable home to settle into. A part-time children's minister at a small church in Indiana spent a considerable amount of time reviewing different children's Bibles and came to the same conclusion I mentioned earlier in this chapter; *The Beginner's Bible* by Karyn Henley and Dennas Davis seems to be best suited for this age. She then decided to write a curriculum based on the stories in *The*

Beginner's Bible, following the order presented in that Bible. She went through craft and other resource books adding centers, crafts, and snacks that went along with each story. She then encouraged the parents to read the stories from that week's lesson at home. This, along with a coloring page or something simple, was the official "take home papers" we parents have come to know and love.

> How many parents of your preschoolers use the "take home papers" you send with them each week as they are meant to be used? How many parents take them home and, when the child is not looking, throw them away? Let me ask you another question: Is this the best use of your church's money? Is this considered good stewardship? Are we sending home "take home papers" just because that is what we have done for the past twenty years? Maybe it is time to stop the tradition.
>
> Parental follow-through in the home aids in the retention and development of the children's spiritual knowledge. I trust, after reading chapter six, you see its importance. How much more effective would it be to send the Bible home with the child, including a simple coloring sheet on the story, asking the parent to read that story as a review during the week? How much more would that child retain if the parent read the stories from the past week over and over to the child during the week? I believe the outcome would be a stronger knowledge of the Bible stories and retention of these stories in the future.

When deciding which Bible stories to use for your Faith Development Plan, you can simply go through this Bible and determine the main stories you want to present to the children. Keep in mind the problem preschool children tend to have with persecution and stay away from stories whose main points are too problematic for preschool children. Often curriculum writers take a Bible story and end with the thought, "God wants us to do right." Looking back on the lesson it's easy to see that "doing right" was not the main point at all! (The Bible was not written so that we could pull a main concept out of each event, but sometimes the message is very clear. For example: Noah was a good man and God blessed him.) Perhaps you would choose

Adam and Eve, Abraham, Noah, and others. Once you have determined the core stories you want to cover in a year, fill in the other Sunday lessons with lessons on the Trinity, Creation, Tithing, Heaven, and other concepts.

If you are uncomfortable with writing your own curriculum, please take time to pray about this, remembering once the curriculum is written it can be used over and over with minor adjustments. Pray that God would lead you in your decision and even bring someone from your congregation to the surface who could help you in this endeavor. Developing your own curriculum is not as hard as you think if you use the resources available and keep in mind the Faith Development goals of your department: What do you want them to know by the time they leave your department and how is this curriculum going to get them there?

Whichever route you choose to take with curriculum, either writing it yourself or choosing a canned curriculum, let me strongly encourage you to use the same story during your Sunday School and worship time. There are few nonnegotiable elements for me in children's ministry and this is one. A preschool or elementary department should never present two different stories on the same Sunday morning.

When we arrived at the church we now serve, the preschool department was using two different curriculums (thus two different stories) due to the fact the teachers were both fond of their respective curriculum sets. After service I would stop the children to ask them what their story was about during class time. The answers were a jumbled mess of confusion. "Daniel and Paul were going down the road to Damascus."

Is this really the best use of your time (1%) with the children in your programs? It would be better to have the story taught one hour and then told in a different way as a reinforcement of the first hour. Perhaps the first hour you could use a drama and the second hour the children could hear the story from a "master storyteller" or with flannelgraph figures and pictures.

Some teachers balk at the idea of teaching the same story twice. They complain that the children become bored with the same story over and over. I have found that to be very far from the truth. Children love to hear the same story when it is presented with creative variety and thrive in all aspects of education through repetition and reinforcement.

In her book *Blue's Clues for Success*, Tracy tells the reader what the in-depth research for their show uncovered: children love and learn more from repetition. "Each *Blue's Clues* episode airs five consecutive days in a week, something that was previously unheard of in children's television. Because the show has so many layers of learning, kids can watch the same episode over and over and not get bored. Children naturally repeat behaviors when they are learning—just like they want to watch the same video or read the same book over and over. *The benefits are learning and mastery.*"[1]

NOTES

1. Tracy, *Blue's Clues*, 39.

Appendix B

CLASSROOM DISCIPLINE AND FAITH DEVELOPMENT

Discipline is an essential part of faith development. The lack of discipline in a classroom can prevent any learning, and therefore any faith development, from taking place. Excessive discipline in a classroom can inhibit a preschool child from coming to class and taint his or her perspective on God and the church.

Discipline is also a touchy subject in the church.

Question: What do you do with children who will not behave in class?

Answer: Have a written discipline policy for your children's ministry including preschool and elementary areas.

Every church should have a written discipline policy. This policy should not only be read and signed by every teacher and assistant in the children's ministry, it should be read and signed by every parent with a child in this department. A discipline policy clearly spells out what events will take place if the child misbehaves in class.

Before writing a child off as a "discipline problem," ask yourself these questions.

1) Are the classrooms child-friendly or are you scolding a child for your lack of safety proofing? (Problem: Two-year-old Jimmy continues to open and close the closet door. Resolution: Lock or childproof the closet doors.)

2) Is the curriculum developmentally appropriate for this specific age? (Problem: Four-year-old Anessa consistently falls off her chair during the story time while the other kids laugh and get rowdy. Resolution: Shorten the story time, recruit a "master storyteller," show more visuals, or add more interaction with the children.)

3) Are you expecting more from this child than he or she is developmentally capable of? (Problem: Two-year-old Steven throws his scissors during craft time. Resolution: Two-year-old children typically cannot manipulate scissors. Try another art project.)

4) Are your teachers prepared? (Problem: Three-year-old Brianna begins running around the room during the transition from singing to story while the teacher stands at the counter looking over her lesson. Resolution: The teacher needs to spend more time on her lesson before Sunday. Transition time for preschoolers must be smooth or discipline becomes a problem.)

5) Do your teachers need a break? Are your teachers cut out to work with children? (Problem: Four-year-old Charlie begins jumping up and down at the wrong point in singing time. The teacher grabs him by the arm and sits him down. Resolution: Evaluate the patience level of this teacher and determine whether or not she may need a break.)

A church classroom discipline policy should contain the exact steps that will be taken for all children in the event of a discipline problem. For example:

1) If the child exhibits inappropriate behavior to the point it affects the class, he or she will be taken aside, in full view of the other adult teacher and encouraged to stop the bad behavior.

2) If the child continues with said inappropriate behavior, he or she will be asked to sit in a "time out" chair for a time equivalent to the year of age (i.e., a three-year-old child will have to sit for three minutes and so on).

3) After the child has completed step number two, he or she will join the class in normal activities.

4) If the child continues the inappropriate behavior, an usher will be called and asked to call the child's mother or father out of the worship service or class time.

5) Upon the parent's arrival at the child's class the parent will

be made aware of the child's specific inappropriate behavior and the steps that had been taken up until that point.

6) After speaking to the teacher the parent must take the child out of the classroom for the duration of the class time.

7) The child may return to the class the next session provided one parent stays with the child the duration of the next class time.

8) At no time will a child be denied a snack for inappropriate behavior.

9) The child will never be turned to face a wall or corner during their stay in "time out."

10) At no time will the teacher strike, grab, push, or physically abuse the child.

11) The teacher and parent must share the same goals:
   A) Wanting the child to return to the classroom as soon as possible with appropriate behavior.
   B) Desiring the child to grow in faith through the activities of the class.
   C) Always letting the child know no matter how he or she acts that God, the teacher, and his or her parents love them very much.

This is simply an "example" of a discipline policy and may sound harsh to some. However, if teachers and parents sign the discipline policy, everyone should be on the same page. Requiring parents to sit with their child in class the next session will upset some parents and inconvenience them enough to make correcting their child's behavior a priority.

Appendix C

PREPLANNING EVALUATION TEST

Here is a sample of the kinds of questions you might ask on a pre-Planning evaluation test.

1. On what continent was Jesus born?
   - ❏ Asia
   - ❏ Africa
   - ❏ Europe
   - ❏ Australia

2. What are the first five books of the Bible called?
   - ❏ The Gospels
   - ❏ The Pentateuch
   - ❏ The Trinity
   - ❏ The Doxology

3. In which part of the Bible is the story of Jonah?
   - ❏ The New Testament
   - ❏ The Old Testament
   - ❏ The Index
   - ❏ The Glossary

4. Which list of these biblical characters is in the correct chronological order?
   - ❏ David, Saul, Absalom
   - ❏ Abraham, Isaac, Jacob
   - ❏ Adam, Esther, Moses
   - ❏ Noah, Cain, Joseph

5. Which of these biblical characters saw the handwriting on the wall?
   - ❏ Daniel
   - ❏ Samson
   - ❏ Jonah
   - ❏ Joseph

6. Who wrote the book of Philippians?
   - ❏ Peter
   - ❏ Philip
   - ❏ Steven
   - ❏ Paul

7. Which Old Testament figure was renamed Israel?
- ❏ Jacob
- ❏ Isaac
- ❏ Moses
- ❏ Joseph

8. What were the twelve tribes of Israel named after?
- ❏ The twelve channels of the Nile
- ❏ The twelve churches of Rome
- ❏ The twelve lions of Judah
- ❏ The twelve sons of #7

9. Can you say all the books of the Bible from memory? (Please be honest)
- ❏ Yes
- ❏ No
- ❏ No. I could when I was younger, but have forgotten since then.

10. Where did Moses lead the children of Israel *from*?
- ❏ Greece
- ❏ Egypt
- ❏ Jerusalem
- ❏ Canaan

11. Which of these persons was not one of the twelve disciples?
- ❏ Matthew
- ❏ James
- ❏ John
- ❏ Paul

12. Whom did Jesus nickname the "Sons of Thunder?"
- ❏ James and John
- ❏ Paul and Peter
- ❏ Peter and Andrew
- ❏ Matthew and Mark

13. In which book of the Bible would you find the story of Joseph?
- ❏ Exodus
- ❏ 2 Kings
- ❏ Genesis
- ❏ Psalms

14. Who is credited with writing most of the book of Psalms?
- ❏ Moses
- ❏ Isaiah
- ❏ David
- ❏ Joseph

15. Match the names with the phrases:

❏ Joseph	❏ Lived in the belly of the whale
❏ Noah	❏ Led the Israelites out of Egypt
❏ Jonah	❏ Was the twin brother of Esau
❏ Daniel	❏ Killed his brother Abel
❏ Jacob	❏ Stoned to death
❏ Adam	❏ Wore a colorful coat
❏ Moses	❏ Was a former tax-collector
❏ Matthew	❏ Survived the lion's den
❏ Stephen	❏ May not have had a belly-button
❏ Cain	❏ Built an ark

16. Primarily, in what language was the Old Testament written?
    ❏ Greek   ❏ Hebrew
    ❏ English   ❏ Latin

17. How many books make up the Gospels?
    ❏ Three   ❏ Two
    ❏ Four   ❏ Five

18. Who wrote the book of Revelation?
    ❏ Paul   ❏ Peter
    ❏ John   ❏ James

19. Which of these is not a major division of the Old Testament?
    ❏ Poetry   ❏ Prophecy
    ❏ Law   ❏ Doctrine

20. In which book of the Bible would you find Jesus' Sermon on the Mount?
    ❏ Mark   ❏ James
    ❏ John   ❏ Matthew

21. In which book of the Bible would you read of Paul's Missionary Journeys?
    ❏ Matthew   ❏ Psalms
    ❏ Acts   ❏ Deuteronomy

22. I believe that the Bible is a historically accurate book and everything contained in it is entirely factual.
    ❏ True   ❏ False
    ❏ I believe that *some things* in the Bible are not entirely factual.

23. Who was the first King of Israel?
    ❏ David   ❏ Saul
    ❏ Josiah   ❏ Ahab

24. The books that were accepted and we now read in the Bible are called the:
    ❏ Apocrypha   ❏ Revelation
    ❏ Canon   ❏ Tribulation

25. Which of these religions believes that Mary, mother of Jesus, never sinned?
    ❏ Judaism   ❏ Presbyterians
    ❏ Catholicism   ❏ Protestantism

26. Which of these religions **does not** believe that Jesus is the Messiah?
    ❏ Judaism   ❏ Presbyterians
    ❏ Catholicism   ❏ Protestantism

27. Which of these best describes the church you attend?
- ❏ Protestantism
- ❏ Calvinism
- ❏ Atheism
- ❏ Pentecostal

28. Esther was a . . .
- ❏ Jewish Queen
- ❏ Prophetess
- ❏ Prostitute
- ❏ Priestess

29. If you are a baptized believer, commit a crime, and die without repenting, will you go to heaven?
- ❏ Yes
- ❏ No
- ❏ I don't know.

30. If I died today, I would go to heaven.
- ❏ Absolutely
- ❏ No way
- ❏ I hope so
- ❏ Only God knows

31. If I had a friend who wanted to accept Christ, I would . . .
- ❏ tell them the basics but couldn't give them any Scripture.
- ❏ have absolutely no idea and tell them to go figure it out on their own.
- ❏ take them to the youth minister.
- ❏ be able to tell them how to accept Christ with scriptural support.

Appendix D

SAMPLE FAITH DEVELOPMENT PLANS

The following pages delineate sample Faith Development Plans for four different age groups over the 2–4 years that children will be in that age group. It is important to remember that this is only a skeleton outline of a formal Faith Development Plan. The most serious mistake you could make at this point is to take this plan and use it verbatim in your ministry.

The plans given make allowance for different meeting hours, as well as such special activities as retreats, mission trips, and service projects. You should use these as suggestions that you will tailor to your own congregation's regular schedule and the needs of your own children and youth.

Before putting your plan together, please take the time to read chapter eleven in detail. You will then understand better how to flesh out these skeletons and make necessary alterations. We encourage you to be imaginative and creative. May God bless you as we strive together to produce spiritually mature arrows for Christ.

Proposed Early Elementary

SS = Sunday School   W = Wednesday

September	October	November	December	January	February
SS—Salvation (2 wks) Heaven (2 wks)	**SS**—Jesus and His Parables	**SS**—Being a Servant (2 wks) Worship (2 wks)	**SS**—The Life of Jesus Christ	**SS**—Prayer (2 wks) Reading God's Word (2 wks)	**SS**—The Life of Moses
W—Creation and the Human Body	**W**—Creation and Animals	**W**—Creation and Nature	**W**—God's Plan for the Family	**W**—People Jesus Encountered	**W**—History and the Bible
SP			**SP**		**SP**
SS—Creation and the Human Body	**SS**—Creation and Animals	**SS**—Creation and Nature	**SS**—God's Plan for the Family	**SS**—People Jesus Encountered	**SS**—History and the Bible
W—Salvation (2 wks) Heaven (2 wks)	**W**—Jesus and His Parables	**W**—Being a Servant (2 wks) Worship (2 wks)	**W**—The Life of Jesus Christ	**W**—Prayer (2 wks) Reading God's Word (2 wks)	**W**—The Life of Moses
SP			**SP**		**SP**

Train a child in the way he should go, even when he

Faith Development Plan

Nights   **SP** = Service Project

March	April	May	June	July	August
SS—God's Plan for Money/ Giving	**SS**—Abraham, Isaac, and Jacob	**SS**—The Great Commission/ Discipleship	**SS**—Oh, Be Careful Little . . . Controlling your • tongue • eyes • ears • hands • feet	**SS**—The Life of King David and other great Kings	**SS**—The Fruit of the Spirit
W—Making Wise Choices	**W**—Heroes of the Faith	**W**—Wednesday Night Review			
		HEAVEN NIGHT	**CHURCH CAMP**	**CHURCH CAMP**	**CHURCH CAMP**
SS—Making Wise Choices	**SS**—Heroes of the Faith	**SS**—Sunday Morning Review	**SS**—Oh, Be Careful Little . . . Controlling your • tongue • eyes • ears • hands • feet	**SS**—The Life of King David and other great Kings	**SS**—The Fruit of the Spirit
W—God's Plan for Money/ Giving	**W**—Abraham, Isaac, and Jacob	**W**—The Great Commission/ Discipleship			
		HEAVEN NIGHT	**CHURCH CAMP**	**CHURCH CAMP**	**CHURCH CAMP**

• The Proposed Faith Development Plan for Early Elementary includes offering a children's choir every Sunday night.

is old he will not depart from it. —*Proverbs 22:6*

PROPOSED LATE ELEMENTARY

SS = Sunday School   **W** = Wednesday Nights

September	October	November	December	January	February
SS—How to Get to Heaven	**SS**—The Life of Joseph	**SS**—Right Choices	**SS**—The Life of Christ	**SS**—Prayer	**SS**—God's Plan for the Family
W—Science	**W**—Self-Esteem	**W**—Jesus' Parables	**W**—Heroes of the Faith	**W**—Spending Time in Devotion to God	**W**—The Life of Moses
SEP		**Giving Thanks Talent Night**			**SEP**
SS—Science	**SS**—Self-Esteem	**SS**—Jesus' Parables	**SS**—Heroes of the Faith	**SS**—Spending Time in Devotion to God	**SS**—The Life of Moses
W—How to Get to Heaven	**W**—The Life of Joseph	**W**—Right Choices	**W**—The Life of Christ	**W**—Prayer	**W**—God's Plan for the Family
SEP		**Giving Thanks Talent Night**			**SEP**
SS—How to Get to Heaven	**SS**—The Life of Joseph	**SS**—Right Choices	**SS**—The Life of Christ	**SS**—Prayer	**SS**—God's Plan for the Family
W—Science	**W**—Self Esteem	**W**—Jesus' Parables	**W**—Heroes of the Faith	**W**—Spending Time in Devotion to God	**W**—The Life of Moses
SEP		**Giving Thanks Talent Night**			**SEP**

I will open my mouth in parables, I will utter hidden things, things from of old
We will not hide them from their children; we will tell the next generation the praiseworthy

Faith Development Plan

SEP = Servant Evangelism Project   **STMT** = Short Term Mission Trip

March	April	May	June	July	August
SS—Jesus' Miracles	**SS**—Worship	**SS**—Esther, Nehemiah, Ruth, and Job	**SS**—The Water Boys: Jonah and Noah	**SS**—The Life of Paul	**SS**—The Life of Daniel
W—Evangelism	**W**—Prophecy	**W**—God's Design for Money			
STMT		**HEAVEN NIGHT**	**CHURCH CAMP**	**CHURCH CAMP**	**CHURCH CAMP**
SS—Evangelism	**SS**—Prophecy	**SS**—God's Design for Money	**SS**—The Water Boys: Jonah and Noah	**SS**—The Life of Paul	**SS**—The Life of Daniel
W—Jesus' Miracles	**W**—Worship	**W**—Esther, Nehemiah, Ruth, and Job			
STMT		**HEAVEN NIGHT**	**CHURCH CAMP**	**CHURCH CAMP**	**CHURCH CAMP**
SS—Jesus' Miracles	**SS**—Worship	**SS**—Esther, Nehemiah, Ruth, and Job	**SS**—The Water Boys: Jonah and Noah	**SS**—The Life of Paul	**SS**—The Life of Daniel
W—Evangelism	**W**—Prophecy	**W**—God's Design for Money			
STMT		**HEAVEN NIGHT**	**CHURCH CAMP**	**CHURCH CAMP**	**CHURCH CAMP**

—what we have heard and known, what our fathers have told us.
deeds of the Lord, his power, and the wonders he has done. —*Psalm 78:2-4 (NIV)*

Proposed Middle School

SS = Sunday School   W = Wednesday Night   SN = Sunday Nights

September	October	November	December	January	February
SS—Salvation W—101 Class—What Do We Believe? SEP SN—Small Groups	SS—Life of Job (Why does God allow bad things to happen?) W—God's Design for Your Body and Sex SN—Small Groups	SS—God's Plan for the Family. W—What the Bible Says about Heaven and Hell GTTN SN—Small Groups	SS—Bible Prophecy and Jesus' Birth. W—Where Did the Bible Come From? (Authenticity) SEP SN—Small Groups	SS—What the Bible Says about Prayer W—The Life of Moses SN—Small Groups	SS—The Fruit of the Spirit W—Creation vs. Evolution CIY's BELIEVE SN—Small Group
SS—101—What Do We Believe? W—Salvation SEP SN—Small Groups	SS—God's Design for Your Body and Sex W—Life of Job (Why do bad things happen?) SN—Small Groups	SS—What the Bible Says about Heaven and Hell W—God's Plan for the Family GTTN SN—Small Groups	SS—Where Did the Bible Come From? (Authenticity) W—Bible prophecy and Jesus' Birth. SEP SN—Small Groups	SS—The Life of Moses W—Evangelism, Missions, and Persecution SN—Small Groups	SS—Creation vs. Evolution W—The Fruit of the Spirit CIY's BELIEVE SN—Small Groups
SS—Salvation W—101 Class—What Do We Believe? SEP SN—Small Group	SS—Life of Job (Why does God allow bad things to happen?) W—God's Design for Your Body and Sex. SN—Small Groups	SS—God's Plan for the Family. W—What the Bible Says about Heaven and Hell GTTN SN—Small Groups	SS—Bible Prophecy and Jesus' Birth W—Where Did the Bible Come From? (Authenticity) SEP SN—Small Groups	SS—What the Bible Says about Prayer W—The Life of Moses SN—Small Groups	SS—The Fruit of the Spirit W—Creation vs Evolution CIY's BELIEVE SN—Small Groups

Even when I am old and gray, do not forsake me, O God, till I declare your power

FAITH DEVELOPMENT PLAN

SEP = Servant Evangelism Project   **GTTN** = Giving Thanks Talent Night

March	April	May	June	July	August
SS—Worship	SS—Evangelism, Missions, and Persecution	SS—The Book of Romans and Grace	SS—The Life of Christ	SS—Right Choices (Ethics)	SS—Made in the Image of God (Self-Image)
W—What Do Other Denominations Believe?	W—God's Plan for Giving.	W—Science and the Bible	W—Armor of God	W—God and the Media	W—Godly Relationships
Mission Trip		**HEAVEN NIGHT**	**CHURCH CAMP**	**CHURCH CAMP**	**CHURCH CAMP**
SN—Small Groups	SN—Small Groups	SN—Small Groups	SN—Book Club WWJD?	SN—Book Club WWJD?	SN—Book Club WWJD?
SS—What Do Other Denominations Believe?	SS—God's' Plan for Giving	SS—Science and the Bible	SS—Armor of God	SS—God and the Media	SS—Godly Relationships
W—Worship	W—What the Bible Says about Prayer	W—The Book of Romans and Grace	W—The Life of Christ	W—Right Choices (Ethics)	W—Made in the Image of God (Self-Image)
		HEAVEN NIGHT	**CHURCH CAMP**	**CHURCH CAMP**	**CHURCH CAMP**
SN—Small Groups	SN—Small Groups	SN—Small Groups	SN—Book Club	SN—Book Club	SN—Book Club
SS—Worship	SS—Evangelism, Missions, and Persecution	SS—The Book of Romans and Grace	SS—The Life of Christ	SS—Right Choices (Ethics)	SS—Made in the Image of God (Self-Image)
W—What Do Other Denominations Believe?	W—God's Plan for Giving	W—Science and the Bible.	W—Armor of God	W—God and the Media	W—Godly Relationships
Mission Trip		**HEAVEN NIGHT**	**CHURCH CAMP**	**CHURCH CAMP**	**CHURCH CAMP**
SN—Small Groups	SN—Small Groups	SN—Small Groups	SN—Book Club WWJD?	SN—Book Club WWJD?	SN—Book Club WWJD?

to the next generation, your might to all who are to come. —Psalm 71:18 (NIV)

S = Sunday Morning   **SN** = Sunday Nights   **W** = Wednesday   **GTTN** = Giving Thanks

September	October	November	December	January	February
S—Salvation/ Grace	**S**—The Holy Spirit	**S**—Self-Image and the Media	**S**—The Life of Daniel	**S**—Spiritual Disciplines/Prayer and Devotions	**S**—Love, Sex, and Dating
W—Electives **SEP**	**W**—Electives	**W**—Electives **GTTN**	**W**—Electives **SEP**	**W**—Electives	**W**—Electives
SN—Small Groups	**SN**—Small Groups	**SN**—Small Groups	**SN**—Small Groups	**SN**—Small Groups	**SN**—Small Groups
S—Salvation/ Grace	**S**—The Life of Moses	**S**—Ethics: Relative vs. Absolute Truth	**S**—The Life of Joseph	**S**—Spiritual Disciplines/Prayer and Devotions	**S**—Love, Sex, and Dating
W—Electives **SEP**	**W**—Electives	**W**—Electives **GTTN**	**W**—Electives **SEP**	**W**—Electives	**W**—Electives
SN—Small Groups	**SN**—Small Groups	**SN**—Small Groups	**SN**—Small Groups	**SN**—Small Groups	**SN**—Small Groups
S—Salvation/ Grace	**S**—The Holy Spirit	**S**—Self-Image and the Media	**S**—The Life of Daniel	**S**—Spiritual Disciplines/Prayer and Devotions	**S**—Love, Sex, and Dating
W—Electives **SEP**	**W**—Electives	**W**—Electives **GTTN**	**W**—Electives **SEP**	**W**—Electives	**W**—Electives
SN—Small Groups	**SN**—Small Groups	**SN**—Small Groups	**SN**—Small Groups	**SN**—Small Groups	**SN**—Small Groups
S—Salvation/ Grace	**S**—The Life of Moses	**S**—Ethics: Relative vs. Absolute Truth	**S**—The Life of Joseph	**S**—Spiritual Disciplines/Prayer and Devotions	**S**—Love, Sex, and Dating
W—Electives **SEP**	**W**—Electives	**W**—Electives **GTTN**	**W**—Electives **SEP**	**W**—Electives	**W**—Electives
SN—Small Groups	**SN**—Small Groups	**SN**—Small Groups	**SN**—Small Groups	**SN**—Small Groups	**SN**—Small Groups

The goal of this command is love, which comes from a pure heart

FAITH DEVELOPMENT PLAN

Talent Night   **HN** = Heaven Night   **MT** = Mission Trip   **SEP** = Servant Evangelism Project

March	April	May	June	July	August
S—The History of Israel/Jews	**S**—The Life of Christ	**S**—What We Believe	**S**—Creation vs. Evolution	**S**—Jesus' Miracles & Parables	**S**—History of the Bible/Canon
W—Electives	**W**—Electives	**W**—Electives			
MT	MT	HN	CIY	CHURCH CAMP	SEP
SN—Small Groups	**SN**—Small Groups	**SN**—Small Groups	**SN**—Book Club	**SN**—Book Club	**SN**—Book Club
S—The Great Commission, Missions, & Persecution	**S**—Prophecy and Jesus' Death	**S**—Cults	**S**—Contemporary Issues	**S**—Old Testament Heroes	**S**—History, Archaeology, and the Bible
W—Electives	**W**—Electives	**W**—Electives			
MT	MT	HN	CIY	CHURCH CAMP	SEP
SN—Small Groups	**SN**—Small Groups	**SN**—Small Groups	**SN**—Book Club	**SN**—Book Club	**SN**—Book Club
S—The History of Israel/Jews	**S**—The Life of Christ	**S**—What We Believe	**S**—Creation vs. Evolution	**S**—Jesus' Miracles & Parables	**S**—History of the Bible/Canon
W—Electives	**W**—Electives	**W**—Electives			
MT	MT	HN	CIY	CHURCH CAMP	SEP
SN—Small Groups	**SN**—Small Groups	**SN**—Small Groups	**SN**—Book Club	**SN**—Book Club	**SN**—Book Club
S—The Great Commission, Missions, & Persecution	**S**—Prophecy and Jesus' Death	**S**—Cults	**S**—Contemporary Issues	**S**—Old Testament Heroes	**S**—History, Archaeology, and the Bible
W—Electives	**W**—Electives	**W**—Electives			
MT	MT	HN	CIY	CHURCH CAMP	SEP
SN—Small Groups	**SN**—Small Groups	**SN**—Small Groups	**SN**—Book Club	**SN**—Book Club	**SN**—Book Club

and a good conscience and a sincere faith. —*1 Timothy 1:5*

Elective Choices for Wednesday Nights

1) Submission/Surrender
2) How to Lead Someone to Christ
3) Giving of Time/Service
4) Giving of Talents
5) Giving Money
6) God's Design for Money/Managing Your Money
7) What Do the Other Denominations Believe?
8) Becoming a Woman of Integrity
9) Becoming a Man of Integrity
10) God's Design for Marriage
11) In the World, Not of It
12) How to Talk to a Suicidal Friend
13) Occupations and College Choices
14) Godly Leadership
15) Girls Only! (Wardrobe, makeup and hair)
16) Sign Language and Worship
17) God's Design for Worship
18) Heroes of the Old Testament
19) Heroes of the Faith – Martin Luther, Corrie Ten Boom, Billy Sunday, and Billy Graham
20) Old Testament Review
21) New Testament Review
22) Creation and Nature
23) Creation and Animals
24) Creation and the Human Body
25) Public Speaking/Preaching
26) Literature and the Bible
27) Old Testament Poetry
28) Visioneering—The Life of Nehemiah
29) Why God Allows Bad Things to Happen
30) The Book of Revelation

ABOUT THE AUTHOR

J. Brackemyre ministers to the Children and Youth at the
Wilmington Church of Christ in Wilmington, Ohio, and
operates Aim Training Ministries (**www.aimtrainingministries.com**).
Brackemyre holds an Associates Arts Degree
in Christian Education, a Bachelor of Science Degree
in Children's Ministry, and a Masters of Arts Degree
in Christian Education from Cincinnati Christian University.